FRAMING EUROPE

FRAMING EUROPE

TELEVISION NEWS AND EUROPEAN INTEGRATION

C. H. de Vreese

aksant
Amsterdam
2003

ISBN 90-5260-080-5

© 2003, Aksant Academic Publishers, Amsterdam

All rights reserved, including those of translation into foreign languages. No part of this book may be reproduced in any form, by photoprint, microfilm, or any other means, nor transmitted into a machine language without written permission from the publisher.

Cover design: Jos Hendrix, Groningen
Type setting: BoekVorm, Amsterdam

Aksant Academic Publishers, Cruquiusweg 31, NL-1019 AT Amsterdam
www.aksant.nl

Contents

	Preface	
1	Introduction	1
2	Towards an integrated process model of news framing	21
3	Europe in the Newsroom	53
4	Europe in the News	77
5	Europe in Public opinion The effects of the conflict and economic consequences frames on issue interpretation, frame salience, and policy support	121
6	The effects of strategic news on political cynicism, issue evaluations and policy support: A two-wave experiment	139
7	Discussion and Conclusion	161
	Notes	185
	References	199
	Appendices	217
	Author index	225
	Subject index	231

Preface

The idea for this book emerged in spring 1998 when, during an internship at the national television news program in the Netherlands, I was dazzled by a seeming paradox: On the one hand, journalists, politicians, and citizens alike rated European integration as one of the most important and wide-reaching changes in post-war Europe. On the other hand, journalists, politicians, and citizens alike also thought about European integration as complex, bureaucratic, inefficient, and decidedly dull. This was enough to intrigue me to undertake the research endeavor reported in this book.

The research was completed as a PhD project in the period 1998-2002 at The Amsterdam School of Communications Research, *ASCoR*, University of Amsterdam. The project was supported by research grants from the The Dutch Organization for Scientific Research [Nederlands Organisatie voor Wetenschappelijk Onderzoek, NWO], the Danish Research Academy [Det danske forskerakademi], the University of Amsterdam, and the Nordic Film Foundation [Nordisk Film Fonden]. I am thankful to all of these institutions.

The book has three key features: interviews with newsmakers in Britain, Denmark, and the Netherlands, content analyses of news in the three countries, and experiments with television news. The latter were conducted in cooperation with the national news program of the Dutch public broadcaster, *NOS* [Nederlandse Omroep Stichting]. This cooperation was exceptional and I am particularly thankful to the (former and current) Editors in Chief Nico Haasbroek, Hans Laroes, and Bernadette Slotboom who granted me the best possible setting for carrying out my research. During the production of the experimental news programs several people were very helpful. From the *NOS Journaal* Jan Talens, Pia Dijkstra, Paul Sneijder, Gijs Wanders, Maryse Ducheine, and Marije Alma all made time and energy available in the midst of their daily work to contribute to the research.

From the Audience Research Department (*NOS-KLO*), I would like to thank in particular Allerd Peeters for a great cooperation and many insights with regard to the logistics of the experimental studies. Several persons contributed to the television stories by providing quotes for the experimental stimulus material. For this I am thankful to Nout Wellink, President of the Dutch National Bank, Dick Benschop, former Secretary of State for Foreign Affairs, Frank Timmermans, MP, and Frans Weisglas, former MP and President of the Dutch

Parliament. Finally, I would like to thank Roland Snoeijer for our cooperation during the first experiment. Without him, this experiment would not have taken place, nor would it have been half the fun to do it.

A second key feature is a series of interviews with newsmakers at the *BBC* and *ITN* (Britain), *DR* and *TV2* (Denmark), and *NOS* (the Netherlands). Editors, journalists, and political correspondents made time available for interviews during hectic periods such as the 1999 European election campaign. In addition, these persons granted me access to the newsroom, making it possible to get an insider's view. I am thankful to all of them for making this possible.

The third key feature of the book is a content analysis of news about European integration in different countries. Several persons in Britain, Denmark, and the Netherlands helped collecting the material and in Amsterdam, I was privileged to work with diligent and meticulous student assistants from the EU member states without whom the content analyses could never have been carried out.

Several persons provided invaluable help without which this Ph.D. project would never have been completed. Most importantly my friends and colleagues at The Amsterdam School of Communications Research provided excellent company, valuable inspiration, and useful feedback. Angela, Hetty, Jochen, Kim, Marjolein, Martin, Moniek, and Roderick all stand out for also being such great persons to be with. Throughout the project, Jay Blumler, Ann Crigler, Wolfgang Donsbach, Esteban Lopez-Escobar, Doris Graber, Stig Hjarvard, Denis McQuail, Paolo Mancini, Tom Patterson, Stephen Reese, and David Weaver all provided input on the ideas and theoretical concepts addressed in the book.

My project resided as part of a larger collaborative research effort directed from the University of Amsterdam. I had the privilege to work together in a team of researchers including Holli Semetko, Klaus Schönbach, Cees van der Eijk, Edmund Lauf, Susan Banducci, and Jeff Karp which was exciting. Member of this group was also my Ph.D. colleague Jochen Peter who has become a much appreciated collaborator and intellectual exemplar. I thank Jochen in particular for inspiring and challenging discussions and for sharing his many insightful comments with me.

The project was supervised by Holli A. Semetko, Professor and Chair of Audience and Public Opinion Research at The Amsterdam School of Communications Research *ASCoR*. In many respects I could not have wished for a better supervisor: Generous, stimulating, challenging, and supportive. Many doors usually closed for a young researcher were made wide open for me. I thank Holli for these qualities that oftentimes made the four years of work a very pleasurable experience. Any shortcomings in the book are, of course, entirely my responsibility.

Claes H. de Vreese
Amsterdam, October 2002

CHAPTER 1

Introduction

The process of European integration constitutes one of the most significant economic and political developments in post-war Europe. The European community is an expanding entity with a common currency and advanced cooperation in a number of areas ranging from economic policies to defense operations. As the European Union moves towards increasingly advanced economic and political integration, media, and especially news media, play an essential role in informing European citizens about the integration process. Given the high level of uncertainty and complexity of European integration, citizens are likely to be dependent on the media for guidance in interpreting developments as well as forming opinions (e.g., Ball-Rokeach, 1985; Gamson, 1996; Gavin, 1998; Herbst, 1998; Page & Shapiro, 1992). With citizens, politicians, and policy makers relying on the news media as the most important source of information when learning about 'Europe' (Eurobarometer, 56, 2002), news media have the potential to influence and alter perceptions and evaluations of 'Europe' by emphasizing potential gains and losses, dangers and benefits of further integration.[1]

This study deals with the role news media play in the process of advanced economic and political European integration. This opening chapter provides a general introduction to the theme and the context of the study, formulates the overarching research question, discusses the key features of the design of the study, and outlines the structure of the book. The project is carried out at a key moment when the European continent is facing fundamental challenges and when the relationship between the political arena, citizens, and media is changing. The examination of the link between news media production, content, and public opinion formation provides insights into the processes directing citizens to either embrace or discard economic and political developments in contemporary Europe.

Setting the scene: From Coal to Coins

The focus of the study is on the *communication processes* in the particular historical, economic, and political context of European integration. A brief introduction to the key issues is warranted.

In the aftermath of World War II, Churchill called for a 'United States of Europe'. Though this idea was not realized immediately, French Foreign Minister, Schuman in 1950 proposed that France and Germany, along with other European countries, pool their coal and steel resources. In 1951 Belgium, France, Germany, Italy, Luxembourg, and the Netherlands established ECSC, the European Coal and Steel Community, and in 1957 treaties establishing the European Economic Community (EEC) were signed in Rome.

In 1972 the EEC expanded with Britain, Denmark, and Ireland. In 1978 the European Council agreed to launch the European Monetary System (EMS) and the European currency unit (ECU). The eight participating member states (Britain stayed outside) were required to maintain their exchange rates within certain fluctuation margins. Almost ten years later, in 1987, the Single European Act (which 'up-dated' the EEC Treaty) was implemented. Its objective was the completion of a frontier-free market by the end of 1992. Jacques Delors was appointed to chair a committee of experts to examine ways and means of completing an economic and monetary union. The first stage of the European Monetary Union (EMU) was launched in 1990 and involved the removal of most of the remaining restrictions on capital movements, increased coordination of economic policies, and more intensive cooperation between central banks.

In 1991 the European Council agreed on The Treaty of the European Union at a meeting in Maastricht. The aim was the completion of the economic and monetary union and introduction of a single European currency. Denmark and Britain did not participate fully in the new Union framework. Britain chose to exclude chapters in the areas of social policy and defense. In a referendum, required by the Danish Constitution, the Treaty of Maastricht was rejected. A year later, following the Edinburgh negotiations, a new Danish referendum fell out in favor of the Europeanists and Denmark was included in the future cooperation of Europe on the basis of the so-called 'Danish exceptions' which pertain to the monetary union, European citizenship plans, and defense cooperation.

Following the Maastricht Treaty, the euro was legally established as a currency and in spring 1998 the decision on participating member states was made. All EU countries joined the euro, except Britain, Denmark, and Sweden that decided to postpone the final decision. Dutchman Wim Duisenberg was appointed President of the European Central Bank (ECB) and by January 1999 the conversion rates of the participating currencies were irrevocably fixed to the euro. The banking and finance industries made the changeover to the euro and the circulation of euro banknotes and coins commenced in January 2002 as the legal tender status of national banknotes and coins disappeared.

The European countries have increased the degree of economic and political integration continuously since World War II. At no point so far have the developments towards integration taken place at such a pace as in the last decade. This study was carried out between the first step (1999) and the full-blown implementation of the euro (2002), witnessed a Danish national referendum on the euro (2000), the lowest turnout ever in European elections (1999), the resignation of the Santer-chaired European Commission (1999), the Irish two-step approval of the Treaty of Nice (2001 / 2002), the launch of an international expert convent addressing the future of the EU (2001), and increased discussions of the EU as an international actor in the aftermath of September 11 (2001) and the intensified situation in the Middle-East (2002). Moreover, the issues of enlargement of the European Union and institutional reorganization stabilized as key points on the EU agenda bringing along debate over issues such as vote distribution and procedures, the democratic deficit of the Union, its budget and finances, and the structure and role of the Commission. In short, the period under study was a period of time with several key events that contribute to shaping the European economic and political landscape.

Public support for European integration

The developments outlined above have generated heated debates in some European countries. Politicians and interest groups have outlined scenarios of Europe in the future ranging from images of a well-united, harmonious financial world player to versions of a politically integrated 'United States of Europe'. News media have played a central role in the debates on Europe, some even advocating clear pro or con European integration views such as the partisan British press.

In Britain, Denmark, and the Netherlands, the three cases examined in this study, Europe has been a 'hot issue' at several points over the last decades. Examples include the large-scale demonstrations prior to the Danish 1972 referendum on joining the EEC and the debates over 'Europe' in recent British (1997 and 2001), Dutch (1998), and Danish (1998) national election campaigns (e.g., Andersen, Borre, Goul-Andersen & Nielsen, 1999; Norris, Curtice, Sanders, Scammell & Semetko, 1999; de Vreese, 2001a). The perhaps most striking examples are the violent riots in the streets of Copenhagen succeeding the 1993 referendum on the Edinburgh Treaty. For the first time since World War II national authorities opened fire on a demonstrating public. Memorable examples of EU-debates include the quota systems for agriculture and the fisheries, guidelines for the production and dissemination of cultural goods, the centralized approval of size and curve of cucumbers and the 1999 resignation of the European Commission based on allegations of fraud, corruption, and incompetence, leaving the European Union without a daily management.

'The European House', as former Chairman of the European Commission, Jaques Santer, labeled the integrating Europe, will neither be truly European nor have any resemblance to a house, if European citizens do not embrace the idea. European citizens have only limited occasions at which directly to voice their view on the on-going integration. Referendums on the key treaties have only been held in a few countries. National and in particular European elections are opportunities for the electorate to show their (dis)content with European politics. However, the legitimacy of this democratic function is challenged by the lack of authority and competences of the European Parliament and representativity is questioned because so few people vote in European elections, most dramatically seen at the 1999 elections where the overall EU turnout dropped below 50% and turnout was 24% in Britain, 30% in the Netherlands, and 50% in Denmark.[2]

Overarching research question

This study takes a cross-national perspective in the investigation of the role of news and information for the process of opinion formation in the context of European integration. A study of this process in only *one* country would not allow for inferences about the situation elsewhere and would hamper the generalizability of the findings. Three European countries are included in the analysis: Britain, renowned as one of the most euro-skeptic countries, Denmark, at best 'lukewarm' towards advanced integration, and the Netherlands, a traditionally pro-European country. These three countries constitute the basis for studying the dynamics between news media production, content, and the formation of public opinion about Europe. Obviously an even more elaborate cross-national design would be preferable. As argued below, however, the combination of investigations of production, content, and effects with any cross-national perspective is an extension of our current knowledge.

The study focuses on the particular role of television news. In terms of audience responses to *television news* about European integration we have only limited knowledge though television is the main source of information for a majority of citizens in Europe (e.g., Eurobarometer, 56, 2002). With the exception of a study of television in the 1979 European election campaign (Blumler, 1983), most studies of the role of media in the process of public opinion formation focus on the written press (e.g., Hoddess, 1997; Kevin, 2001; Werder, 2002). The impact of television news on public attitudes towards European integration has been largely neglected in previous research, as Gavin (2000) recently concluded.

The concept of *framing* is central to the research project. Events have little intrinsic value unless embedded in a meaningful framework that organizes and lends coherence to the interpretation of events. Framing, on the one hand, refers to the packaging of information that takes place in the newsroom where journalists must unavoidably select and prioritize to tell a story in the news. Framing, on the other hand, also refers to the ability of message attributes to organize experiences of situations and issues for citizens and rendering certain patterns of thoughts available for the expression of attitudes and opinions. The central research question links the study of television news production processes with analyses of news coverage and investigations of effects on public opinion formation:

What characteristics of the television news production process influence the framing of Europe in the news and what influence does the news have on public opinion about Europe?

This overarching research question is divided into a number of sub-questions. The formulation of expectations and the specific theoretical rationale for each of these questions is discussed after a review of the literature. For now it suffices to say that the study has three main components: the process of framing in the production of news, frames in the news, and framing effects on public opinion. 'Europe in the newsroom' investigates the role of framing in the newsrooms of European broadcasters. The organization of the production of news about European affairs, the constraints and challenges facing journalists covering 'Europe', and the considerations that go into selecting and packaging news are investigated. 'Europe in the news' aims at identifying recurrent structures and frames in news about European integration in a cross-national, comparative fashion. 'Europe in public opinion' finally refers to the analysis of the influence of news frames on public perceptions of European affairs.

Trends in public opinion

In democratic systems where decision-makers are kept accountable at elections, surveys and polls have become important ad-hoc indicators about opinions of the electorate (Lavrakas & Traugott, 2000). Public opinion polls are tools to adjust political strategies and policies (Brettschneider, 1997). The issue of European integration is no exception to this pattern and public opinion is monitored closely. Beyond media commissioned polls, regular aggregate-level data on public opinion about issues of European integration is available from, for example, the Eurobarometer reports.[3] These data show considerable variation and fluctuation in the levels of support for European integration, both in a between-country comparative perspective and in a within-country temporal perspective. Britain, Denmark, and the Netherlands are three interesting cases in terms of public support for integration.

In terms of *general support for membership* in the EU, the overall EU average approval rating has fluctuated from 50% to 70% over the past two decades and has been around 50-55% in the past few years (Eurobarometer, 56, 2002). Britain is considerably below the EU average with an aggregate-level support for membership of around 40%, reaching a high 50% around 1990 and in the past years being around 30% (Eurobarometer, 56, 2002). In Denmark, public support for membership of the EU was below the EU average up until 1992 and has since been equal to the overall EU average so that support currently is around 55-60% (Eurobarometer, 56, 2002). Public support in the Netherlands is high, with a stable approval rate of about 70%, which is 15-20 percentage points above the overall EU average.

Looking specifically at *support for the common currency*, the euro consistently had an overall EU wide approval rating of approximately 50%. Between 1998 and 2002 a considerable increase in the approval rating was matched by an equal drop in the opposition to the currency so that the average currently is about 60-70% in the twelve countries participating in the euro (Eurobarometer, 56, 2002). The current level of support in the Netherlands is 71%, Denmark 47%, and Britain 27% (Eurobarometer, 56, 2002). On the issue of the euro, however, public opinion may change rapidly (de Vreese & Semetko 2002a) and in Britain and Sweden, public opinion is monitored closely in advance of the up-coming referendums on the common currency.

Turning to public *support for the enlargement of the Union*, there is an overall EU average support of about 50% for the enlargement plans (Eurobarometer, 56, 2002). Denmark is among the strongest supporters with 69% favoring enlargement while the Netherlands is at 58%, and the British are the most skeptical at 41% (Eurobarometer, 56, 2002). Evidence from countries on the ascension list shows support for inclusion in the EU, but a decrease in support in recent years is noticeable (Eurobarometer Candidate, 1, 2002; Kolarska-Bobinska, Doblinska et al., 2001).

In sum, on the aggregate level, the three countries relevant to this study can be situated on a 'Europe Warm – Europe Cold' scale. In Britain, public opinion is divided and the country is among the most Europe-skeptic members of the EU, both in general terms and with regard to specific key EU policies such as the common currency and the enlargement. Denmark is 'lukewarm' towards advanced integration. On the aggregate level, the support for membership is similar to the EU average. The support for the euro is lower than in most other countries, which was demonstrated in the 2000 rejection of the euro in a national referendum, but support for EU enlargement is higher than in most other countries. The Netherlands is pro-European, both in terms of general support and in terms of support for key EU policies.

Factors influencing public opinion about Europe

Beyond descriptive summaries of developments in public opinion on key European issues, the Eurobarometer reports also outline a number of bi-variate relationships between attitudes towards European integration and, for example, social-demographic characteristics such as gender, age, and education. These analyses suggest main effects of gender (men being more supportive of European integration) and education (higher levels of education are associated with being more positive towards the EU). Over time, differences in terms of age, gender, and education have decreased, suggesting that explanations of attitudes towards European affairs must include other predictors than social-demographic data. Extant research investigating the antecedents of attitudes towards European integration can be classified in three groups:[4]

Political sophistication and values. The first group of studies examines the relationship between support for European integration and value orientations with regard to economic and political issues (Inglehart, 1970; 1990). Inglehart's work suggests that political attitudes are shaped by the socio-economic environment during the formative years. The social-economic environment is translated into values and attitudes that persist in adult life. According to Inglehart, Rabier, and Reif (1991), the European Union is a vehicle for economic, political, and social change towards a more egalitarian society which is more attractive to citizens with post-materialist values. In addition, these studies suggest that high levels of political sophistication and awareness enable citizens to identify with a supra-national entity such as the European Union (Inglehart, 1970). This argument is partly supported by Eurobarometer data that suggest that higher levels of knowledge are associated with support for European integration.

Economic experiences and expectations. The second group of studies posits that "EU citizens from different socio-economic situations experience different costs and benefits from integrative policy" (Gabel, 1998, p. 336). These studies explain support for European integration in terms of income, education, occupational skills, and proximity to border regions (e.g, Anderson & Reichert, 1996; Gabel & Palmer, 1995).[5] The proposition that attitudes towards integration, including the common currency, is driven by economic experiences and evaluations is also shared by Pepermans and Veleye (1998) who found national economic pride and satisfaction to be the a key explanatory variable for support for the euro across the 15 EU-countries. However, Bosch and Newton (1995) did not find any coherent pattern in their 12-country study of how economic variables may explain support for European unification.

Domestic politics. The third group of studies focuses on the effects of domestic political considerations for attitudes towards European integration. This research suggests that attitudes towards European integration are a function of citizens' partisanship and the degree to which their preferred political party is supportive of integration (Franklin, Marsh & Wlezien, 1994; Franklin, van der Eijk & Marsh, 1995). These studies in essence suggest that support for integration is *mediated* by party affiliation. Along these lines, studies have also suggested that voters' support for integration is conditional upon their support for and evaluation of the incumbent government (Franklin et al., 1995).[6]

Gabel (1998) examined the explanatory value of the different theories of support for European integration using Eurobarometer data from 1978-1992. The data substantiated the claims of all of the theories, but he found 'utilitarian consequences', that is the expected economic benefits of integrative policy, to provide the most robust explanation. Political values and sophistication, as proposed by Inglehart (1970, 1990), received only limited support as predictors of support for European integration, while domestic political considerations, in the form of partisanship and government evaluations, were the second most important predictors.

In a study specifically investigating voting behavior (as opposed to general attitudes) in the 1994 European Parliamentary elections, van der Eijk, Franklin, and Oppenhuis (1996) assessed the simultaneous influences of several theories traditionally used to explain party choice. They specified a model where the likelihood of voting for different political parties was regressed on the influence of social cleavages, post-materialist values, ideology, issue voting, government performance, and EU evaluations. They found that preferences for political parties in the European Parliament elections were driven by "parties' political stances and voters' preferences in terms of left/right ideology, issues, and government approval" (van der Eijk et al., 1996, p. 359).

None of the previous studies specifically address the impact of campaigns (in the context of European elections) or news and information (in the context of understanding general attitudes towards the EU). By and large, the impact of media in understanding variation in support for European integration has been neglected. Some studies allude to the impact of the media, such as Hewstone (1986) who discusses the role of the press or Anderson and Weymouth (1999) who analyze the British press coverage of the EU. None of these studies, however, have attempted to formally model the impact of media and communication variables. Moreover, the discussion so far has been focused on the role of the press.

THE ROLE OF THE MEDIA. The key question for this study is what role television news plays in shaping public opinion about 'Europe'. Available data suggest that citizens who consult several different media sources are generally more positive towards, for example, the euro than citizens who rely on only one source (Eurobarometer, 50, 1999). Such observations, however, say nothing about the causality of this relationship. Do interested and pro-European citizens turn more to the news media for information? Or does the use of multiple information sources contribute positively to interest and enthusiasm for integration? In addition, such general observations fail to say anything about *what* information citizens obtain when turning to the news media and about the types of effect this information may have.

Previous work discussing support for integration has speculated about the role of the media in this process.[7] Norris (2000) offered initial insights into the contribution of news media for, for example, public support for the euro and EU membership. Drawing on survey data from several EU countries, she found a significant effect of the tone of press coverage about the euro on support for the euro and EU membership. This study is an initial indication of a relationship between tone of news and, for example, support for the EU. This investigation, however, focused on the bivariate relationship between the slant of the news and aggregated expressions of public opinion. Controls were only made for cross-national differences, but there was no individual-level investigation. The study was not designed to address the crucial issue of causality in the relationship between media content and citizen responses.

One study investigated how the information environment, in particular the news media, in a referendum campaign served to crystallize opinion on an issue within the context of a number of other hypothesized influences on the vote (de Vreese & Semetko, 2002c). Drawing on a nationally representative two-wave panel survey and a content analysis of news coverage of the Danish 2000 euro referendum campaign, it was found that exposure to certain media outlets, and the tone of the coverage, influenced how voters made their decision, when controlling for other predictors.[8] These findings emphasize the importance of considering the news and information environment during a campaign and provide a direct link between exposure to the content of specific news outlets and electoral behavior.

The aforementioned study of a referendum campaign on a European issue considered the role of media content in a specific campaign in *one* country. With the exception of a study of the 1979 European elections, cross-national investigations of the role of media are rare. The study of the 1979 campaign addressed, for example, the relationship between exposure to different media and campaign evaluations (Cayrol, 1983) and media exposure and learning (Schönbach, 1983). However, these studies offer only discussions of the bivariate relationships between media exposure and a variety of dependent measures. In sum, studies of attitudes towards European integration have been negligent of the role of the media in this process. Given the characteristics of previous research, cross-national investigations of media production, content, and effects in the context of European integration are important extensions to the research field.

Three political systems, three media systems, three journalistic cultures

The three countries in this study are interesting cases in terms of their varying role in the history of European integration. They also vary substantially with respect to aggregate-level support for future European integration as discussed above. In addition, the countries have several system-level characteristics that define the context in which news about European affairs is produced and consumed. In this perspective it is important to consider key features of the political system, the media landscape, and the 'journalistic culture' in which the process takes place (Semetko, de Vreese & Peter, 2000).

POLITICAL SYSTEM. Although Britain, Denmark, and the Netherlands are parliamentary democracies in which the Prime Minister is almost always the leader of the largest party in parliament, they represent different political systems. The traditional British de facto two-party system is fundamentally different from the multi-party systems of Denmark and the Netherlands where governance is a coalition issue. The political system in the three countries is characterized by continuity and change. In domestic politics, studies suggest that the alignment between political parties and their voters is decreasing while the number of vote switchers, undecided voters, and strategic voters is increasing (e.g., Andersen et al., 1999; Franklin, Mackie & Valen et al., 1992). In the context of European integration, little is different from the national systems. The party systems in the EU are still essentially organized along the lines of national politics, and no European-level party system has emerged as the result of advanced integration (Mair, 2000).[9]

In addition to the developments in the political system, the relationship between politics and the media has evolved over the past decades. Broadly speaking a transition has taken place in which more assertive journalism was paralleled by politicians' use of streamlined communication strategies, PR, news managers, and spin-doctors. Journalists have adapted by making the 'exposure' of professional political tactics the focus of news stories (Bennett & Entman, 2001; Blumler & Kavanagh, 1999; Esser, Reinemann & Fan, 2001; Farrell, 1996; Mancini, 1999; Mazzoleni & Schulz, 1999; Newman, 2000; Norris, 2000; Swanson & Mancini, 1996).

While these developments have been addressed in the context of national-level elections in both Europe and the US, little is known about changes in the political culture at the European level. Though a European party system has not emerged, changes at the national level provide reason to believe that the European political institutions have also adapted new strategies and that the media have responded accordingly. Only few studies, however, have investigated the efforts made by EU institutions to deal with public relations and media attention. One study argued that in the wake of the Maastricht treaty, the EU was alarmed by its inability to 'get its message across' and launched a program of providing background information and press briefings and increased accessibility to documents (Tumber, 1995). A second study provides a picture of the European Commission's media communication as poor and incompetent suggesting that 'fragmented political authority', a 'pervading technocratic mindset', and 'inadequate staffing' result in severe communication deficits (Meyer, 1999). The study suggests that the degree of professionalization of politics at the European level might be less prominent compared to the national level. However, the general tendency in a number of European countries is to adapt more advanced technical and organizational modes of communication as well as strategic parameters of professional campaigning (Plasser, Scheucher & Senft, 2000).

MEDIA SYSTEMS. The changes in political communication discussed above coincide historically with significant changes in the European media landscape in general and broadcasting in particular. Today all countries have full-blown competition in broadcasting and all operate in a dual system, far from earlier public service broadcasting monopolies (McQuail & Siune, 1998).[10]

Britain represents a European frontier in terms of broadcasting and has known a dual system since 1954. The British television news market is highly competitive and dominated by *BBC News* and *ITN*. The main evening *BBC* news bulletin was traditionally at 9 p.m. but moved to 10 p.m. in 2002. It competes head-on with *ITN* which, after a rescheduling to 6.30 p.m., appeared at 10 p.m. again in 2002.

Denmark was a 'late arrival' in the era of deregulated broadcasting. The monopoly of national public broadcaster – the *BBC* equivalent *Denmark's Radio*, *DR*, (which also broadcasts television) - was challenged as late as 1988 by the launch of the semi-public, semi-private *TV2*.[11] The national channels have daily news with *DR's 'TV-Avisen'* at 9 p.m. and *TV2's* 7 p.m. *'Nyhederne'* being the market leaders.

Broadcasting in the Netherlands is a product of Dutch society's traditionally pillarized structure and is entirely different from Britain and Denmark. Broadcasting associations are organized around religious and societal segments in the population and are allocated air time according to membership volume (Brants & McQuail, 1997). Commercial television was de facto introduced in the Netherlands in 1989 with *RTL* broadcasting in Dutch from Luxembourg. The public broadcasters and private *RTL4* and *RTL5* lead the news market with the public 8 o'clock *NOS* bulletin and the 7.30 p.m. '*RTL Nieuws*' being the most widely watched.[12]

To understand the context in which news about European affairs is produced an important question is whether the structural changes outlined above have affected content and the way audiences respond to the diversity in news provision. Over time, from 1971 to 1996, it seems that the share of news and information might have gone down slightly, at least in Denmark and the Netherlands (Norris, 2000, p. 108). However, there are no comparable data available to suggest whether these changes have also been paralleled by changes in the amount of time audiences spend on political and international news. The specific impact on the volume of political news and audiences' exposure and attentiveness to such news notwithstanding, the fully competitive media market is the backdrop against which news production and content about Europe must be seen.

JOURNALISM. A third and final aspect to consider in cross-national news research is 'journalistic culture' (Semetko, 1996). The orientation towards politics and politicians by news people varies greatly in Europe. In two comparative studies of the British and German press, Köcher (1986) suggested that German journalists place more value on opinion whereas their British counterparts see themselves more as transmitters of facts. This finding dovetails with Blumler and Gurevitch's (in Semetko et al., 1991) description of British television journalists as cautious and reactive. In Spain, a comparative analysis of public service and commercial television news during the 1996 general elections found profound differences in the attitude and approach taken by the two competing news organizations with the public broadcaster being descriptive and non-evaluative and the private broadcaster being analytic and interpretative (Semetko & Canel, 1997). This suggests that news peoples' orientations differ not only between, but also within countries.

While there is some evidence of how British journalists compare in their orientations towards national politics, this is absent when looking at attitudes towards EU politics. One study investigated the British press corps in Brussels (Morgan, 1995), but this study does not allow for any tentative comparative expectations. In the Danish case, virtually nothing is known about the professional culture and attitudes of journalists. In the Dutch case, recent research suggest that Dutch journalists consider 'being analytical' and providing 'interpretation of the news events' important when covering politics (Deuze, 2002).

But this general observation tells us little with respect to journalists' attitudes towards covering European affairs.

In sum, this study of television news and public opinion about European integration takes place in a context of transition. The political system is faced with changes in electoral behavior and internationalization of governance. The media landscape has become a competitive market led by a quest for audiences, also for television news. The journalistic approach to politics has evolved parallel with the changes towards professionalization of politics (Blumler & Gurevitch, 2001). Within these general trends, Britain, Denmark, and the Netherlands represent considerable variation on each of the variables. This is the context in which the findings must be interpreted.

Designing the study

An important impetus for this study is to provide initial insights in to how news media may affect public opinion about European integration. Equally important, however, are the questions how news about European affairs is produced and how European affairs are represented in the media. Both questions have received only limited attention in previous research (Gavin, 2000; Semetko et al., 2000). There is little known about the structure and content of economic and political news in a cross-national perspective, let alone in the specific context of European integration. And there is even less known about the effects such coverage might have on public opinion.

CROSS-NATIONAL COMPARATIVE DESIGN. Our understanding of the relationship between news media and public opinion is largely based on national studies, suffering somewhat from "naive universalism" (Gurevitch & Blumler, 1990, p. 308) by making generalizations of theoretical propositions and single-country data to different political, cultural, and media systems. Comparative research is labeled communication science's "extended and extendable frontier" (Blumler, McLeod & Rosengren, 1992, p. 3) and has gained in scope and frequency, though comparative designs are still the exception rather than the rule.[13]

Comparative research knows several dimensions, most notably time and space. Comparative studies often contrast findings at different levels, including system-level variables, individual-level variables, and aggregated within-system observations (Przeworski & Teune, 1970). Longitudinal comparative research is often faced with severe problems of comparability. The lack of control over data collection poses great challenges. Researchers are often forced to make concessions and establish "equivalencies" rather than comparing "identical measures" (Gurevitch & Blumler, 1990). Comparative research with a cross-national design (comparisons in space and between cultures) is less vulnerable to these problems. Researchers often have more control of the (systematic) collection of data, though this may be a highly resource demanding matter. Research comparing across countries is faced with other pitfalls in the attempt to interpret findings.

The three countries in this study represent interesting cases in terms of public support for European integration as well as in terms of the differences in political systems, media landscape, and journalism. Whereas it has been argued elsewhere that it will be "more productive to compare dissimilar than similar things – and much more fun" (Blumler et al., 1992, p. 280), the perspective applied in this project is that comparing 'pears with apples' may indeed be both interesting and valuable in an exploratory phase, but a certain degree of similarity is required to make comparisons worthwhile and interpretable. Nonetheless, dissimilarity and cross-national variation, as found in the political and broadcasting systems in Britain, Denmark, and the Netherlands is of course an essential premise for any insightful comparison. By using the differences in political and media systems, and the knowledge about aggregate-level public opinion as the backdrop for understanding the findings, in other words as independent systemic variables, the investigation of television news' role in the European integration process is potentially enhanced beyond the level of national parochialism.

MULTI-METHODOLOGICAL APPROACH. Beyond the cross-national design, a second feature of the study is the multi-methodological approach. The project integrates the study of news content with studies of production and effects. Based on investigations of the persuasive effects of media, Hovland (1959) concluded that the effects found depended on the method of measurement. He demonstrated how differently collected data (in that case survey versus experimentation) could be used as evidence of exact opposite hypotheses about the effects of media. He concluded that a test of media effects would need to balance and integrate the strengths of measurement precision and validity offered by each methodological approach (Hovland, 1959).

The plea for multi-methodological designs also refers to investigations combining different phases of communication processes in single studies. Shoemaker and Reese (1996), for example, call for more studies integrating production and effects in an attempt to look at the general picture and not over-simplify the actual communication process. "We cannot fully understand the effects of that version of social reality if we do not understand the forces that shape it" (Shoemaker & Reese, 1996, p. 258). One example of an integrated design is Neuman, Just, and Crigler (1992, p. 25) who used "content analyses to study media coverage of issues and depth interviews, surveys, and experiments to study individual conceptualizations and mediated learning".

The current study draws on interviews and observations in the newsroom to study the production process of news about Europe, content analysis to study the media coverage, and experiments to study the effects of news on public opinion. In the following sections, the various research methods used to address the central research question are introduced. Each method is briefly defined and its relevance to this study is discussed. The specific applications of the different methods as well as the operationalization of key concepts and measures used are discussed in the relevant chapters.

INTERVIEWS. The processes underlying news stories are essential for understanding patterns and conventions found in the content, not only during elections, but also in relation to everyday coverage of political and economic issues. Interviews with journalists and editors and newsroom observations are valuable sources for understanding the journalistic sense-making of political affairs, and interviews provide exclusive information about news production processes, work routines, and attitudes held by newsmakers. This stream of research using newsroom observations and interviews has not been at the core of research agendas. Holtz-Bacha (1999, p. 59) argued that this is because "both journalists and politicians do not appreciate people looking over their shoulder". This observation touches the nerve of research in this tradition. Access to newsrooms is a prerequisite for enhancing our knowledge about news production and the interaction between politicians and the media. Newsroom observations and interviews have merit in themselves, but they are particularly relevant in addition to the 'content and effects research paradigm' that prevails in election studies, because they contribute with specific insights about why election news is shaped as it is.

Most European newsroom observations have been carried out in Britain with studies of the *BBC* coverage of British elections (e.g. Blumler, Gurevitch & Ives, 1978; Blumler, Gurevitch & Nossiter, 1989). Research outside Britain offers comparisons between the production of different national news programs, for example in Germany (Semetko & Schönbach, 1994) and in Spain (Semetko & Canel, 1997). As argued above and elsewhere (Gavin, 2000) there is hardly any previous research available investigating the production of news about European integration-issues. One exception was Noël-Aranda's (1983) survey of broadcasters during the 1979 European elections, but this is the only reference point with regard to the approach by television journalists and editors to news about European integration. The current study makes an attempt to fill some of this gap by drawing on interviews with journalists and editors in a cross-national perspective. 'Europe in the newsroom', the first dimension of this study, is investigated by means of structured interviews with news practitioners in the three countries to examine the organization of the coverage and the key challenges perceived by journalists and editors when reporting Europe, and to investigate how the framing of Europe emerges within the newsroom.

CONTENT ANALYSIS. Content analysis of the news coverage of European affairs is the central component of the 'Europe in the news' dimension of this study. A content analysis is a systematic method of research which aims at "making replicable and valid inferences from data to their context" (Krippendorf, 1980, p. 21). To do so, an appropriate sample of material must be identified and reliable procedures and measures are required.[14]

In this study data were collected during multiple periods in Britain, Denmark, and the Netherlands. The multiple rounds of data collection enable comparisons of the coverage of European affairs during key events, elections, and routine periods. To reliably analyze and compare findings across countries and periods, the content analysis is systematic and deductive in nature. That is to say the features of the content analysis were formulated in advance of the analysis on the basis of the existing literature and consequently applied in the analysis. This approach is different from, for example, an inductive approach where content is used to illustrate latent meaning that emerges during the research and is not based on a priori expectations (McQuail, 2000).

The content analysis identifies general and specific characteristics of the news coverage of European affairs. The analysis serves several purposes in the overall study. First, it provides a systematic, cross-national comparative examination of the news coverage with particular attention paid to the framing of European issues as well as the visibility of themes and the presence of different actors in the news. Second, the content analysis provides a valuable data base and source of inspiration for creating stimulus material to be used in experiments (see below). The findings from the content analysis validate and guide the operationalization of the independent variables in the experiments.

PUBLIC OPINION. Although the premise of most studies in political communication is that news media have the ability to influence public opinion, there is little agreement on the nature of these effects (McQuail, 2000). The relative contribution of news to the formation of public opinion is dependent on other media coverage and available information as well as a variety of audiences' characteristics such as the antecedents of support for European integration discussed above. Opinions consist of newly acquired information meeting a set of predispositions in terms of, for example, values and knowledge. Zaller (1992, p. 6) states it succinctly: "every opinion is a marriage of information and predisposition". Public opinion about Europe is the sum of the influence of new information, as provided for instance in news media, and existing predispositions, values, and knowledge. To investigate the effects of television news on public opinion about European affairs, experiments were conducted.

EXPERIMENTATION. The essence of an experiment is the manipulation of the experimental variable under investigation and observation of changes in a dependent variable. Brown and Melamed (1990, p. v) summarize the key principle of experimentation as "the *manipulation* of a treatment variable (X), followed by observation of a response variable (Y)" (italics in original).[15]

The advantage of experimentation over alternative methods is the knowledge of causation it ideally provides (Jackson, 1992; Kinder & Palfrey, 1993; Neale & Libert, 1986). Correlations found in survey data between, for example, television news viewing and the belief that unemployment is the nation's most important problem, are insufficient to establish a direct causal relationship between the two observed phenomena. By creating different conditions in experiments, the researcher can isolate and test one variable at a time. To assure that any variation found between the conditions is not caused by differences between the individuals in the conditions, randomization procedures are used. By randomly assigning participants to different conditions, the contaminating influence of other variables is ideally ruled out. Differences in the dependent measures can then with more confidence be ascribed to the systematically manipulated, independent variable.[16]

As a result of the extensive degree of control, internal validity in experimentation is high. One potential disadvantage of experiments is the essentially unnatural environment in which experiments often take place. Problems such as test effects, forced exposure, and alterations in behavior and responses are recognized. However, given the absence of research investigating the effects of news coverage of European integration on the individual level, experimentation is an appropriate and valuable method of investigating such effects. Experiments provide a rigorous test of the impact of particular structures in news coverage on, for example, public perceptions and evaluations of European policies.

CHALLENGES IN EXPERIMENTAL RESEARCH WITH TELEVISION NEWS. Beyond the more generally applicable criticisms of experimentation, including forced exposure, artificiality, and low external validity, an additional number of challenges pertain to experimental framing research and experimentation with television news. Scholars are often not able to exercise full control over the creation of the stimulus material, i.e. specifically manipulating the independent variable which implies jeopardizing the experimental design (Reeves & Geiger, 1994; Slater, 1991).

Experimental research on the effect of news frames in *print* news requires attention to the construction of the frames in the composition and wording of a news article. Such studies of effects of press, however, have a number of advantages compared to experimental research involving *television* news. For print media, the production costs and efforts involved in producing stimulus material are lower than for television news. News articles can be drafted by researchers and validated through supervision of, for example, senior journalists (e.g., Valentino, Buhr & Beckman, 2001a). Most importantly, however, the researcher can meet one of the requirements for genuine experimental research: full control over the manipulation of the stimulus material.

Television production, on the contrary, is expensive, labor intensive, and requires specific technical skills. Scholars have addressed these challenges differently in previous research on framing effects. Iyengar, for example, used news stories that were "actual news reports that had been previously broadcast by one of the thee major networks" (Iyengar, 1991, p. 20). Cappella and Jamieson (1997, p. 90) utilized both segments already broadcast, and when these "were clearly of one type or the other, they were left unchanged". For other stories, the experimental manipulation was created by retaining the original visual material, but changing the introduction and voice-over (Cappella & Jamieson, 1997). Yet other scholars have utilized already broadcast stories that were deemed to be representative of a specific news frame (e.g., McLeod & Detenber, 1999; Nelson, Clawson & Oxley, 1997).

The drawback when opting for already broadcast news stories deemed to represent a particular form of framing is that the researcher does not have complete control over the manipulation. While a frame may indeed vary between two news stories, so too may a number of other aspects such as texts, use of footage, valence of the story etc. In other words, a successful isolation of the manipulation of the *one* independent variable, the news frame, is jeopardized because potentially confounding variables are not kept constant.

An important goal of this project is to address the potential shortcomings of previous research by fulfilling the requirements for conducting experimental research with television news. The news stories used in this study are *produced* rather than *selected* as being representative of a particular frame. This ensures full control over the stimulus material, i.e. variation in the manipulation only and exclusion of other, unintended, variation in the material. In addition, it also ensures that participants in the study had not been exposed to the news story in advance of the study. Finally, the experimentally manipulated news story is inserted into a simulated bulletin of the national main evening news which addresses the challenge of using a single stimuli design (Slater, 1991). The specific design of the stimulus material used to address these potential shortcomings in television news research is discussed in chapter 5 and 6.

Outline of the book

In the next chapter (Chapter 2) the concept of framing is introduced. The chapter reviews previous research in the field. A typology and an approach to studying the production, contents, and effects of news in a framing perspective are proposed. Following this chapter, the book continues with its three empirical components. These are reported in chapters 3 to 6. Chapter 3 discusses the production of news about European integration and draws on interviews with newsmakers in Britain, Denmark, and the Netherlands. Chapter 4 reports the findings of a content analysis of the television news coverage of European affairs in the three countries. Chapter 5 reports an experiment conducted to investigate the effects of framing a European issue in the news. Chapter 6 also deals with the effects of framing Europe and reports a second experiment. Chapter 7 summarizes the key findings, attempts to draw both theoretical and practical lessons, and proposes avenues for future research.

CHAPTER 2

Towards an integrated process model of news framing

Introduction

The ability of news to "provide perspectives, shape images [...] and highlight issues" is succinctly stated by Lippmann (1922, p. 226). His observations about the impact of news on our perception of the world from the beginning of the last century have been the natural starting point for many investigations into the influence of news.[1] The mediating role of news is also the focus of this study. With the news media and in particular television being European citizens' most important sources of information about European affairs (Eurobarometer, 56, 2002), news is an essential resource for citizens' thinking about 'Europe'.

One concept giving guidance to investigations of how news influences public opinion that has gained substantial scholarly attention in recent years, is *framing*. Framing is a multi-dimensional concept and has the potential to inform research on news production, contents, and effects (Entman, 1993; McQuail, 1994). The increased scholarly interest in the framing concept is reflected in overviews and meta-analyses that have been published recently (see e.g., D'Angelo, 2002; Reese, Gandy & Grant, 2001; Scheufele, 1999; 2000; Simon, 2001).

A first step in understanding how Europe is framed in the news is to specify the framing process. In this chapter, relevant literature is reviewed and critiqued before an integrated process model of framing is proposed. The chapter consists of six elements. First, the notion of framing is discussed from a multidisciplinary perspective that traces antecedents of framing research in communication science to studies in psychology, political science, and sociology. Second, framing is outlined as a process with interchanging independent and dependent variables. Third, three co-existing traditions and approaches in framing research are identified. This leads, fourthly, to a definition of frames and a review of previous studies of frames in the news. Fifth, existing framing effects hypotheses are summarized and previous effects studies are classified according to a proposed typology. Finally, an integrated approach to studying framing is proposed and specific research questions are formulated.

Framing: An interdisciplinary introduction

Contemporary framing research is indebted to studies in several disciplines. In the following section a number of central studies is revisited to consider the sources of inspiration. The review focuses on key studies with relevance for understanding research on news framing effects.

In his seminal work from a *sociological* tradition, Goffman defined a frame as "an arbitrary slice or cut from the stream of ongoing activity" (Goffman, 1974, p. 10). His work on frame analysis is not concerned with mass media specifically, but discusses the organization and classification of life experiences in general. The use of frames in processing and interpreting unmediated events helps individuals to "locate, perceive, identify, and label" (p. 21).[2] While Goffman's work pertains to the human processing of *real life* experiences by means of frames, other research has focused on how subtle alterations in the *contextual cues* about reality may impact the perception, comprehension, and recollection of events.

In a study of eyewitness testimonials, Loftus (1979) demonstrates how subsequent information supplied about an event significantly alters the retrieval of knowledge and the perception of that event (Loftus, 1979; Loftus, Klinger, Smith & Fielder, 1990). In an experiment participants watched the recordings of a traffic accident and were subsequently asked to estimate the speed of the cars. In one condition, the question read: "About how fast were the cars going when they *smashed* into each other?" and in a second condition, the question read: "About how fast were the cars going when they *hit* each other?" (Loftus, 1979, p. 77, my italics). Not only did the cue in the question influence the perception of actual speed, the information provided (i.e. the framing of the event) also influenced respondents' retrieval of information about this event. In a second post-test, held one week later, respondents exposed to the 'smash condition' reported a much more violent recalled perception of the accident than respondents from the 'hit condition' (Loftus, 1979). This experiment suggests that only minor differences in the provision of information about an event may have major implications for the perception of this event.[3]

The framing research tradition is also indebted to Kahneman and Tversky's (1983) seminal studies demonstrating framing effects on the perception of a pre-defined problem. They sketched two hypothetical scenarios concerning an unusual Asian disease, expected to kill 600 people. In two experiments they offered two scenarios for the participants to choose from: If program A is chosen, 200 people will be saved. If program B is adopted, there is a one-third probability that 600 people will be saved and a two-thirds probability that no people will be saved. 72 percent chose Program A, 28 percent Program B. In the second experiment the scenarios were: If Program C is chosen, 400 people will die. If program D is adopted, there is one-third probability that nobody will die and a two-third probability that 600 people will die. The preference for scenarios was reversed by the framing: Program C was chosen by 22 percent, though the identical Program A was chosen by 72 percent. Program D was chosen by 78 percent, though the identical Program B received only 28 percent. The experiments provide the basis of *prospect theory*, stating that people are risk seeking when considering losses and risk averse when considering gains (Kahneman, Tverksy & Slovic, 1984).

Several studies have replicated Kahneman & Tversky's findings (see e.g. Frisch, 1993; Kuhberger, 1995). Another study further substantiated the evidence of framing effects on preferences by adding a contextual information dimension to Kahneman and Tversky's initial design (Bleiss, Betch & Franzen, 1998). Replicating Kahneman and Tversky's findings, they additionally framed the problem as a 'medical problem' in one condition and as a 'statistical problem' in another condition. Respondents from the 'medical problem' condition replicated earlier findings whereas respondents in the 'statistical problem' condition showed no variation in their preferences. This implies that subtle cues about the *context* may influence the degree of reflection shown by respondents and the extent to which they 'accept' or 'reject' a frame (Bleiss et al., 1998; Wang, 1996). In addition, the study suggests that *issue involvement* is a potential mediator of framing effects (see also Rothman & Salovey, 1997).

Studies in *economic psychology* and *health psychology* have addressed the impact of framing of information on choices and decision-making. Financial decision-making is traditionally considered an area of ultimate *rational* decision-making. One strand of research demonstrates how contextual information in the form of 'anchoring', i.e. providing a point of reference, in situations of uncertainty affects choices (e.g., Fang & Marky, 1982; Stephan, 1998). When estimating uncertain quantities, the provision of anchor values from which the estimation process starts largely defines the range of estimations (Stephan, 1998). Similarly, decision-making about personal health is regarded a high salience issue. Research has demonstrated that gain-framed messages (emphasizing, for example, the benefits of obtaining mammography) were less effective than loss-framed messages (emphasizing the risks of not obtaining mammography) in both immediate post-tests and on behavior (actual obtaining of mammography) (Banks, Salovey, et al., 1995).

As the previous examples suggest, research on framing effects in other disciplines has, despite great diversity in topics explored, methods applied, and operationalization used, shown evidence of framing effects on both information processing, attitudes, decision-making, and behavior. Overall, the perhaps most influential antecedent of framing research in political communication research is the study of schemas. A schema is "a cognitive structure that represents knowledge about a concept or type of stimulus, including its attributes and the relations among those attributes" (Fiske & Taylor, 1991, p. 98). Much research has focused on the use of schema in *person* perception, but findings from social psychology also suggest that schemas affect the processing of information and perception of *objects* (Fiske & Taylor, 1991).

This line of research is very influential for the study of news and public opinion and has contributed to the emergence of different approaches to framing research. Since most citizens rely on the media for information about politics, the framing of issues in the news is a key resource for forming, altering, and expressing opinions and political attitudes.

Framing: A process with independent and dependent variables

In political communication, framing may be perceived as a process that includes *media frames* and *audience frames*, a distinction much akin to Kinder and Sanders' (1996) discussion of 'frames in political discourse' and 'frames as structures of the mind'. Entman (1993) noted that frames have several 'locations', including the communicator, the text, the receiver, and the culture. *Communicators* make ((un-)conscious) judgments about *what* to express and *how* to express something. The *text* contains frames that are expressed in the presence or absence of certain words, phrases, images, and sources. The *receiver*'s thinking, interpretation, and evaluations are influenced by these frames and (s)he makes inferences that "may or may not reflect the frames in the text and the framing intention of the communicator" (Entman, 1993, p. 53). Finally, the broader '*culture*' is the 'stock of commonly invoked frames' which are exhibited in the discourse and thinking of social groups. These components are integral to the process of framing that consists of distinct *frame-building* and *frame-setting* stages (D'Angelo, 2002; de Vreese, 1999; Scheufele, 1999; 2000).[4]

Frame-building refers to the process and factors that influence the structural qualities of news frames. Scheufele (1999) points to factors internal to journalism that determine how journalists and news organizations frame issues (see also Shoemaker & Reese, 1996). Equally important, however, are factors external to journalism. The frame-building process takes place in a continuous interaction between journalists and elites (Gans, 1979; Tuchman, 1978) and social movements (e.g., Cooper, 2002; Snow & Benford, 1992). The outcomes of the frame-building process are the frames manifest in the text. Compared to frame-setting (discussed below), frame-building has been investigated only peripherally (e.g. Durham, 1998).

Frame-setting refers to the interaction between media frames and individuals' prior knowledge and predispositions. Frames in the news may affect learning, interpretation, and evaluation of issues and events. This part of the framing process has been investigated most elaborately, often with the goal to explore the extent to which and under what circumstances audiences reflect and mirror frames made available to them in, for example, the news (see discussion of these studies below). The *consequences* of frame-setting can be considered on the individual and the societal level.[5] Individual-level consequences include altered attitudes about an issue based on exposure to certain news frames. Societal-level consequences refer to, for example, how frames contribute to shaping social processes such as political socialization, decision-making, and collective actions.

In sum, the framing process can be thought of with frames being both the independent variable (IV) and the dependent variable (DV) (Scheufele, 1999). For example, media frames may be studied as the DV, i.e. the outcome of the news production process including organizational pressures, journalistic routines, and elite discourse. Media frames may also be studied as the IV, i.e. the antecedent of audience responses.

Cognitive, critical and constructionist approaches: Three traditions of framing research

Framing has for more than a decade been considered a promising theoretical contribution which, however, lacks structure and paradigmatic unity (Entman, 1993). Much of the conceptual and terminological inconsistency in research on framing within communication science stems from the different approaches taken by researchers to the study of framing. A recent meta-theoretical overview of framing as a research program concluded that most studies – often without explicating this – reside within one of three approaches (D'Angelo, 2002). The three approaches – the *cognitive*, the *critical* and the *constructionist* approach – are adopted from Rosengren's (1993) general classification of different perspectives in the communication science discipline.[6]

The premise of the research in the *cognitive* approach is that by means of activation of certain constructs, news can "encourage particular trains of thoughts about political phenomena" (Price et al., 1997, p. 483). This may lead citizens to make use of the considerations and beliefs emphasized by the news in subsequent judgments (Druckman, 2001a; Nelson et al., 1997). Research in the cognitive approach primarily addresses how, to what extent, and under which circumstances frames in the news find resonance with individuals and lead them to accept and reproduce, negotiate and reinterpret or reject the frame.

In the *constructionist* approach, framing is investigated as part of a system of articulations of public opinion and political socialization (Crigler, 1996; D'Angelo, 2002; Gamson & Modigliani, 1989). Constructionists are less concerned with the information processing effects of news frames, but focus more on frames as one of many resources available when formulating opinions and as part of socialization processes (Gamson, 1992). The idea that individuals negotiate the meaning of frames to derive at their own ideas is emphasized in this perspective.

In the *critical* approach, framing is inherently related to a notion of power. Frames in the news are considered articulations of power embedded in a hegemonic world (Reese & Buckalew, 1995). Scholars in the critical tradition see news selection and news framing as intentional exclusion of some information and intentional inclusion of other (D'Angelo, 2002). Within the critical approach much emphasis is placed on *sponsors* of frames suggesting that, for example, elite frames dominate media coverage.

The distinction and demarcation of the three research approaches serves to understand differences in the terminology used in the framing literature. For example, if we contrast how the role of journalists in the framing process is discussed in the framing literature, framing appears as an incoherent research paradigm. However, when applying the distinction between the different approaches, these differences are put in perspective. Research in the cognitive tradition tends to conceive of journalists and news organizations as responding to journalistic professional norms and values (e.g., Price et al., 1997). Critical scholars see journalists as active players in the frame-building process where political power is not distributed in a pluralist way (e.g., Reese & Buckalew, 1995). Studies in both traditions speak to the role of journalism, but the research agendas vary. The three traditions can be used to locate both existing and new research as tying in with one of the three paradigms.[7]

Frames in the news: broad and narrow definitions

Having established *framing as a process* and having distinguished different traditions and approaches to studying framing, the question still remains what a *frame* is. The variety of definitions of news frames in both the theoretical and empirical literature is considerable. Gitlin (1980, p. 7) defines frames as "persistent patterns of cognition, interpretation, and presentation, of selection, emphasis and exclusion by which symbol-handlers routinely organize discourse". Gamson and Modigliani (1989) refer to frames as 'interpretative packages' that give meaning to an issue. At the core of this package is "a central organizing idea, or *frame*, for making sense of relevant events, suggesting what is at issue" (Gamson & Modigliani, 1989, p. 3, italics in original). By virtue of emphasizing some elements of a topic above others, a frame provides a way to understand an event or issue. In this vein, Cappella and Jamieson (1997, p. 47) suggest that frames activate knowledge, stimulate "stocks of cultural morals and values, and create contexts".

As discussed above, political communication research into framing is indebted to other disciplines. One obvious predecessor is the series of studies by Kahneman and Tversky (e.g., 1984). Their framing manipulation – reversing information by altering the wording of a scenario – was appropriate to explore the psychological process of framing effects, but this definition of framing is rather *narrow* for application in political communication research. Simple question wording differences are not easily compatible with more complex communicative situations and politics (Sniderman & Theriault, 2002). Though some theoretical arguments support the use of the narrow conceptualization in framing research (e.g., Scheufele, 2000; Shah, Domke & Wackmann, 2001), hardly any empirical studies in political communication have investigated the 'reversed information' phenomenon. The vast majority of framing studies, more or less explicitly, apply a *broader* definition of frames. *Conceptually*, a broader notion of news frames is indebted to a definition of a frame as "a central organizing idea or story line that provides meaning to an unfolding strip of events, weaving a connection among them. The frame suggests what the controversy is about, the essence of the issue" (Gamson & Modigliani, 1989).

A broader definition of frames is in line with the thoughts offered by scholars working on specific aspects of the communication of politics (e.g., Cappella & Jamieson, 1997; Entman, 1993; Iyengar, 1991; Kinder & Sanders, 1996, Nelson et al., 1997). In short, a frame, then, is *an emphasis in salience of some aspects of a topic*. This conceptualization is commonly applied in studies of news frames and makes more intuitive sense than a narrow definition of frames because most issues – political and social – cannot be meaningfully reduced to two identical scenarios. Political, economic, and social events and issues are presented to citizens – by journalists and elites – as *alternatives* (Sniderman & Theriault, 2002) whereby issues are constructed and presented with emphasis on different aspects.

Zaller (1992) provides a compelling illustration of such a concept of frames. When discussing oil drilling, for example, citizens are presented with frames such as economic costs of gas prices, unemployment, dependency on foreign energy sources, and environmental considerations. Such frames are alternative ways of defining and constructing an issue, endogenous to the political and social world, and distinguish themselves from a narrow conception of framing.

A typology of news frames

While newsmakers may employ many different frames in their coverage, scholars agree that in spite of this abundance in choice in how to tell and construct stories, distinctive and particular frames dominate. In order to synthesize previous research, a general typology with reference to the nature and content of the frame is suggested here. A useful distinction can be made between *'issue-specific news frames'* and *'generic news frames'* (see also de Vreese, 1999; de Vreese, Peter, & Semetko, 2001). Issue-specific frames pertain only to specific topics or news events. Generic frames transcend thematic limitations and can be identified in relation to different topics, some even over time and in different cultural contexts.[8]

The advantage of an issue-specific approach to the study of news frames is that it allows for a profound level of specificity and details relevant to the event or issue under investigation. This advantage, however, is inherently disadvantageous. The high degree of detail and issue-sensitivity make analyses drawing on issue-specific frames difficult to generalize, compare, and use as empirical evidence for theory building. The lack of comparability has led researchers to "too easily finding evidence for what they are looking for" and to contribute to "one of the most frustrating tendencies in the study of frames and framing [being] the tendency for scholars to generate a unique set of frames for every study" (Hertog & McLeod, 2001, pp. 150-151).

In the following section, studies of frames in the news are reviewed and classified.[9] The review of studies of frames in the news is not exhaustive. Framing is a 'buzzword' in political communication and during the past years, numerous studies making use of the term frames have appeared.[10] Table 2.1. classifies previous content analyses of frames in the news according to the distinction between issue-specific and generic frames and according to the focus of the study (press versus television news).

Table 2.1. Overview content analyses of frames in the news

Medium	Issue-specific News Frames	Generic News Frames
Press	Durham, 1998	D'Haenes & de Lange, 2001
	Entman, 1991	Lawrence, 2000
	Jasperson et al., 1998	Pan & Kosicki, 1993
	Simon & Xenos, 2000	Patterson, 1993
Television	Norris, 1995	Iyengar, 1991
	Mendelson, 1993	De Vreese et al., 2001
Both	Gamson & Modigliani, 1989	Cappella & Jamieson, 1997
	Martin & Oshagan, 1997	Neuman et al., 1992
	Shah et al., 2002	Semetko & Valkenburg, 2000

ISSUE-SPECIFIC NEWS FRAMES. One study of issue-specific news frames focused on the presentation of US national budget deficits in the press (Jasperson et al., 1998). Drawing on a content analysis of several major US newspapers four frames were identified, and these were labeled 'talk', 'fight', 'impasse', and 'crisis'. The frames deduced were highly issue-sensitive and pertained specifically to the chronology of the topic examined. Another example is Entman's study of the news media coverage of two airline accidents. He demonstrated how a US accident was framed in terms of "tragedy" and "mistake" whereas a comparable Soviet accident was framed in terms of "attack" and "deliberate" (Entman, 1991, pp. 18-19).

Two studies investigated US news media framing of labor conflicts. In one study of press and network news coverage of the closing of a General Motors plant, it was found that a 'no option' frame dominated the news coverage above an 'alternative frame' that challenged and offered alternatives to the closing of the plant (Martin & Oshagan, 1997). In an analysis of elite US newspapers' framing of a national labor strike, it was concluded that a 'disruption' frame dominated the news coverage of the strike above, for example, a 'bargaining' frame (Simon & Xenos, 2000).

In the realm of elections, Shah, Watts, Domke, and Fan (2002) identified three frames recurrent in the news during the final stages of the Clinton presidency. They identified 'Clinton behavior scandal', 'Conservative attack scandal', and 'Liberal response scandal'. Mendelson (1993) identified three frames used in the television news coverage of the 1993 Canadian general election. He suggested 'tactical motivations', 'performance', and 'leaders' moods' as the most prominent frames in the election coverage. These frames reflected themes present in this specific election campaign.

Some of these studies of frames in the news move beyond the level of issue specificity. Elements of the frames in Mendelson's (1993) study, for example, may also apply to other situations and contexts than the Canadian election. Similarly, Gamson and Modigliani's (1989) analysis of network news broadcasts, news magazines, and newspapers identified a 'progress media package'. This package "frames the nuclear power issue in terms of the society's commitment to technological development and economic growth" (p. 4). They argue that the dominance and persistency of the progress frame is due to the frame's resonance with a larger cultural theme of technological progress. In addition to the 'progress package', which Gamson and Modigliani (1989) specified prior to doing their study, they also found media packages such as 'public accountability' and 'runaway', which emerged during the analysis process. A final example is an investigation of Cold War and post-Cold War US television news where Norris (1995) identified a 'cold war' news frame. This frame "cued journalists and viewers about friends and enemies" (Norris, 1995, p. 357) by suggesting stereotyped, interpretative categories in which international power struggles could be placed. The study demonstrated how a dominant news frame as the 'cold war frame' evolved over time, creating a 'frame vacuum' after the end of the Cold War.

The frames suggested by Gamson and Modigliani (1989), Mendehlson (1993), and Norris (1995) are all examples of issue-related, context bound frames. However, given the persistency of, for example, the 'progress frame' and the 'cold war frame', we take a step beyond the purely single issue-specific news frame towards a more *generic* notion of news frames.

GENERIC NEWS FRAMES. Generic news frames are general and not confined to a specific issue. This increases the possibilities for making comparisons. A potential shortcoming of generic news frames is that certain issue-specific details may less easily be captured in an analysis. However, generic news frames that are structural and inherent to, for example, the conventions of journalism may prove more useful for understanding general features of news reporting beyond the issue-specific limits. Studies examining generic news frames essentially fall into two categories. The first group of studies concentrates on the coverage of politics, in particular election campaigns.

Cappella and Jamieson (1996, 1997) investigated the consequences of strategically framed news on political cynicism. Strategic news is defined as news that (1) focuses on winning and losing, (2) includes the language of war, games, and competition, (3) contains 'performers, critics and audiences', (4) focuses on candidate style and perceptions, and (5) gives weight to polls and candidate standings (Jamieson, 1992). According to Cappella and Jamieson (1997), strategic news dominates American news coverage of not only election campaigns, but also of policy issues. Their study, however, provides only a limited discussion of the design of the content analysis of news media reports, which forms the basis of their conclusions concerning the dominance of the strategy frame. In addition, they do not address whether some of the five elements constituting the strategy frame are more or less prevalent in the news and the study does not offer any discussion as to whether the strategy frame is more or less prominent in relation to certain topics. It is therefore difficult to estimate the extent to which the frame pervades US news coverage of politics.

Lawrence (2000) elaborated on the strategy frame and investigated the conditions under which the strategy frame is likely to emerge. She found that the news frame is most likely to be applied to public policy issues when discussed in national election news and when Washington policymakers are engaged in conflicts. The strategy frame is less likely to be applied when public policy issues are discussed in news about state-level political debates (Lawrence, 2000).

The focus on winning and losing and polls bears close resemblance to Patterson's (1993) discussion of the use of 'game schema' in election news.[11] Game refers to strategies and (predictions of) electoral success, emphasizing candidates' position in the electoral race. Patterson (1993) provides evidence of the historical increase in the use of the game or horse race frame in the press coverage of US elections from 1960 until 1992.[12]

An often-cited study of the presence and effects of generic news frames is Iyengar's (1991) investigation of the 'episodic' and 'thematic' news frames. In an analysis of the US network coverage of social issues such as poverty, crime, and unemployment from 1981 to 1986 he found that daily news coverage was strongly biased towards an *episodic* interpretation in which news depicts social issues as limited to events only and not placed in a broader interpretation or context (the *thematic* frame). Iyengar (1991) suggested that norms and standards within news organizations and news production reinforce episodic framing. This practice "simplifies complex issues to the level of anecdotal evidence" (Iyengar, 1991, pp. 136-137) and induces a topical, disorganized, and isolated, rather than general and contextual, understanding of public affairs and social issues.[13]

The categories applied in Iyengar's content analysis to identify thematic and episodic focus in news stories are not mutually exclusive. As Iyengar notes (1991, p. 145), "very few stories were exclusively thematic or episodic", and though news stories tended to 'tilt clearly' in the direction of one or the other frame, the content measures suffer from imprecision. A further problem is the fact that the content analysis was based on the Vanderbilt abstracts with some real news stories from *one* network analyzed in addition to validate the analysis. Utilizing the Vanderbilt archive for content analyses aiming at assessing subtleties in media content has been criticized for lack of depth (Althaus, Edy & Phalen, 2001). Given these gaps in the content analysis it is difficult to appropriately assess the merit of the content analytic distinction between episodic and thematic news. This is problematic since this analysis forms the core of the argument of the effects of the episodic and thematic mode of news coverage (see below).

A second group of studies also shares a conceptualization of news frames as being 'detached' from any specific issue. These studies link news frames to more general features of news coverage such as journalistic conventions, norms, and news values. Though not referring to 'generic news frames', Neuman et al. (1992), based on in-depth interviews with audience members, derived a typology of frames used by the audience when discussing current affairs.

They found that the frames deduced from the interviews were also present in the news media coverage of a series of current issues. In their exploratory study they identified 'human impact', 'powerlessness', 'economics', 'moral values', and 'conflict' as common frames used by the media and the audience (Neuman et al., 1992). The human impact frame focused on descriptions of individuals and groups affected by an issue. The powerlessness frame referred to "the dominance of forces over weak individuals or groups" (1992, p. 67). The economics frame reflected "the preoccupation with 'the bottom line', profit and loss" (1992, p. 63). The moral values frame referred to the often indirect reference to morality and social prescriptions by e.g. including certain quotations or inferences. The conflict frame referred to the journalistic practice of reporting stories of clashing interpretation and it was found to fit well with news media's "game interpretation of the political world as an ongoing series of contests, each with a new set of winners and losers" (1992, p. 64). These frames were found in relation to different issues which suggest that the frames are more generally applicable than issue-specific news frames.[14]

Neuman et al.'s (1992) study refers to the framing concept as part of the journalistic packaging of events in a broader social and historical context as well as individuals' attempt to interpret news in terms of their own lives. The study, however, does not provide a description of the measures that were used to assess and compare the framing of different issues in television news, newspapers, and magazines and there is no discussion of the reliability of these measures.

Semetko and Valkenburg (2000) developed this line of research and identified five generic news frames: 'conflict', 'human interest', 'attribution of responsibility', 'morality' and 'economic consequences'. Each of the five frames was measured by multi-item scales to assess the relative visibility of the different news frames. The conflict frame emphasizes conflict between individuals, groups, institutions or countries. The human interest frame brings a human face, an individual's story, or an emotional angle to the presentation of an event, issue or problem. The responsibility frame presents an issue or problem in such a way as to attribute responsibility for causing or solving to either the government or to an individual or group. The morality frame interprets an event or issue in the context of religious tenets or moral prescriptions. The economic consequences frame, finally, presents an event, problem or issue in terms of the economic consequences it will have on an individual, group, institution, region or country.

The study found that the attribution of responsibility frame was the most commonly used followed by the conflict and economic consequences frames based on an analysis of national print and television news coverage surrounding an EU summit with European Heads of Government (Semetko & Valkenburg, 2000). A subsequent study of Dutch regional newspapers' framing of asylum seekers using the same indicators found that the responsibility, human interest, conflict, and economic consequences frames were all used by the newspapers though with varying intensity (d'Haenens & de Lange, 2001).

Expanding the research on generic news frames to a cross-nationally comparative setting, de Vreese et al. (2001) found that although the conflict and economic consequences frames were used in television news in Britain, Germany, the Netherlands, and Denmark, national news organizations provided a significant local or national 'spin' to the news stories. This is important because it links the generic quality of the frames with a specific resonance that in this case was national in focus. The use of similar news frames in different political and journalistic cultures nevertheless emphasizes the *generic* nature of such news frames.[15]

Identifying frames in the news

Previous research on frames in the news shares little conceptual ground and most studies draw on tentative working definitions or operational definitions of frames designed for the purpose of the specific study. Therefore there is little consensus as how to identify frames in the news. Most studies, however, address how frames in the news are measured, though in some exceptions this is not sufficiently explicated (e.g., Neuman et al., 1992). One approach is *inductive* in nature and refrains from analyzing news stories with a priori defined news frames in mind (e.g., Gamson 1992: Neuman et al., 1992). Frames emerge from the material during the course of analysis. Studies taking an inductive approach have been criticized for relying on too small a sample and for being difficult to replicate (Hertog & McLeod, 2001; Semetko & Valkenburg, 2000). A second approach is rather *deductive* in nature and investigates frames that are defined and operationalized prior to the investigation.

Empirical scholars in political communication research have argued in favor of applying concise, a priori defined operationalizations of frames in content analyses. Cappella and Jamieson (1997) state that considering *any* production feature of verbal or visual texts as a candidate for news frames is a too broad view. They suggest four criteria that a frame must meet. First, a news frame must have identifiable conceptual and linguistic characteristics. Second, it should be commonly observed in journalistic practice. Third, it must be possible to distinguish the frame reliably from other frames. Fourth, a frame must have representational validity (i.e. be recognized by others) and not be merely a figment of a researcher's imagination (Cappella & Jamieson, 1997, pp. 47; 89).

When working with a deductive approach, the relevant question is: *what* (which components) in a news story constitutes a frame? Entman (1993, p. 52) suggested that frames in the news can be examined and identified by "the presence or absence of certain keywords, stock phrases, stereotyped images, sources of information and sentences that provide thematically reinforcing clusters of facts or judgments". Along these lines Shah et al. (2002, p. 367) refer to "choices about language, quotations, and relevant information". Gamson and Modigliani (1989) identify 'framing devices' that condense information and offer a 'media package' of an issue. They identify (1) metaphors, (2) exemplars, (3) catch-phrases, (4) depictions, and (5) visual images as framing devices. Pan & Kosicki (1993) suggested dividing news texts into four empirically operationalizable dimensions. First, a 'syntactical structure' including for example the classic inverted pyramid of news stories. Second, a 'script', such as for example the dramaturgy of news stories. Third, a 'thematic structure' that consists of logically related propositions. Fourth and finally, Pan & Kosicki (1993) suggest 'rhetorical structures' which include Gamson and Modigliani's (1989) five framing devices. The most comprehensive empirical approach is offered by Tankard (2001, p. 101) who suggests a list of 11 framing mechanism or focal points for identifying and measuring news frames: (1) headlines, (2) subheads, (3) photos, (4) photo captions, (5) leads, (6) source selection, (7) quotes selection, (8) pull quotes, (9) logos, (10) statistics and charts, and (11) concluding statements and paragraphs.

In sum, scholars within the empirical approach to measuring frames agree that frames are *specific textual and visual elements* or 'framing devices'. These elements are essentially different from the remaining news story which may be considered *core news facts*. Price et al. (1997, p. 488) operationalized a frame by varying "introductory and concluding paragraphs to establish a unique journalistic frame" with information exclusive to the frame while the other paragraphs in the news articles were kept identical. In the same vein, Neuman et al. (1992, p. 126) in their content analysis divided news articles in to sections containing 'frames' and sections containing 'facts'. The distinction between *core elements* and *frame-carrying elements* has effectively been applied in the operationalization of news frames in most studies of framing effects (e.g., Cappella & Jamieson, 1997; Iyengar, 1991, Price et al., 1997; Valentino et al., 2001a; Valkenburg et al., 1999) and will be explored further in this study (see Chapter 5 and 6).

Framing effects: A typology

In this section the primary attention shifts from the *framing* of issues in the news to the *effects of frames*. An individual's way of understanding, interpreting, and evaluating an issue or problem is now the dependent variable, typically investigated in a study with media frames as the independent variable. To organize and systematize previous research a typology is proposed that distinguishes between effects of frames on (1) cognitive information processing, (2) attitudes, affection, and opinions, and (3) behavior (Fishbein & Ajzen, 1975; McLeod, Kosicki & McLeod, 1994; 2002).[16] Previous research has documented framing effects on cognitive and affective dependent measures, political attitudes, political evaluations, and vote intention. Table 2.2 provides a brief introduction to key findings of framing effects studies. These studies are discussed in detail below.

Table 2.2. Overview of framing effects studies

Effect type	Key findings
Cognitive responses / information processing:	
	• Frames may affect the topical focus and evaluative valence of thoughts generated in response to a news story (Price et al., 1997),
	• Frames may influence the kind and direction of thoughts produced by news readers by eliciting thoughts mirroring the frames used in the news (Valkenburg et al., 1999),
	• Frames may affect individuals' interpretations of election campaigns (Rhee, 1997)
Attitudes / evaluations:	
	• Frames may generate cynicism about election campaigns and politics (Cappella & Jamieson, 1996, 1997),
	• Frames may alter public opinion towards trade organizations and health care (Cobb & Kuklinski, 1997),
	• Frames may alter the perception of national economic issues (Jasperson et al., 1998),
	• Frames may influence citizens' perception of an issue, including the level of tolerance towards the Ku Klux Klan (Nelson et al., 1997),
	• Frames may impact the ways people ascribe responsibility for social, political, and economic problems (Iyengar, 1991; 1996),
	• Frames may affect public reactions towards a social protest (McLeod & Detenber, 1999)
Behavior (intention)[17]:	
	• Frames may affect the type of decision-making strategy voters employ when choosing candidates (Shah et al., 1996),
	• Frames may marginally depress turnout intention for citizens with lower educational levels (Valentino et al., 2001a).

Framing effects: a review of the literature

The vast majority of studies investigating effects of framing rely on experimentation. However, a few *survey* and *interview* based studies have investigated news framing effects. A seminal study by Graber (1988) drawing on *depth-interviews* with a panel consisting of 21 persons selected to cover a range of standard demographics (as well as high and low interest in politics and easy and difficult access to media) functioned as an empirical baseline to identify a number of recurrent schemata used by citizens to 'process the news'. This study may be considered a predecessor of later framing studies. The 'thinking categories' found by Graber (1988) have several similarities with the audience frames identified by Neuman et al. (1992). The 'human interest/empathy' thinking category suggested by Graber can be equated with Neuman et al.'s 'human impact' frame, Graber's 'cultural norm' to their 'morality' frame, and

Graber's 'institution judgments' to their 'powerlessness' frame. The 'human interest/empathy' category, for instance, described the incentive for citizens to follow news to "learn about the personal lives, joys, tragedies, and varied activities of other people" while processing stories with a direct human relevance (Graber, 1988, p. 213). Graber identified her thinking categories in relation to several issues in the news which suggest that people may make use of similar strategies when processing different types of news.

Both studies emphasize that media reports are one of several resources available to citizens when thinking and talking about politics. Neither of the studies assesses in detail the specific relationship between news content and, for example, audience attitudes. The designs and sample sizes do not allow making a compelling link between, for example, exposure and attention to specific media contents and subsequent cognitive and attitudinal responses. Such a design could have answered questions such as whether citizens that rely heavily on the media for information make more use of this resource than other citizens when making sense of the political world.

Utilizing *peer/focus group discussions*, Gamson (1992, 1996) in his work on framing suggested that media discourse is one among several resources that citizens use in constructing political issues. He specifically investigated frames as mental constructs created to understanding current issues. Persons may choose different resource strategies on which to base their thinking including 'cultural resources', 'personal experiences', and 'media discourse'. For some issues media induced information play a more important role than 'personal resources', suggesting that issue type may be an important moderating factor of framing effects.

Gamson (1996) and Gamson and Modigliani (1989) stress that citizens employ multiple resource strategies, drawing on media discourse, popular wisdom, and experienced knowledge, when making sense of issues in the news. This approach is closely related to Graber (1988) and Neuman et al. (1992) who point out that any effects of frames is likely to be moderated by individuals' existing predispositions, socialization, and prior knowledge which may lead citizens to either accept, reinterpret, or ignore the frames offered by the media.

Turning to *survey* based investigations of framing effects, one study, based on a two year long content analysis linked with 12 opinion polls, concluded that changes in attribute salience in the news coverage of the national US budget was followed by changes in public opinion (Jasperson et al., 1998). More specifically they found that an increase in the 'fight frame' (a frame that focused on the conflict between political elites) boosted the public's perception of the salience of the issue (Jasperson et al., 1998). In an innovative study of public approval of US president Clinton, Shah et al. (2002) linked data from analyses of news coverage to public opinion data on support for the president. The study suggested that the media framing of the scandal – which was specific to the chronology of the situation – explained changes in mass evaluations of Clinton during this presidency. In particular the framing of the scandal as 'Conservative attacks' led to a backlash and explained the sustained support for Clinton.

EXPERIMENTAL FRAMING RESEARCH. Experimentation is the most commonly used method in framing studies. Below experimental studies of effects of frames in the news are discussed. Appendix 2.1 provides a more detailed overview of the studies. The appendix specifies the design, independent (experimentally manipulated), and dependent variables, and summarizes the main findings of each study. Table 2.3 provides a brief overview of experimental framing effects studies. The distinction between different types of effects (cognitive information processing, attitudinal, and behavioral) and different types of news frames (issue-specific versus generic) is used.

Table 2.3. Overview experimental news framing effects research

		FRAMES	
		Issue-specific	*Generic*
EFFECT	Cognitive / information processing	Domke et al., 1998 Domke et al., 1999 Druckman, 2001b Nelson et al., 1997 Nelson & Oxley, 1999 Shah et al., 2001	Cappella & Jamieson, 1997 Rhee, 1997 Tewksbury et al., 2000 Valentino et al., 2001ab Valkenburg et al., 1999
	Attitudinal / Affective	Cobb & Kuklinski, 1997 Druckman, 2001b McLeod & Detenber, 1999 Nelson et al., 1997 Nelson & Oxley, 1999 Shah et al., 1996 Tewksbury et al., 2000	Cappella & Jamieson, 1997 Iyengar, 1991 Price et al., 1997 Valentino et al., 2001ab
	Behavioral (intentional)	Shah et al., 2001	Valentino et al., 2001a

Note. Studies with multiple table entries indicate dependent measures on different levels.[18]

EFFECTS OF ISSUE-SPECIFIC NEWS FRAMES. Turning first to studies investigating the *effects of issue-specific news frames,* a series of experiments investigated the ability of news frames to influence respondents' degree of tolerance towards the Ku Klux Klan. Nelson et al. (1997) tested this in two experiments with a Ku Klux Klan group's right to rally framed as either a 'free speech issue' or a 'disruption of public order'. In the first experiment un-doctored versions of television news stories taped directly from real news programs were used. Participants who viewed the free speech television news story expressed more tolerance towards the KKK than participants who watched the public order story. In the second experiment, relying on the same design, constructed newspaper articles allowing full control over the stimulus material were used. The results of the second experiment were supportive of the first and the authors concluded that the two studies show how alternatives in the journalistic framing of an issue "can exert appreciable influence on citizens' perception of the issue" (Nelson et al., 1997, p. 576).

Drawing on the same design, Druckman (2001b) replicated Nelson et al.'s (1997) findings. He argues that certain considerations and beliefs are made more important by frames in the news and consequently used by citizens when making evaluations. Specifically it was found that a newspaper story framed in terms of 'free speech' consequently made free speech and opposing racism the most salient considerations for expressing the degree of tolerance towards the KKK. Conversely, participants exposed to a news story framed in terms of 'disruption of public order', rated public safety and opposing racism as the most salient beliefs when making their assessments of tolerance.[19]

Nelson and Oxley (1999) manipulated news frames in a dispute over land development. Contrasting an 'environmental' versus an 'economic' framing of the issue, they found that participants exposed to the economic frame considered economic beliefs more important which lead to endorsement of the land development plan. Conversely, participants exposed to the environmental frame considered environmental beliefs more important which lead to an unfavorable evaluation of the plan.

In a series of experiments, Shah and colleagues found that frames had significant influence on voters' issue interpretation and subsequently on their decision-making strategy for choosing electoral candidates (Domke et al., 1998; Domke et al., 1999; Shah et al., 1996; Shah et al., 2001). More specifically they found that news framed in an 'ethical' rather than a 'material' way lead to an ethical interpretation of the issue of health care. They also found evidence of a "strong, consistent, and robust relationship between an ethical issue interpretation and use of a 'non-compensatory' decision-making strategy" whereby candidates that do not share participants' values are discarded (Domke et al., 1998, p. 315). The experimental studies make a direct link between media frames and voting intention. The studies make use of an 'ethical' frame which, for example in the case of abortion, meant pitting "the sanctity of an unborn child's life against the personal liberty of a woman to control her body and destiny" (Domke et al., 1998, p. 306). While this frame, as the authors emphasize, has considerable appeal given the 'layman' nature of the frame, the studies do not provide any evidence or discussion of the use of the frame in actual news reports. The important shortcoming is that we cannot infer from these effects studies whether the 'ethical' and 'material' frames are in fact, in the words of Cappella and Jamieson (1997, p. 47), "commonly observed in journalistic practice".

A study by McLeod & Detenber (1999) introduced a new dimension to experimental research on the effects of news frames. Rather than contrasting the effects of competing frames on an issue, they varied the level of presence of *one* news frame across their experimental conditions. Investigating the balance of status quo and protest group support in the framing of a social protest, they found a negative relationship between emphasis on social status quo in the news frame and public criticism of protesters. The study relies on already broadcast news stories as the stimulus material, but, as the authors acknowledge, the news reports varied in ways other than the framing of the event which makes it difficult to attribute the findings to the news frames exclusively.

Another study also addresses the effects of *weight* given to a frame. At the level of local politics, the effects of an 'advocate frame' – that is a frame advocating the viewpoint of an interest organization – were investigated in a news story about the size and regulation of local hog farms (Tewksbury, Jones, Peske, Raymond & Vig, 2000). Contrasting the effects of moderate versus strong degree of presence of the advocate frame, the study suggested that the *weight* given to a frame in the news was reflected in students' interpretation of the issue. Participants exposed to the strongest framing condition showed the strongest effects. The study included a delayed post-test three weeks after initial exposure and found significant, though muted effects of exposure to the frame used in the experiment.

The common element in the studies discussed above is the use of exposure to *issue-specific frames* as the independent variable. The studies investigate the effects on a number of dependent measures, but the frames that drive these effects pertain specifically to the issue in question. While this evidence tells us much about the effects of news and information in a particular context, none of the studies were designed to address whether the effects on, for example, issue interpretation and evaluation can be expected to generalize to other situations.

EFFECTS OF GENERIC NEWS FRAMES. Turning next to studies investigating *effects of generic news frames*, Cappella & Jamieson (1996, 1997) investigated the effects of strategically framed news on public cynicism about politics. In a series of experiments, carried out during the 1991 Philadelphia mayoral race and the 1993 health care reform debate in the US, participants received news about the election and the debate framed as problems and proposed solutions (issue framing) or news emphasizing how a candidate's position either provided an advantage or disadvantage in securing votes (strategy framing). Overall, they found that participants watching news segments framed strategically reported higher levels of political cynicism.

The study is broad in scope and involves different political contexts (mayoral election campaign and health care debates) and different media (newspapers and television). The study has been criticized for relying on unconventional measures of political cynicism (e.g., Valentino et al., 2001a), but Cappella and Jamieson (1997) argue that unlike more commonly used measures of cynicism – such as those used in the American National Election Studies – their items tap cynical responses to politics and not general measures of trust. The study investigated the effects of the strategy frame, but it remains vague with regard to which elements of the strategy frame were manipulated. The strategy frame consists of five elements (see discussion of news frames above), but the stimulus material used in the experimental studies were already broadcast news stories that were either left unchanged or edited with some alterations to the audio-track if the story was not deemed to be a clear example of the strategy frame. The study is consequently not able to assess *which* aspects of the strategy frame cause the political cynicism.

Drawing on data from the Cappella and Jamieson (1997) studies, Rhee (1997) investigated the effects of strategic versus issue news coverage of the 1991 Philadelphia election. He found that strategic news coverage of the campaign, focusing on the strategic electoral drama, influenced audiences' interpretation and perception of the campaign. Issue coverage, focusing on substantial elements of the campaign, generated more responses focusing on content aspects of the campaign. Rhee (1997) also concluded that not only the frames in the news contributed to shaping audiences perception of the campaign. Respondents' level of knowledge was also found to have explanatory value so that knowledgeable participants were more likely to make use of the frame suggested by the news when formulating their perceptions of the campaign.

A further exploration of the effects of the strategy news frame suggested that the strategy frame fuels negative campaign evaluations and reduces recall of information in the news (Valentino et al., 2001b). Data from the same study also suggested that the strategy frame depresses vote intention and feelings of civic duty for citizens with low levels of education, as well as reduces trust and sentiments of political meaningfulness for non-partisan citizens (Valentino et al., 2001a).

Iyengar (1991, 1996) focused on the effects of episodic and thematic framing in network news coverage of five current issues (crime, terrorism, poverty, unemployment, racial issues). Based on a series of experiments, he tested the impact of such framing on the attribution of responsibility for these issues. He compared news on unemployment, for example, as a social and political phenomenon (thematic framing) with news on unemployment that emphasized the shortcomings of unemployed individuals (episodic framing). It was found that episodic news influenced the ways people ascribed responsibility for social, political, and economic problems, so that episodic news led people to attribute responsibility to individuals whereas thematic news fuelled system-level attributions of responsibility (Iyengar, 1991, 1996).

Turning to studies investigating the effects of generic frames with a link to journalism, Price et al. (1997) explored the differential impact of *three* news frames: 'conflict', 'human interest', and 'personal consequences'. The authors conclude that "by activating some ideas, feelings, and values rather than others, then, the news can encourage particular trains of thought" (Price et al., 1997, p. 3). In two experiments the effects of these news frames on thoughts and feelings were investigated. Students responded to a fictitious newspaper story about state funding of universities. All stories contained the same core of information, but varied in their opening and closing paragraphs according to the frame employed. Post-test thought-listing procedures revealed that the different news frames used in the stimulus material significantly affected both the topical focus and evaluative implications of the thoughts generated.

An experimental study elaborated on this research, and served as a pilot study to the studies discussed in this book (Valkenburg et al., 1999). The study investigated the impact of four different news frames (conflict, human interest, attribution of responsibility, and economic consequences) in relation to two different real-life issues. One story was about an issue that was more salient (increasing crime rates), and the other was about an issue that was less salient (European integration). The study showed that the way in which a news story was framed had a significant and consistent influence on the kind of thoughts produced by participants. Participants who had just read a story framed in terms of human interest, for example, emphasized emotions and individual implications in their responses. Similarly, respondents who had just read a story framed in terms of economic consequences focused on costs and financial implications in their thoughts (Valkenburg et al., 1999).

Framing: Towards an integrated approach of studying news

The chapter both serves to organize and summarize a diverse research field and to describe the contours of the key theoretical concept for this study. Thus far the chapter has (1) reviewed the antecedents of framing research in other disciplines, (2) outlined different approaches to studying framing, (3) explicated the differences and consequences of narrow and broad definitions of frames, (4) described framing as process, (5) developed and subsequently applied a typology of frames in the news, and (6) proposed a typology for an overview of framing effects. It enables us to place the approach taken to framing in this study in the light of these considerations.

The current study is an attempt to integrate the entire process of framing into a single project. The study links news production, content, and effects investigations and thereby follows the recommendations made in previous reviews of the framing literature (Entman, 1993; Pan & Kosicki, 1993; Scheufele, 1999; 2000). Indeed, considering framing as a *process* involving both production, content, and effects is a perspective gaining support in the literature as McLeod et al. (2002, p. 230) recently concluded: "For framing to meet its full potential, audience research needs to be tied carefully to the work of journalists in meaningful ways". To study the process of framing in its entirety, framing must be conceptualized as both dependent and independent variables and must be examined in the newsroom of news organizations, as frames in the news, and as expressed public opinion.

The study is indebted to the *cognitive paradigm*. Most studies within this approach focus primarily on the frame-setting phase of framing and generally pay less attention to elaborate content analyses or investigations of frame-building. However, the process by which frames in the news come into existence is the antecedent for understanding any of the consequences frames may have. The production of news determines the frames in the news so that the production process is an independent variable for news frames as dependent variables. News frames in turn are resources available to audiences and can thus be seen as independent variables for dependent audience responses. Central to the perspective on framing in this study is an *integrated process model of news framing* which is discussed in the next sections.

Figure 2.1. An integrated process model of news framing

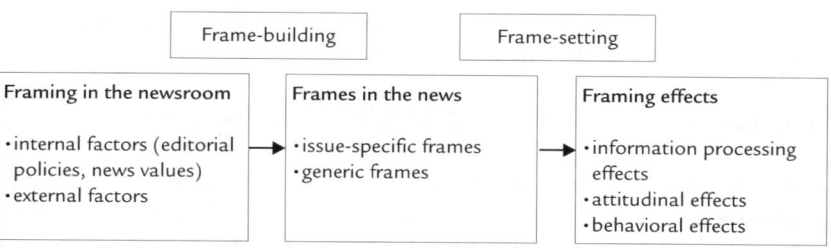

FRAMING IN THE NEWSROOM. 'Framing in the newsroom' is the starting point. With journalists forced to select and prioritize to tell a story in the news, framing plays a central role in the production of news. Journalists have to tell a story within a limited time or space, so they need certain frames to simplify and give meaning to the flow of events, and to keep audiences interested. Frames guide journalists, editors, and news executives to structure and organize news stories and framing helps audiences to make sense of the information provided.

As McQuail (1994, p. 355) notes "much news is presented within frameworks of meaning which derive from the way news is gathered and processed". Standard organizational procedures, work routines, and news values all function as 'guidelines' in the quest for fast and regular news output. News in itself has little value unless embedded in a meaningful framework which organizes and structures it. A news frame is a template for journalists to compose a news story in order to optimize audience accessibility.

The process of news production is influenced by factors both internal and external to news organizations and journalism. *Internally*, norms and values of individual journalists, specific media routines, and organizational constraints are important (see Bennett, 1996; Schudson, 1995; Shoemaker & Reese, 1996; Tuchman, 1978; Weaver and Wilhoit, 1996). *External* factors for understanding the production of news content and the way news is presented are ownership, funding, political affiliation, and the degree of competition in the news market. A key factor is also the role played by, for instance, interest groups, spin-doctors, and officials. They contribute to the process of message framing as they give stories a "spin" congenial with their goals (e.g., Esser et al., 2001; Neuman et al., 1992). Previous research in this field, however, tends to follow a static input-output model in which, for example, the arguments put forward by interest organizations is compared to the portrayal in the news (e.g., Cooper, 2002). Such studies do not analyze the *process* in which this interaction takes place and thereby neglect the role of news production.

Internally, in the selection and packaging process, news values play a central role. Stephens (1980) (c.f. Shoemaker & Reese, 1996, p. 111) identifies 'human interest', 'conflict', and 'controversy' as central news values. McManus (1994, p. 119) lists 'human interest', 'conflict', 'proximity', 'consequence', and 'unusualness' as important criteria in his synthesis of research on newsworthiness. Much along these lines, Price and Tewksbury (1997) identify 'conflict', 'shared narratives' (e.g. Good versus Evil), 'human interest', 'proximity', and 'timeliness' as key news values. Consequently, an event containing conflict, controversy and/ or proximity is likely to be covered by a news organization.

In this study, the frame-building part of the integrated process model of framing is closely linked to the news selection process. A link is made between news values and framing. News values guide which events and issues are considered sufficiently newsworthy for media attention. From previous studies of news production there is little evidence to provide direction to expectations about the frame-building process in the newsroom. However, news values not only influence the *selection* of events and issues, they also affect the *presentation* of issues (e.g., Gamson, 1992; Price & Tewksbury, 1997). Framing a story in terms of conflict, for example, is a translation of a key news selection criterion into a template for organizing the news story in a way that is familiar to journalists, sources, and audiences. This frame-building phase of the framing process is comparatively understudied and deserves attention (Scheufele, 1999) and is a key focus in the current study.

Linking the production perspective to research specifically dealing with European integration, previous studies offer analyses of either EU institutions' communication efforts (e.g., Meyer, 1999) or a discussion of the attitudes of, for example, the British press corps in Brussels (Morgan, 1995). These studies, however, tell us little about the processes of news selection and subsequent framing and presentation of issues in the news.

FRAMES IN THE NEWS. The second dimension in the *integrated process model of framing* concerns frames in the news. As discussed throughout this chapter, multiple conceptualizations and methods have been applied in previous content analyses of frames in the news. In the review of previous research a distinction between *issue-specific* and *generic* news frames was proposed.

In this study the emphasis is on generic news frames. Following Price and Tewksbury (1997), Price et al. (1997), and Semetko and Valkenburg (2000) the study centers on the framing of news in terms of *conflict* and in terms of *economic consequences*. These frames are generic in the sense that they have been found in relation to news coverage of a broad variety of political, economic, and social issues. The frames fall within the broader definition of frames in which framing the news implies making elements of an issue more salient than others (Pan & Kosicki, 2001).

In addition, this study explores elements of strategic news coverage. Thus far, the study of strategic news coverage has been limited to the United States and has most frequently been conducted in relation to election campaigns, but studies also suggest that the type of news reporting may be found in the coverage of policy issues (e.g., Cappella & Jamieson, 1997; Lawrence, 2000). It remains, however, an open question whether news in European context also contains traces of strategic coverage and what effects such news may have.

Looking at the topic of European integration, previous research offers little in the way of systematic cross-national comparisons of media content about Europe or European affairs (Gavin, 2000; Semetko et al., 2000). While news coverage of European integration is likely to have a number of unique characteristics that are particularly relevant to European issues, this study focuses on investigating *generic* frames. This is because issue-specific frames have no reference point which makes it impossible to investigate the degree to which the framing of an issue is deviant from or similar to, for example, framing of other economic and political news. Generic frames can be investigated both in general economic and political news and in the coverage of particular events in order to analyze differences and similarities. Second, investigations of issue-specific frames do not contribute substantially to theory-building. Notwithstanding the insights an analysis of specific 'Europe-related frames' could contribute with, it is problematic to generalize from such findings to other contexts or issues. Third, generic news frames can be seen as part of the integrated process model of studying the framing process. Generic news frames are linked theoretically and conceptually with our knowledge of news production processes as discussed above.

The approach taken to the study of news frames is theory-based, deductive, and designed so that the reliability of measurement can be determined (Tankard, 2001). The frames under investigation are closely related to and can be addressed in the light of journalistic practice. The frames have unique, identifiable conceptual and linguistic characteristics (Cappella & Jamieson, 1997).

Beyond these theoretical considerations related to the integrated process model of framing, the analysis can be seen in the light of the issue of European integration. Given recent discussions about fraud and corruption in the European Union, we might ask whether news media coverage of EU affairs has become more critical and is framed in terms of strategy. If so, we might expect such coverage to fuel public cynicism as has been documented in the US (Cappella & Jamieson, 1997). Given tension between countries and within groups over advancements in European integration, we may ask whether news coverage of European affairs is focused on conflict or perhaps the economic implications of further integration. In either case, it is important to assess what the implications of such news coverage are for citizens' processing of information about and perception of European integration.

FRAMING EFFECTS. The frame-setting part of the integrated process model refers to the effects of news frames and the interaction with individual characteristics. Specifically, the study links the effects of generic news frames to the issue of European integration and investigates a variety of cognitive information processing and attitudinal effects of the conflict and economic consequences frame and of strategic news reporting.

An important question for the integrated approach to framing research is the psychological base for framing effects. Graber (1988) provided an introduction to information processing that gave guidance to the cognitive paradigm in framing effects research. Inspired by schema theory, she identified four steps. Schemata (1) determine what information is noticed, processed, and stored, (2) they serve to organize and evaluate new information to be fitted into established perceptions, (3) they help to provide extra information to complete information, and (4) they provide information about scenarios and how to cope with them (Graber, 1988).

Early empirical studies of framing effects conceive the framing process almost entirely as an *accessibility* effect (Iyengar, 1991). Given the key role of news media for the provision of information about politics, news is a key determinant of accessibility. Television news, for example, makes accessible or retrievable information from memory and easily retrieved or accessed information then dominates "judgments, opinions, and decisions" (Iyengar, 1991, p. 131). The concept of framing then "refers to subtle alterations in the statement or presentation of judgment and choice problems, and the term 'framing effects" refer to changes in decision outcomes resulting from these alterations" (Iyengar, 1991, p. 11).[20]

Another perspective has emerged in the framing literature. Scholars have argued that framing effects occur in 'on-line' processing of information, independently from accessibility or memory-based activities. The effects stem from the *weight* and salience that citizens attach to certain considerations when making political judgments. News frames affect opinions and attitudes, not by mere accessibility, but by stressing specific values, facts or other considerations, endowing them with greater relevance to an issue than under an alternative frame. Selectively enhancing the psychological salience and relevance or weight to specific beliefs can be accomplished without accessibility of these concepts in memory (Druckman, 2001a; 2001b; Nelson & Kinder, 1996; Nelson & Oxley, 1999).

Determining the psychological antecedents of framing effects is important, though not at the core of this study. An important aspect, which is argued by several scholars (e.g., Gamson, 1992; Graber, 1988; Iyengar, 1991; Neuman et al., 1992), is that framing effects are general, but not omnipresent effects. Frames interact with individuals' predispositions and knowledge, so that framing effects are conditional upon finding resonance with its audience. In this respect, scholars from the *cognitive* and the *constructionist* approaches share common ground by arguing that not all individuals are necessarily affected similarly and that news frames are 'negotiated' with prior knowledge and individual predispositions (e.g., Crigler, 1996; Gamson, 1992, Neuman et al., 1992). Following this argument, it is necessary to model and control for a number of factors that may moderate the effects of frames. Previous research on effects of news frames is primarily experimental and (implicitly) deals with the impact of individual characteristics by means of randomization, which ideally eliminates the structural impact of individual differences to randomly distributed noise. However, randomization does not necessarily eliminate the effects of all influences and therefore theoretically driven intervening variables may be introduced in the analysis.

MODERATORS, MEDIATORS AND INDIVIDUAL DIFFERENCES: SUSCEPTIBILITY TO FRAMING EFFECTS. Despite the fact that most previous studies of framing effects acknowledge the importance of individual characteristics, few have modeled and assessed the impact of these differences. In addition, previous research offers little in terms of whether these characteristics have an independent, direct effect in the framing process or whether they *moderate* or *mediate* the framing effects. *Moderators* partition an independent variable into subgroups to illustrate differential effects on a dependent variable (Baron & Kenny, 1986). For example, political knowledge may moderate the effect of exposure to a news frame so that differences in the dependent variable vary according to the level of knowledge. *Mediators* function as the indirect mechanism through which an independent variable influences a dependent variable (Baron & Kenny, 1986). For example, if the magnitude of an effect of an independent variable (for example exposure to a news frame) on a dependent variable (for example support for environmental restrictions) decreases when introducing a mediator (for example political ideology) this suggest that the newly introduced variable mediates the framing effect.

In recognition of the fact that news frames are but *one* resource that citizens rely on when forming attitudes, a number of additional influences are considered in the effects studies discussed in Chapter 5 and 6. In the media effects literature, there is little consensus concerning *which* variables play a moderating or mediating role, how these should be *operationalized* and *measured*, and in which *direction* these variables may contribute, that is whether they enhance or diminish the main effect. Framing research resides in a stage of infancy in this respect while agenda-setting and priming research is more advanced in terms of identifying moderating variables.[21]

In *agenda-setting*, McCombs (1981) more than twenty years ago called for an investigation of mediators and moderators of the agenda-setting process.[22] Previously, McLeod, Becker & Byrnes (1974), for example, specified a number of contingent or contributory audience orientations affecting the agenda-setting function of the media including partisanship, newspaper dependency, and political interest. Non-partisans, frequent newspaper readers, and persons with low political interest, for example, were found to be more susceptible to agenda-setting effects. In another study the perceived *credibility* of a source was found to exert a positive influence on the agenda-setting process, so that, for example, the *International Herald Tribune* was more likely to set the agenda for an audience that the *National Enquirer* (Rogers & Dearing, 1988). Weaver (1977) suggested that a high *need for orientation*, that is high uncertainty, leads individuals to consult more information in the media to reduce their uncertainty, and thereby enhancing the agenda-setting effect as a function of the greater exposure and reliance on news.

There is mixed evidence concerning the role of *personal experience* with issues. Some evidence suggests that little or no direct experience with an issue is likely to enhance the impact of the media on public opinion on that issue (e.g., Zucker, 1978). Other studies suggest that personal experience may 'sensitize' a person to that issue and thereby increase the probability of being affected by media attention to that issue (e.g., Iyengar & Kinder, 1987). Finally, there is also mixed evidence concerning the effect of *political knowledge*. Weaver, Graber, McCombs and Eyal (1981), for example, found that knowledge diminished agenda-setting effects while Smith (1985) found a stronger effect for more sophisticated individuals.

Political knowledge is a much-debated concept given different operationalizations and measurement and the empirical evidence on the effects of political knowledge is inconclusive. Political knowledge is an indicator of the availability of cognitive resources a person has (Fiske, Kinder & Larter, 1983; Fiske & Taylor, 1991). A number of studies use political knowledge as a *dependent* variable in addressing questions about media effects in terms of political learning (e.g., Graber, 2001). Although there is little known about the differential impact of different media on political knowledge, recent European research suggests that the type of news provided by public broadcasters or commercial television has differential associations with knowledge so that public television exposure is related to higher levels of knowledge (Aarts & Semetko, 2003; Holtz-Bacha & Norris, 2001).

In more general theories of media effects, some scholars have advanced the argument that political knowledge – which is referred to as 'political awareness' – is superior to other indicators as an *explanatory* variable (Zaller, 1992). The argument is that given the inherent measurement errors in, for example, self-reported media exposure and attention measures, general political knowledge questions function as better and more accurate predictors of learning and attitude change. Price and Zaller (1993) accordingly found that political knowledge was a strong predictor of learning from the news when controlling for education and volume of news exposure. There has been considerable criticism, however, by researchers of the actual value or relevance of these general knowledge measures in capturing what they claim to measure (e.g., Graber, 2001; Mondak, 2001).[23]

While political knowledge in the studies discussed above is equated with and taken as a proxy of media exposure and attention, political knowledge in *priming research* has generally been investigated in terms of its moderating effect, but the evidence is this respect is inconclusive.[24] Krosnick and Kinder (1990) found politically knowledgeable persons to be *less* susceptible to priming effects. Iyengar and Kinder (1987) found no systematic differences between 'experts' and 'novices' in the magnitude of priming. Krosnick and Brannon (1993) found that political expertise facilitates priming effects. The latter argument was elaborated by Miller and Krosnick (2000) who found the strongest priming effects for politically knowledgeable citizens who also trust media sources.

In *framing* research, the influence of individual characteristics is often not explicated or is omitted in analyses. Scheufele (2000) points out that default control for demographics and pre-exposure orientations should be incorporated in models of framing effects. Others suggest that theoretically motivated or situational factors are more important, but there is no consistency concerning which variables may moderate or mediate framing effects, how these should be measured or whether these can be expected to enhance or dilute framing effects. McLeod and Detenber (1999), for example, included gender, age, political interest, and media use measures in their study of framing effects, but did not report whether or in which direction any of these moderators performed.

Druckman (2001b) suggests that source credibility can both enhance and limit framing effects, so that frames sponsored by a less credible source is less convincing and influential compared to frames endorsed in highly credible sources such as, for example, the *New York Times*, a finding which dovetails with previous research on agenda-setting (see above). Cobb and Kuklinski (1997) found 'political inattentive' participants to respond more strongly to pro-arguments suggested in a news story about the *NAFTA*. Domke et al. (1998) modeled gender, education, income, party identification, and issue importance in a multivariate analysis to distinguish the effects of these control variables and their framing manipulation on decision making strategies. They found a main effect of framing, but no consistent patterns with regard to the individual-level control variables.[25]

Looking specifically at the effect of political knowledge (or equivalents hereof), the findings are mixed. For example, Kinder and Sanders (1990) found that persons with lower levels of political information were more susceptible to framing effects, while Nelson et al. (1997) found persons with higher levels of political information to be more susceptible. Valentino et al. (2001a) included education (which they called 'political sophistication') in their study and found exposure to the strategic frame to be associated with lower levels of turnout intention for participants with lower levels of 'sophistication'.

Iyengar (1991) concluded that the greater the discrepancy between the attributions suggested by the frame and audience members' predispositions (in this case party identification), the weaker the influence of the news frame. He additionally included 'political involvement' and social-demographic characteristics as moderators with the expectation that politically involved viewers (which was operationalized as an index of political participation, political interest, political knowledge and frequency of media exposure) would be more 'immune' to framing. Though there was some evidence that persons who participated frequently in political activities and were politically interested and knowledgeable, were more likely to consider societal level treatment for problems of crime and terrorism (Iyengar, 1991, p. 121) no consistent pattern emerged.

Cappella and Jamieson (1997) addressed the impact of 'political sophistication' which was measured as factual political knowledge. They found political sophistication to be the strongest positive predictor of accuracy of recall of news content in their field experiment, and that this effect overrides any effects of the experimental manipulation (Cappella & Jamieson, 1997, p. 193). Based on panel data about health care reform they also found political knowledge to positively predict political cynicism.[26]

Price et al. (1997) found that knowledgeable students produced more responses to their open-ended measure of issue interpretation. They found no systematic influence of knowledge on the topical focus or valence of participants' thoughts.[27] Rhee (1997) found knowledge to significantly contribute to participants using an experimentally induced news frame in their interpretation of a political campaign so that "knowledgeable people were better able to take the thoughts and ideas in the news materials and to integrate them into their interpretations" (Rhee, 1997, p. 43).

In sum, there is little agreement in previous research as to what variables exert influence in the framing process, either independently and directly or through mediation or moderation. Moreover, the measurement and operationalization of these variables differ per study and the hypothesized direction of the effects is often mixed and contradictory. Based on previous priming, agenda-setting, and framing research (see Druckman (2001a), Miller and Krosnick (2000), Nelson et al., (1997), Price et al., (1997), and Rhee (1997)), political knowledge (that has elsewhere been labeled 'political awareness' and 'political sophistication') is included in the investigation of the frame-setting process (see Chapter 5 and 6).

In conclusion, bringing together the last part of the process model of framing and the discussion of framing effects and mediators and moderators, and linking this specifically with the context of European integration, key questions emerge. We may, for example, ask whether the conflict and economic consequences frames affect audiences' associations with European issues? Similarly, does a strategic mode of reporting affect levels of political cynicism and support for EU policies? And if frames in the news affect audience responses *what*, if any, role does political knowledge and other individual-level characteristics play in this process?

Specifying the research questions

Following the integrated process model, framing is investigated as inherent to *news production*, as manifest in *content*, and as an *effect*. Throughout the book this theoretical model is at the core. However, a second aim of the study is to provide a baseline of information about 'Europe' and television news. Therefore several aspects are addressed in the investigation.

The broader question of 'Europe in the newsroom' is both aimed at (1) establishing a baseline of how journalists cover Europe which has been neglected previously (Gavin, 2000) and at (2) addressing the role of framing in news production by investigating the application of news values and news selection criteria. To fulfill the first aim, the *organization* of the news coverage of European affairs, the *constraints* and *challenges* newsmakers perceive when covering European affairs, and the *editorial policies* are investigated. To fulfill the second aim, the *news selection criteria* used when choosing European events and issues for attention in the news are investigated. As argued above, these criteria are likely to also affect the presentation and framing of European issues in the news. The specific sub-questions guiding this part of the investigation are:

– *How is the coverage of European affairs organized?*

– *What are the constraints and challenges for newsmakers when reporting European affairs?*

– *What are the editorial policies applied by journalists and editors in the reporting of European economic and political affairs?*

– *How are news selection criteria applied in the reporting of European economic and political affairs?*

The 'Europe in the news' component of the study also serves as (1) a baseline for understanding the presentation of Europe in the television news and (2) an analysis of the specific framing of European affairs. For the first aim, the *visibility* of news about European affairs is assessed, the extent to which news about European affairs is *focused domestically* or on the *EU-level* is investigated, and the *visibility* and *evaluation* EU actors is compared to other actors in political and economic news. These aspects provide an overview of the coverage. The theoretical rationale and expectation for each of these questions is elaborated in Chapter 4. The second aim of the 'Europe in the news' component is to investigate the extent to which news about European affairs is *framed* in terms of conflict, economic consequences, and strategy. The specific design and operationalization of these frames are discussed in Chapter 4. The specific sub-questions guiding this part of the investigation are:

– *How visible is European news on the national television news agendas?*

– *To what extent is news about European affairs focused domestically or on the EU-level?*

– *To what extent is news about European affairs framed in terms of conflict?*

- *To what extent is news about European affairs framed in terms of economic consequences?*
- *To what extent is news about European affairs presented strategically?*
- *How visible are European actors in national television news compared to other actors?*
- *To what extent and how are European actors in national television news evaluated in comparison with other actors in the news?*

Turning finally to the 'Europe in public opinion' component of the study, this is investigated by means of two experiments. These investigate the effects of the conflict and economic consequences frames on the one hand, and strategic reporting about Europe on the other. The experiments are designed specifically to investigate effects of news frames (as independent variables) on a number of cognitive and attitudinal dependent measures and the potential moderating role that, for example, political knowledge (see above) plays in this process. The research questions focus on the following aspects and are dealt with in more detail in Chapter 5 and 6.

- *What are the effects of reporting about European affairs in terms of conflict and economic consequences on audiences' thoughts?*
- *How salient is the news frame compared to other information in the news story for the audience?*
- *What are they effects of news frames on support for European integration?*
- *What are the effects of strategic reporting about European affairs on political cynicism?*
- *What are the effects of strategic reporting about European affairs on issue evaluation?*
- *What are the effects of strategic reporting about European affairs on political mobilization?*

In the following chapters the empirical studies are discussed. Chapter 3 addresses the production and framing of Europe in the newsroom and Chapter 4 analyses the framing of Europe in the news. Chapters 5 and 6 deal with the effects of news about Europe on public opinion.

CHAPTER 3

Europe in the Newsroom

> "It is difficult to 'sell' an EU story. It must either contain an exceptional scandal about the EU and how they once again exceed limits on spending, or it must be events that have an impact such as summits, and Finance and Foreign Minister meetings." *(Editor-in-Chief)*

Introduction

Research in political communication has generally emphasized effects of news coverage on public perceptions of politicians, parties, institutions, and issues over the equally important question addressing the antecedents of such effects:[1] the factors that influence news media content (Shoemaker & Reese, 1996).[2] One important, but comparatively understudied question is: what role do news organizations play in shaping the coverage of political and economic events?

This chapter investigates the role of television news organizations in shaping the coverage of European affairs. The previous chapter argued that there is a close link between the *selection* of events for the news and the *presentation* and *framing* of these events in the news. The frame-building phase of the integrated process model of framing – in which the coverage is shaped by the interaction between, for example, politicians and news media, is currently underdeveloped, both empirically and theoretically, and investigations of the framing process from within the newsroom are virtually unrepresented in the literature (Scheufele, 1999).[3] This chapter investigates the criteria applied by newsmakers in Britain, Denmark, and the Netherlands when selecting and presenting news about European affairs with the aim of enhancing our understanding of the framing-building process.

The study of the production process is not limited to investigating framing in the newsroom. The chapter also provides a baseline for understanding the organization of television news production in relation to European affairs and the constraints and challenges facing journalists when reporting about the EU. A main focus of the study of the production of news is the June 1999 European Parliament (EP) elections. Election campaigns are pivotal moments for democracy and the campaign provides a key event to study.[4] Most of the issues raised, however, are also discussed in more general terms beyond the specific context of the election campaign.

The production of news

What shapes the content of news? The answer to this question is found in a multiplicity of factors. News content is the result of a process involving influences from both within and outside the news organization. Previous research has approached the investigation of the production of news from political economy, ideological, and sociological perspectives while focusing on, for example, notions of the newsworthiness of events, issue management, and organizational routines (see Shoemaker & Reese (1996) and Schudson (2000) for overviews).

Factors *internal* to the news organization have been investigated in several classical studies (Breed, 1955; Ettema & Whitney, 1982; Gans, 1979; Tuchman, 1978; White, 1950). These studies explore the impact of attributes and activities of either individual journalists and editors or the impact of routines embedded in the organizational structures. This line of work is referred to as the sociological perspective on news production (Reese & Ballinger, 2001; Schudson, 2000). Factors *external* to the news organization include the financial control and ownership structure of media organizations as well as the relationship between, for example, news and the larger political and economic culture (Golding & Elliott, 1979; Schudson, 2000).[5]

Both internal and external factors have direct implications for political journalism, the production processes, and the interplay between the institutional context, politicians, political parties, and intermediaries. While the assumptions and approaches vary in studies of the news production process, one important element brings them together, namely the observation that the news organization is a crucial player in the interaction between politics and citizens (e.g., Manheim, 1998; Tuchman, 1978).[6]

COVERING ELECTIONS. In discussions of news organizations' approach to covering politics, Blumler and Gurevitch proposed a continuum between *sacerdotal* and *pragmatic* approaches (Semetko et al., 1991).[7] The typology refers to the status attributed to political news. In a sacerdotal approach, political processes are perceived as the fundament of democracy and politics is considered newsworthy *per se*. The attitude towards politicians is respectful, cautious, and reactive. In a pragmatic approach political news is evaluated against conventional news selection criteria and is not automatically given special attention. The pragmatic orientation implies that the "amount of time or space allocated to [political events] will be determined by strict considerations of news values, in competition with the newsworthiness of other stories" (Semetko et al., 1991, p. 6).

Based on research in Britain in the 1980s, four roles for political journalists were discerned: prudential, reactive, conventionally journalistic, and analytical (Blumler, Gurevitch & Nossiter, 1986; Blumler et al., 1989). The *prudential* approach prescribes an 'invisible' and minimal role for the journalist and refers to a concern to "ensure that television journalism [is] politically beyond reproach, perhaps even politically innocuous" (Blumler et al., 1989, p. 162). The *reactive* approach looks predominantly to the agenda of the political parties as evident in press briefings, press releases, political speeches etc. which television is believed to be obliged to cover. The *conventionally journalistic* approach suggests filtering election events and issues through professional criteria "looking for events that would be strongly laced with elements of drama, conflict, novelty, movement, and anomaly" (Blumler et al., 1989, p. 163). The *analytical* approach suggests that events and issues are analyzed and interpreted by reporters, leading to coherence in the reporting whereby journalists contrast arguments for the viewer.

Few studies have investigated the role of news organizations in covering politics and most of them focus on the role of news organizations during election campaigns. One study of the 1990 German election campaign helped to explain why so little news was devoted to the elections and why the incumbent chancellor was able to continue 'governing as usual' during the final days of the campaign (Semetko & Schönbach, 1994). Another study in Spain during the 1996 general election campaign compared competing news organizations and found the public service channel and its main competitor at the time to utilize quite distinct approaches in their election coverage (Semetko & Canel, 1997).

The series of interviews and newsroom observations by Jay Blumler and Michael Gurevitch at the BBC during general elections in Britain allows for unique over-time comparisons of the developments in the news. In a temporal comparative perspective it seems that journalists in Britain have become more assertive and that journalists have assumed a more central role in election news coverage at the expense of politicians. Blumler and Gurevitch (2001) conclude that in some respects political journalism in Britain has moved closer to an American model of political communication so that in the 1997 election "sacerdotalism was conspicuously absent from the approach to political institutions, parties and the political establishment" (Blumler and Gurevitch, 2001, p. 398).

Also in other European countries public broadcasters were found to adhere to a more sacerdotal approach in the 1980s (Meurs, van Praag & Brants, 1995; van Praag & van der Eijk, 1998; Semetko et al., 1991). Similarly, more recent studies suggest that public broadcasters increasingly make use of a combination of the sacerdotal and pragmatic approaches in their coverage of national elections (van Praag & Brants, 2000; de Vreese, 2001a).

Cross-national comparisons of this type of research are rare, with one notable exception. In an analysis of the 1983 British general election and the 1984 American presidential election, it was found that *BBC* journalists were prudential and cautious, concerned about ensuring that political journalism could not be reproached. In comparison journalists at the US network *NBC* were more analytic and committed to a conventional journalistic approach including searching for, for example, political conflicts and drama (Semetko et al., 1991).

In addition to the Europe-US comparisons one comparative study in Europe investigated the role of broadcasters in relation to the 1979 EP elections. Noël-Aranda (1983) conducted the presumably only cross-national study addressing the attitudes of broadcasters towards their role in the campaign. Based on a survey of broadcast journalists in the then nine member states of the European Community, it was found that about half of the broadcasters saw no need for them to play a part in defining the issues of the European elections. The study concluded that many of the broadcasters were adhering to the agenda proposed by politicians and that they "appeared fearful of advancing into a territory they considered to be reserved by the politicians" (Noël-Aranda, 1983, p. 97), suggesting the presence of 'sacerdotal' sentiments among the journalists.

Taken together, there is only fragmented evidence available about changes over time in news organizations' approach to national elections. The evidence from cross-national comparisons is virtually absent (Schudson, 2000) and turning to EP elections, the 1979 campaign is the only baseline from which to compare. As Blumler and Gurevitch (2001) acknowledge their findings *may* generalize and be part of an international trend, but their data do not allow for such inferences. Without formulating formal hypotheses, however, based on evidence from single-country studies it seems reasonable to expect that European broadcasters today would approach European elections differently than in 1979, so that sacerdotal attitudes and prudential approaches have been replaced by pragmatic attitudes and analytic stances.

COVERING 'EVERYDAY' POLITICS. Outside the campaign context we know little about the way journalists approach and cover European politics. A recent study succinctly concluded that "little or no work has been done on how television journalists deal with European issues" (Gavin, 2001, p. 305). For the press, studies have examined the role of journalists and their interaction with key European institutions, referred to as the 'Brussels beat' (Morgan, 1995; Slaatta, 1998). The notion of a 'beat' in journalism is well established and the 'Capitol Hill' and the 'Supreme court beat', for example, are institutionalized in American journalism (Shoemaker & Reese, 1996). The Brussels beat is organized as a bureau with many large news organizations having permanent correspondents assigned in Brussels.

Morgan's (1995) profile sketch of the British press corps in Brussels reported frequent clashes between members of the British press corps and, for example, EU information officers over the negative and 'agnostic' approach taken by the Britons. A different type of tension was found in the relationship between the Brussels bureau and the London editors. Journalists stated considering what the London headquarters would accept rather than what they wanted to convey to the British public and found themselves in a position of writing and rewriting "to suit changing London demands" (Morgan, 1995, p. 324).

The scope of the Brussels bureau is dependent on the state of the on-going European integration. In Norway, outside the EU, it was found that in 1996/97 only three newspapers had permanent correspondent presence in Brussels (Slaatta, 1998, p. 217). In the wake of the 1994 national referendum on joining the EU, when the Norwegian public voted 'no', two-thirds of the permanent correspondents were pulled back from Brussels (Slaatta, 1998). Reporters from the political, economic, and domestic desks were expected to cover the EU when news was in their respective fields. This suggests that news organizations and journalists redefine their considerations of newsworthiness according to the political and institutional context. In sum, however, studies to date have primarily focused on the press and the Brussels beat and have not addressed the editorial policies and production processes in television news.

Elements of the production study

The goals of this chapter are to establish a baseline for understanding the news coverage of European affairs, to extend previous research on the approach of television news organizations to European politics with a cross-nationally comparative dimension, and to investigate the frame-building process in the newsroom. This is investigated both in relation to pan-European events, such as the European elections, as well as during 'everyday' politics. The organization of EU coverage and general constraints and challenges in the telling the 'European story' are identified. The editorial policies and the application of news selection criteria are investigated. The notion of 'balance' in news reporting is discussed as this is a key feature of political communication, particularly in the news coverage of election campaigns (Beck, Dalton, Greene & Huckfeldt, 2002; Blumler et al., 1986; 1989; Gurevitch & Blumler, 1981; Semetko, 1996).

THE ORGANIZATION OF COVERAGE OF EUROPEAN AFFAIRS. The first dimension addresses the organizational structure and efforts invested in the coverage of European affairs. Logistics is a key component of political news with activities in national campaigns often taking place simultaneously in various locations. Previous studies have noted the tension that can emerge between the 'periphery', the field where political actors operate, and the 'center', where news is produced (Gurevitch & Blumler, 1981). For European politics this challenge is even greater because of the additional level of European governance (Siune, 1983). To assess the organization of the coverage of European affairs, the set-up of the coverage within the newsroom, the degree of advance preparations for stories, the allocation of budgetary means, and the staffing of the political unit is investigated.

CONSTRAINTS AND CHALLENGES. The second dimension addresses the challenges and potential constraints that television journalists perceive when covering European affairs. So far there is only speculation about how television journalists think about and deal with 'Europe' (Gavin, 2001). When it comes to the press, however, a clearer picture emerges, at least in the British case. The strongly partisan British press is overly skeptical about the EU and advanced European integration and is often exaggerated and stereotyped in its coverage (e.g., Anderson & Weymouth, 1999; Morgan, 1995). No comparable studies are available in either Denmark or the Netherlands and for television journalism such studies are entirely absent. It is interesting to consider what journalists consider challenging and potentially different when reporting European affairs since answers to this question may help understanding actual news output.

EDITORIAL APPROACH. The third dimension addresses the formally defined organizational and editorial approach to covering European affairs. Here a distinction should be made between editorial policies concerning European *elections* and policies concerning the *daily* coverage of European politics. The essential question at stake is the degree of *discretion* that news organizations and journalists exert when covering European affairs. Key indicators for evaluating the editorial approach include officially formulated policies, the use of reactive or pro-active strategies by the news organization, and the policy regarding coverage of issues brought forward by politicians and parties. The editorial policy can be placed in the sacerdotal – pragmatic continuum and the journalistic approach can be discussed in terms of Blumler and Gurevitch's role typology of political journalists (see above).

European broadcasters have traditionally covered national elections in a cautious way, adhering largely to the agenda of parties and politicians (e.g. Asp, 1983; Blumler et al., 1989; Hjarvard, 1999; Semetko et al., 1991; Siune & Borre, 1975). While this journalistic role may be labeled 'reactive', recent research suggests that this may no longer be the case (e.g., Blumler & Gurevitch, 1998; 2001; Hjarvard, 1999; Norris et al., 1999; Semetko & Canel, 1997; de Vreese, 2001a). News organizations and journalists have been found to be more pro-active in their coverage of national politics and to exert more discretion when choosing which stories to bring in and how to cover these issues. This may, in Blumler and Gurevitch's terminology, more appropriately be labeled 'conventionally journalistic' and 'analytical'. It remains an open question if this development also applies to European-level elections where the only available benchmark is the 1979 EP elections when broadcasters were found to be primarily reactive and adhering largely to the agenda of the political parties (Noël-Aranda, 1983).

NEWS SELECTION CRITERIA. The fourth dimension addresses the use of news selection criteria. These criteria have a dual function. They are criteria for selection of material available and they are guidelines for the presentation of the news by "suggesting what to emphasise, what to omit, and where to give priority in the preparation of items" (Golding & Elliott, 1979, p. 114). News selection criteria are linked to the frame-building part of the integrated process model of framing as discussed in Chapter 2. Key indicators to assess the application of selection criteria are editors' and journalists' formulations of the qualities that events and issues must have to make it into the news. An important question is then also whether standard criteria for evaluation of the newsworthiness of events and issues are applied or whether special criteria are applied for evaluation of European stories. In other words, does news about European affairs compete equally against all other news?

BALANCED REPORTING. The fifth dimension addresses the notion of impartiality and balanced reporting. Though there is no single definition of bias in television news (Gunther, 1997) and impartiality is operationalized and applied differently in different countries (Semetko, 1996), fairness and balance are crucial concepts in political journalism, in particular during election campaigns. During the late 1970s it was concluded about the *BBC* that 'fairness is all' (Hardiman-Scott, 1977 c.f. Gurevitch & Blumler, 1981). Producers of news were determined to achieve an appropriate balance when reporting the activities of the principal election contenders. The *BBC*, like other European public broadcasters, is legally obliged to present issues with 'due impartiality'. One interpretation dominating previously is the quantitative interpretation of fairness, the so-called 'stopwatch culture' (McQuail, 1992; 1994). The balance obligation is translated so that the allocation of time in the news is distributed according to the size of political parties in a country.

Today the fairness concept is typically applied less rigorously. However, balanced reporting is still important to the work in the newsroom (Semetko, 1996; Semetko & Canel, 1997). In the case of European integration, impartial reporting of the election campaign applies not only to striking a balance between exposure of different political parties, but also between pro- and con- EU arguments in the debate about European integration.

Research Questions

With the five dimensions outlined above as the interpretative background, the general question that guides the investigation is: How do television news organizations approach the coverage of European affairs? This question is addressed by studying the 1999 European elections as well as more general aspects of the coverage of European affairs. The study (1) maps how the coverage is organized, (2) identifies specific constraints and challenges related to 'covering Europe', (3) analyzes and locates the editorial approaches along the sacerdotal – pragmatic continuum, (4) investigates how news values are applied, and (5) explores how the notion of balanced reporting is interpreted. In the next chapter (Chapter 4) the 'outcome' of the choices made by the news organizations, the actual news coverage, is analyzed.

Method

The study draws on structured interviews with senior political and economic correspondents, senior editorial staff members, editors and Editors-in-Chief.[8] Given the logistic constraints of cross-national research, most interviews were made with representatives from the public broadcasters (*BBC, DR*, and *NOS*). A total of twelve face-to-face interviews (five in Britain, four in Denmark, and three in the Netherlands) with a duration of 60-90 minutes on average were conducted with members from these three organizations. In addition, five interviews were conducted with representatives from the private networks (*ITN* in Britain and *TV2* in Denmark) and two interviews with editors of news programs at Channel Four and Channel Five in Britain.[9] The journalists and editors were affiliated with the following programs: *BBC Nine o'clock News,*[10] *ITN News at Ten,*[11] *DRTV TV-Avisen, TV2 Nyhederne, NOS Journaal,* and *RTL4 Nieuws.*

The total number of editorial staff involved in formulating and implementing policies about the coverage of European affairs at the sampled programs is limited. The interviewees therefore cover a significant part of the total population of journalists and editors covering 'Europe'.[12] The interviews followed a common interview protocol with questions pertaining to the organizational structure and effort, interviewees' role perception, perceived constraints and challenges, the editorial approach, and the application of news selection criteria. The interview protocol was designed to address, on the one hand, the role of the news organization in covering the European elections in 1999 specifically, and, on the other hand, more general features of the coverage of European affairs.

In the interviews, individual perceptions and interpretations of the campaign coverage policy were investigated and the editorial strategies elaborated.

Themes such as priority of and approach to the topic were addressed in each interview. In addition, the role of the political agenda, changes in policies over time, and differences between coverage of national and European politics were explored with senior news executives and reporters.[13]

Results

THE ORGANIZATION OF EUROPEAN NEWS COVERAGE: THE DAILY LOGISTICS. Turning first to the organization of the news production, it is important to note that all television news programs included in this study broadcast several bulletins a day. Television news is continuously updated which has implications not only for the production routines, but also poses new demands for journalistic skills. Television journalists are increasingly stakeholders in multimedial production modes and some produce news not only for television news, but also for radio and on-line outlets (Bierhoff, Deuze & de Vreese, 2001).[14]

To give an example, *NOS Journaal* daily produces several short morning bulletins, two lunch-time editions, early evening bulletins and in addition to the 8 o'clock flagship they also have bulletins at 6 p.m., 10 p.m. and a late midnight edition. Typically, individual crews are assigned to produce one of the main news bulletins and a few shorter ones. These crews work simultaneously towards 'their' bulletins throughout the day. The 'workday' is therefore still scheduled towards deadlines, but these have become multiple and rolling. At *DR* in Denmark, for example, bulletin editors meet in the morning after having scanned the dailies to start preparations for the main thirty minutes 9 p.m. news program. They are briefed by the early crew, survey the agenda, and make a 'short list' of potential stories that are discussed at a central editorial morning meeting. The afternoon is spent with continuous updates with reporters and coordination with the editors of other bulletins as well as meetings with, for example, the news graphic department. Towards the end of the afternoon, when reporters return from the field, the editing process commences, and the final news bulletin script is made.

The other news programs have schedules that resemble this pattern though, for example, *NOS* and the *BBC* have their most important newsroom meeting in the early afternoon where the topics of the day are discussed and yesterday's program evaluated. A key task for a *BBC* bulletin editor is to coordinate with the large number of other news outlets. The *BBC* newsroom is centrally organized and all *BBC*-gathered material, both for radio, television, and on-line is available (via a large server) to all journalists in the newsroom so that, for example, a quote collected by a television reporter can be used on the radio.

The proliferation in daily outlets also has implications for the work of reporters and correspondents with European affairs in their portfolio. In most organizations it is the exception rather than the rule that EU correspondents join the meetings via teleconferencing. The bulletin editors brief the Brussels crew while the Head of the political unit briefs members of the domestic political unit.

BRUSSELS, LONDON, COPENHAGEN, THE HAGUE AND HILVERSUM. The coverage of European affairs is organized very similarly at all programs studied here. All news organizations operate with a *triadic organization* with respect to EU coverage. The studio headquarters and central newsroom work together with the political unit (at Westminster in Britain, The Hague in the Netherlands, and Christiansborg, Copenhagen in Denmark) and the news organization's Brussels desk. This set-up is more complex than the traditional set-up for news coverage of domestic politics where the central headquarter works together with the parliamentary unit only (Blumler et al., 1978).

Most of the coverage is organized from the central newsroom at the headquarters of each program. Here the selection of news stories most often takes place. Reporters at the Brussels desk conversely pitch their stories at the central newsroom. If a European theme has domestic political and economic implications, these aspects are typically covered by members of either the central newsroom or the domestic political desk. Reporters at the political desk more often communicate directly with the central newsroom and less frequently with the Brussels bureau. Some organizations also have 'EU reporters' in the domestic political units (such as *BBC*, *DR*, and *NOS*). The structure of the EU coverage is represented in the figure below.

Figure 3.1. Organization of production of news about European affairs. Full lines represent the most significant communication lines.

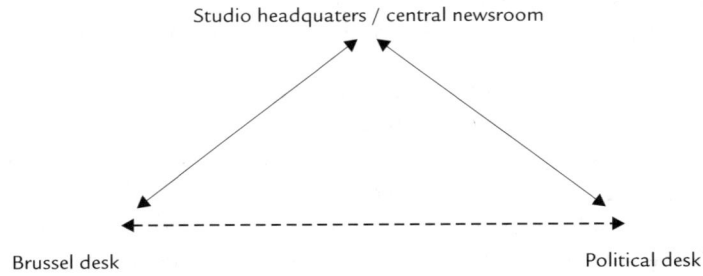

The *BBC* has a fairly large bureau in Brussels with a Bureau Chief and four full-time correspondents employed. They are permanently covering the 'Brussels beat' for the whole range of *BBC* outlets (BBC1 and 2, BBC World, BBC 24, BBC Radio). The central London-based *BBC News Gathering* automatically covers large events such as European summits to meet the demands of the different outlets. The *9 o'clock News*, along with the other programs, can commission stories to be produced by the Brussels bureau by making use of an allocated budget per program. As discussed above, the scope of a Brussels bureau may change and its size is defined on the basis of a continuous review of the political context. As the Editor of the *BBC 9 o'clock News* put it:

> "Earlier we compared ourselves to America, today we are much more likely to compare ourselves to another European country such as Germany or France [...] We now have bureaus in Brussels, Frankfurt, Paris, Berlin and Rome, and we can tap onto BBC World's correspondents in such places as Warsaw and Vienna".

Danish *DR* has two correspondents in Brussels, one that primarily follows the news beat of the institutions (e.g., the Parliament and the Commission) and one that covers EU news from various locations in Europe, but operates out of Brussels. The correspondents work together with the newsroom in Copenhagen and a Parliament-based political reporter who covers the potential domestic political consequences of EU news.

Very similarly *TV2*, *NOS*, and *RTL* all have one correspondent in Brussels who works primarily with the Odense and Hilversum-based headquarters and, often indirectly, with the political units in Copenhagen and The Hague respectively. *ITN* has an integrated bureau in Brussels with correspondents also working for Channel 4 and 5. As the Editor of Channel 5 news said:

> "When setting up the program, we had to decide whether to have a bureau in Washington DC or in Brussels. We opted for Brussels as almost anything that comes out of there has importance, directly, for Britain, much more so than what comes out of Washington".

The planning of European news takes place within this triadic structure. Prior to larger events, ad-hoc groups and teams are formed often consisting of members from the Brussels bureau, the political and economic units, and the central newsroom.

During the fall of 1998, prior to the introduction of the euro, *DR* and *BBC*, for example, created special units specifically designed to prepare the euro launch coverage. The *DR* group consisted of members of the economy desk, the foreign news desk, the political unit and included reporters from television, radio, and the *DR Online News* group. Similar preparations took place at the *BBC* with members of the Brussels desk preparing the coverage of the launch with members of the economy desk and political unit in Britain.

For the European elections, none of the news programs implemented a special daily campaign segment in their bulletin which has been tradition during national election campaigns (Blumler & Gurevitch, 1998). The elections were covered within already existing structures of political and economic coverage. However, all programs allocated additional budgets for covering the elections and all initiated advance planning in specialized ad-hoc units. Prior to the European elections, a few stories dealing with Europe were commissioned by the Editor-in-Chief of *9 o'clock News*:

> "I chose thematic issues rather than saying 'let's go to Germany and see what they think about the European elections'. I had two issues basically: Where was Europe heading politically now with all these center-left governments in power, so different from a few years ago? And similarly for the economy: The economy of Europe, by then nearly six months into the euro, what conclusions could be drawn on that relatively short time scale?".

As acknowledged by the BBC Editor-in-Chief these stories eventually played only a marginal role in the actual coverage:

> "Without Kosovo I might have done more. I would certainly have done more in Europe, I would have sent more people around, maybe to Greece capturing the world outside the currency [...] I would have done more under normal circumstances, but I scaled it back a bit".

Danish television (*DR*) started preparations for covering the elections six months prior to Election Day. Specifically, the two correspondents from the Brussels bureau, and reporters from the Copenhagen based political unit and the Domestic desk prepared the elections in a small 'working group'. The Head of the Political Unit functioned as a daily coordinator for the election coverage. One important managerial and editorial choice guiding the coverage was to carry out a national survey with the Gallup polling institute. This survey was designed to investigate the electorate's agenda for the elections. As the Editor-in-Chief put it:

> "As the kick-off for our campaign coverage, we wanted to know what issues, what themes are interesting to the public prior to these elections. A very unambiguous answer emerged. What came back was that at the top of the agenda was fraud."

The survey led *DR* to assign two additional reporters from the central newsroom full time during the campaign to investigate issues of fraud and malpractice in EU-related institutions.

In anticipation of the European elections the Dutch *NOS Journaal* also created a 'Europe Unit'. The group consisted of the program's Brussels correspondent, editors, and political reporters based in The Hague. Preparatory research was carried out for a number of issues, such as the competence of the European Parliament, fraud, the EU budget, and voter apathy. However, in the actual coverage of the campaign, these advance preparations were never used and the internal organizational structures developed to cover the campaign were not implemented.

In the daily coverage of European affairs the news is planned and produced within the triadic structure. The triangle also forms the backbone of ad hoc groups. *NOS Journaal*, for example, planned and broadcast historical pieces in advance of the December 2000 Summit in Nice where the enlargement of the EU was a key issue. Similarly, Danish *DR* and *TV2* both formed units consisting of political correspondents and members of the central newsroom in their coverage of the 2000 national referendum on the euro.

CONSTRAINTS AND CHALLENGES: COMPLEXITY AND INADEQUACY. The second focal point of the study deals with the potential constraints and challenges experienced by journalists and editors when covering European economic and political issues. Based on the interviews with members of the newsroom at all channels, the following challenges were identified: (1) 'distance and time', (2) 'access and terminology', (3) 'internal disagreement', and (4) 'audience competences'.

The first challenge is inherent to the EU decision-making process. Despite the fact that Britain, Denmark, and the Netherlands are all geographically relatively close to centers of power such as Brussels and Strasbourg, the distance is experienced as a constraint when composing an EU story. In addition, the time frame in EU decision-making procedures is often longer than in domestic politics. As the Head of the Political Unit at *DR* said:

> "The difficulty is that we are quite far from the decisions in the European system. Physically because it takes place in Brussels, but also because it can take years before you have a real decision".

The perception of the Parliament as an institution that is both physically and mentally far away from most voters and which requires a certain critical reflection was also found at the Danish *DR*. The Head of the Political Unit described the perception of the Parliament in these words:

> "The difficulty of covering 'Europe' is that, in the eyes of our viewers, it is still something very distant. I do not believe that many people are too concerned about the competences of that Parliament. And throughout the years an image has been created that it is not a real Parliament, like the national one".

Time constraints are also perceived by newsmakers in their work when making stories dealing with European affairs. A senior political correspondent at the *BBC* noted:

> "The more abstract, the more difficult, the more potentially 'boring' that a story is, the longer duration it needs in order for it to be clear [...] You need more padding, more breathing space for people to take the point. But an editor fearing that you are putting in something that would be a turn-off for the audience will offer you less time. The you get 'over compression' instead of a nicely packaged story that somebody can find their way around."

The time constraints are inherent to the news format of main evening news bulletins that typically have between 20 and 30 minutes available. This conclusion is supported by the Editor of Channel 4's daily 50-minute news magazine who has more time available for 'the European story' and therefore sees less of challenge in covering European issues:

> "I can't think of an example where we said 'no, let's not do the story, it's too complicated'. The stories are interesting, take Austria: the prospects of neo-nazis getting into Parliament in continental Europe. That is a good story by anyone's yardstick. Clearly there will be a little to do to spell out the arithmetic of how the coalition in Austria works, but that is OK as long as the story is a good one".

Another challenge perceived by the newsmakers is related to the institutions of the EU that are perceived to be non-transparent and bureaucratic. This impression of the EU institutions dovetails with both Meyer's (1999) critical analysis of the Union's 'communication deficit' and Morgan's (1995) discussion of the tension between members of the Brussels press corps and the EU spokespersons. The Head of the *DR* Political Unit said:

> "There is the terminology and the language used in the EU. The treaties are more complex than any Danish legislation [...] There is a big difference in terms of culture when comparing Brussels and Strasburg to Denmark. Take the Commission, it is virtually impossible to get access through the system of spokespersons to a Commissioner while we in Denmark have almost unlimited access to our ministers".

A third challenge is internal to the news organization. Concurrent with the findings by Morgan (1995), journalists identified tension between their wishes for a story and the terms and conditions for a story defined by the central newsroom. A senior political correspondent noted this type of intra-organizational conflict while stressing that this was a personal rather than organizational point of view:

"The sad and embarrassing fact is that the biggest difference between reporting Westminster and reporting European politics, is actually not the audience, but my colleagues. I can approach an editor of a program with a Westminster story and they know what I am talking about. [...] But I am engaged in a much more detailed process of explanation and persuasion before I can get a piece, which is significant in European terms, through to my colleagues."

The view was echoed by an Editor-in-Chief who estimated to reject 75% of the 'offers' made to him by correspondents and bureaus: "*They have to make a pitch and have it accepted before they can do the piece [...] it is kind of an internal market*".

The fourth and final challenge emerges from the lack of audience interest in and knowledge about European affairs. The challenge was discussed both in relation to covering domestic politics and in more general terms as problem of inadequate audience competences. As a senior *BBC* political correspondent said about the difference between covering domestic politics and European politics:

"Here we have our 'Punch and Judy rows'. They are easy to cover because they fall into that 'British-wish-to-have-two-sides'. They are neat because they are told briefly, only need two bits of actuality, and require very little explanation, because people are familiar with the ideas, and you don't have to explain too much. [...] Now things are more complicated and we are still learning to accommodate a more sophisticated story in relation with the EU".

The Editor-in-Chief of *BBC 9 o'clock News* offered this view:

"There is always constraints of resources, money, and time. One eye is on the audience all the time and you don't want to do anything that people find boring. The European stories are quite difficult to explain and to illustrate in television terms. [...] You need to infuse people. If you ask someone who watches the 9 o'clock news whether they wanted a piece on how the euro goes down in Bavaria, they would say 'no thank you very much, can we please get some football instead."

The complexity of the topic and the lack of audience knowledge were also stressed by the Editor-in-Chief of *ITN*:

"We believe in having specialist economics and political reporters. We have Europe correspondents working in Brussels and we turn to them to cover these stories, because they are complex stories. They require reporters who have got authority [...] who can use graphics, and 3D animations in trying to explain economic factors in a narrative. [...] People in Britain are not very well informed about European institutions and we devote quite a lot of air time to analytical pieces. To explain things: what is the euro? How is it going to work? What are the potential benefits?"

EDITORIAL APPROACH: WHITHER SACERDOTALISM? When the sacerdotal – pragmatic continuum suggested by Blumler and Gurevitch (in Semetko et al., 1991) is used to analyze the approach taken to European political affairs by the different news programs, we see that all programs cluster towards the 'pragmatic' end of the continuum. 'Sacerdotal' policies that suggest a cautious, respectful, and subordinate approach to politics are not found to crystallize in the policies of any of the news programs in covering the EU.

Turning specifically to the 1999 EP elections, the news organizations' editorial policies were formulated in, for example, internal memos in which the role of the news program in initiating own stories and dealing with the advance scheduled political agenda was addressed. For the EP elections the editorial approach to covering the elections by the *BBC*, *DR*, and *NOS* varied considerably.

One observation, however, overrides other comments about the European election campaign. The period leading up to the EP elections was influenced by the conflict in Kosovo. During the course of the election campaign NATO carried out bombings, peace negotiations were initiated, and on Election Day, a peace agreement was reached. The highly unusual news environment had implications for the editorial politics concerning the European elections.

The *BBC's* original pro-active plans of initiating a number of political and economic themes were only marginally implemented. In fact the *BBC* ended up following the political agenda to a greater extent than initially planned. According to a senior political reporter covering the EP elections this was a result of two things: the competitive news environment with Kosovo dominating and the pro-active Tory campaigning versus the passive government campaigning:

> "We did attempt, before the campaign had really got rolling, from this unit, to sell ideas for features setting up what would be the main issues and main questions [...]. When it came down to it, that wasn't really available to be done, so we ended up following the stories of the day. That also arose out of the fact that they [9 o'clock] really didn't want to take any pieces they didn't have to have, and ended up having to take a piece every day at the end of the campaign in order to feel that they had done the job properly. This means that they had to take the 'story of the day' out of the press conferences".

A sacerdotal approach 'prescribes' a respectful perception of political institutions, including the European Parliament. At the *BBC* the EP was considered an institution in transition, but not a strong political authority. According to the Editor-in-Chief:

> "The European Parliament is becoming a more powerful body, and had new powers this year. Therefore it is potentially more influential and therefore potentially more important who goes there. There was in the past a kind of

unwritten feeling that Members of the European Parliament were actually just kind going over there talking, declaring their expenses, doing not very much [...] It was a bit of talking shop and not totally relevant. Leading up to the European elections, because the Parliament had given the Commission a very bloody nose only three months previously, it was seen to have scored some kind of a victory and asserted its position against fraud, plus it was taking on the new powers."

In line with the pragmatic approach *DR* assumed a distinct proactive and agenda-setting role in the campaign, which was a debated decision in the campaign. As the Editor-in-Chief noted:

"If you ask the politicians what the agenda is, then it is totally different. Then you get big, abstract things like the enlargement [of the European Union] to the East, very diffuse themes that in terms of news coverage have been extremely difficult to make some concrete political stories about 'what is this election all about?' [...] What you have here is a gap between what the voters think is interesting, what they would like to see addressed – corruption which we have done a number of stories on – and what the politicians want. This has meant that we have all the Members of the European Parliament criticizing us, saying that we have derailed the debate".

NOS Journaal in the Netherlands intended to assume an active role and initiate topics of their own in relation to the European elections. This policy was, however, never implemented, and Dutch news largely neglected the elections. The Deputy Editor-in-Chief elaborated:

"[T]here was no campaign. Even the political parties reduced their campaign activities to an absolute minimum".

When comparing the editorial policies of the different news programs there is considerable variation. However, all programs took a pragmatic approach to covering the elections though this manifested itself in different ways. The pragmatic approach in the Netherlands crystallized as selectivity and neglect of the elections. In Britain, it was partly neglect, partly reporting the euro theme played up by the Tories in a distanced and reflexive manner. In Denmark it was by defining the fraud issue as the key agenda point at the expense of issues put forward by politicians.

The conclusion based on the European elections may hold also across other issues where most editors at the different news programs express the acceptance of a critical and analytical role that goes far beyond a 'sacerdotal' orientation towards political events. In response to the news coverage of a promotion event by the European Parliament where a hot air balloon was launched to fly across Greater London, *ITN* Editor-in-Chief said:

> "There is a great fondness in British politics to have the photo ops or 'balloons'. Our view is that we should not take them too seriously, wherever they come from. [...] I think the European Parliament was perfectly entitled to try and interest people, but I do not think we should report it 'straight'. It was a stunt like any other stunt and we are not taking it at its face value. It is a part of political marketing and we are not part of that, so we are objective and detached from it, and, if you like, a little skeptical and cynical and amused by it."

The pragmatic approach is characterized by 'conventionally journalistic' and 'analytical' roles by political journalists. In the policy for covering European affairs, editors acknowledged this position and defined their role in distinct 'pragmatic' terms. As the Editor-in-Chief of *ITN* said:

> "We analyze what they are doing far more than we used to. We analyze their tactics, who they try to appear to be. We try to deconstruct what is going on and try to explain to the viewer what is really happening".

At Danish *TV2*, a senior political correspondent was used as a commentator during the 2000 national referendum campaign on the euro. His role during the campaign was to interpret, bring coherence to, and comment on the broader implications of a day's events on the campaign trail. This suggests a reflexive and analytical type of reporting. To the Editor-in-Chief at the *BBC*, the analytical mode of covering European affairs is also a function of the fact that many European news stories are highly specialized:

> "Just telling what has happened or what somebody said is of no use to the audience at all unless you give them some background and context, a bit of explanation, where it all comes from and where it is all leading. [...] We employ journalists with specialist knowledge to give that sort of information and guidance. They lay out the arguments for you by saying why a person is saying this or that."

NEWS SELECTION CRITERIA: BUSINESS AS USUAL. To explore the link between news selection criteria, such as conflict, proximity, and consequences, on the one hand, and the framing of issues in the news on the other, all interviewees were asked to identify qualities that a 'European' event or issue must have to select that event or issue for the news. In addition they were asked whether special selection criteria were applied during the 1999 EP elections. The application of news selection criteria is an indicator of the weight and importance given to elections. While broadcasters have traditionally extended the news bulletins or designated daily campaign segments at national elections (Blumler & Gurevitch, 1998), this was not done by any of the news organizations during the 1999 European elections.

Turning first to the qualities that European events and issues must have to be included in the news, the Head of the Political Unit at *DR* succinctly stated that "*the good story is one that has consumers. What does this mean for me?*" Similarly, the Editor of *BBC* said that practical stories, for example, "*what exactly are British firms doing to adapt the euro and why are they ahead of the political process?*" would make for a good story. The key qualities mentioned by editors and journalists were: domestic relevance and political tension, either within the country of the news outlet or between European countries or actors. Bulletin editor at *DR* summarized these points in her characterization of what an issue or event must contain:

> "Two things are important: First, what does this mean for ordinary Danes? That is to say, what are the consequences, financially, politically, personally? Second, who are the domestic political stakeholders? Do the EU countries agree? Is there unanimity? Any vetos, why and how?"

The presence of conflict, either domestic or international was also confirmed by the Editor-in-Chief of *ITN* who said a key aspect in the EU coverage was "*to continue to look at the arguments both between the parties and within the parties*". In the same vein, a senior political reporter at the *BBC* said about the conflict impediment:

> "In political stories, domestic and European, we like to focus on tension between two sides. We have a bipolar, very confrontational Parliament, and that is the structure we use for our political stories. [...] Of course that means simplification, but you sometimes have to take decisions that it is easier to tell this as a 'nasty little stitch-up' between Germany and Spain".

On occasions, the 'European story' was upgraded and devoted additional attention. One reason, for the public broadcasters, was pedagogical and stems from the ideal (and obligation) of providing 'enlightening' civic information. *DR*'s Head of the Political Unit put it this way:

> "In the case of the euro, it would be perfectly legitimate, according to our news criteria to say: 'here is this euro, Denmark is not in, so we will make one or two stories'. But we chose very consciously to say that the euro is more than what happens once it gets here, so we gave the issue extra priority, almost a kind of pedagogical news provision".

Turning next to the application of news selection criteria during the 1999 campaign for the European elections, the networks varied in the degree to which standard criteria were applied for evaluating the newsworthiness of events and issues.

The *BBC* applied fairly standard news criteria in evaluating the EP campaign news. Contrary to, for example, the coverage leading up to the introduction of the euro in 1999 and 2002, *9 o'clock News* did not commission a series of stories focusing on the elections and important European themes. News about the 'euro-elections' was not given extra priority. *DR* devoted extra attention to the fraud issue during the campaign. This up-grade of the campaign pertained only to the fraud issue and not other issues such as candidates on the campaign trail. The Editor-in-Chief elaborated on this:

> "Given the fact that we give European issues the same news priority as all other issues and given the fact that we had a period of Kosovo War and peace negotiations that largely influenced the news agenda, then our coverage of the European elections has to some extent been damaged [...] A news story about the European Parliament must compete equally with a story about peace or not in Kosovo. We cannot enter that process and say: we must have four such stories in the beginning of our program every day. We don't do that, we select according to normal news values."

The Head of the Political Unit at *DR* elaborated on the rationales for the news program not to cover the campaign more closely:

> "One reason is logistical. One can say 'why don't we go out and cover one of the election rallies / evening meetings?' We have done that. But if you want to cover the content of such a meeting then you cannot bring it the same evening and already then it is 'dead' in terms of news. It is difficult to go on air and say to the viewers: 'Yesterday evening there was a rally and this is what the candidates said…'. To be quite frank: not many people find that very exciting, it is old news. What we have done is to cover a couple of meetings, but within the time available to us, dealing with the interest for the election which is almost absent".

News about the EP elections was evaluated against conventional news values and selection criteria at *NOS Journaal*. The Deputy Editor-in-Chief noted that this policy was both an advance choice and a pragmatic function of the general news environment during the campaign:

> "The threshold for the European elections to get in the news was extremely high. These Parliamentary elections are a 'non-issue'. It means nothing to the voters. Added to this were a number of factors: the war and peace negotiations in Kosovo, our governmental crisis, the resigning Minister of Agriculture, and the elections in Indonesia and South Africa which in other countries may not

receive much attention but are important here in the Netherlands [...] Under more normal circumstances we would have covered the European elections more, but even then we would not have extended the coverage very far".

In sum, conflict and tension between elites as well as events and issues with significant domestic political and/ or economic consequences were among the key qualities that European events and issues according to the newsmakers should have to get in to the news. This pattern was found at all news programs in the three countries. A strong cross-national difference emerged between the different news programs in the way they applied news selection criteria in relation to the 1999 European elections. *NOS*, for example, was very selective and hardly mentioned the elections, while *DR* paid specific attention to the issues defined by the news program's audience in a survey. Subsequently one would expect differences in the actual priority given to the campaign in the bulletins of the different networks. This is aspect is addressed in Chapter 4 that deals with the content of news.

BALANCED REPORTING: SLEAZE ON ALL. The final dimension addresses concerns about balanced and impartial news coverage. The notion of equal access and balanced reporting of different political parties prevails in Britain, Denmark, and the Netherlands. Editorial staff emphasized this when evaluating the 1999 election campaign coverage, but the interpretation of balance differed. At all programs, time was a key feature of the interpretation of balance, but while this was limited to monitoring by means of a stopwatch in Britain and the Netherlands, balance was also interpreted in terms of substance in Danish news.

With the shift to proportional representation in Britain, new challenges met the news organizations, and influenced the coverage of the elections. As a senior political reporter noted:

"At BBC we set our own guidelines that are more stringent than the laws demands. But all those rules we are familiar with are thrown up in the air by proportional representation. With this, all kinds of middle groups have to be taken a lot more seriously than they ever would have been under the old system. For television, it was a big nightmare to construct a piece because there were too many voices that needed acknowledging. And because the 'Euro-elections' were deemed to be intrinsically boring, they [editors] would be offering you 1 minute and 45 seconds, but ask you to include the viewpoints of six political parties."

As mentioned earlier, 'balance' in the case of European integration also includes weighting and giving access to both pro- and con-European arguments. The Editor-in-Chief of ITN said:

> "We believe Europe is important news and we report about it impartially. It is not our job to counteract the euro-skepticism in the press. But it is our job to ensure that we are not contaminated or tainted by the political prejudice or by others, whether they be pro or anti".

At Danish *TV-Avisen* the notion of political balance was prominent. At editorial meetings, effort was made to structure the coverage to include the whole range of the Danish parties running for the elections (11 parties in total). During the making of a piece on fraud with salaries in the EU, aired only two days prior to Election Day, great caution was taken to criticize both ends of the political spectrum equally in order not do be accused of unbalanced reporting. In fact the story was ready to be broadcast one day, but was postponed until the next day so that 'comparable sleaze' would be available about the contending political parties.[15]

Discussion

This chapter explored the editorial approaches and role of television news organizations in the coverage of European affairs. The coverage of European affairs is organized in a very similar triadic structure in the three countries. The scope of, for example, the Brussels bureau is dependent upon the size of the news organization, the strategic alliances with other programs (such as between *ITN* and Channel 4 and 5 news), and an estimation of the political relevance of 'Brussels' which may change over time (see the example of Norway in Slaatta (1998)).

Editors and journalists at the different news programs varied in their estimation of the ways in which reporting European news poses a challenge different from the challenge of reporting, for example, domestic political news. The most important constraints and challenges were along four areas: (1) 'distance and time', (2) 'access and terminology', (3) 'internal disagreement', and (4) 'audience competences'. In particular, the perceived complexity of the issue, the lack of interest from peers and editors internally and the audience externally as well of the lack of background knowledge were considered key challenges.

The editorial policy of the different news programs may all be characterized as pragmatic and rather 'conventionally journalistic' and 'analytical' in Blumler and Gurevitch's terminology (1989). However, the pragmatic approach took different forms. For example, during the 1999 EP election campaign Dutch news programs were highly selective and did not by any means consider the political event of interest *per se*. British news programs devoted more time to the elections than the Dutch, but they relied on 'auto-pilot' and took over the issue of the euro put forward by the Tories as a key agenda-issue. However, this topic was covered in a distanced and critical manner. Danish news programs assumed a pro-active, highly analytical and even interpretative editorial policy by focusing on the fraud and corruption issue. These findings suggest that the approach taken by television journalists in the coverage of European affairs has changed considerably since the first EP elections in 1979. Noël-Aranda (1983) concluded that broadcasters during the 1979 campaign were cautious and adhered largely to the agenda put forwards by politicians. This is no longer an appropriate description when assessing the approach taken by broadcasters in the 1999 elections.

With respect to the application of news selection criteria, conflict and tension between elites as well as events with significant domestic political and/ or economic consequences were among the key qualities that European events and issues should have to get in to the news. In addition, some difference was found in the application of news selection criteria at the different news programs in the 1999 European elections. The political event was not considered to have sufficient intrinsic importance or interest to yield coverage *per se*. The European Parliament was evaluated critically and did not enjoy any privileges as a political authority. In general, the elections were not 'up-graded' and events in the campaign were mostly evaluated according to normal news selection criteria.

The pragmatic approach and choice to opt for the application of conventional news selection criteria in most instances did not negatively affect the notion that television news, in contrast to for example the press, should remain balanced and impartial. Despite the selective and at times assertive journalistic style, editors and reporters at all programs were, according to themselves, still concerned with balance.

The cross-national design of the study suggests a strong similarity in terms of work routines, logistic organization of the coverage, and criteria for selecting events to become news. However, the cross-national perspective also stresses differences in the editorial policy defined by the different news programs. The findings from the Netherlands illustrate this point since the approaches taken by, for example, *NOS* and *DR* become interesting in a comparative perspective. Both programs can be said to have been pragmatic about the elections by not considering them relevant *per se*. However, one program as a consequence decided to neglect the elections (*NOS*) whereas the other chose to set a different agenda than the one put forward by the political arena (*DR*).

In future research to further elaborate on the 'frame-building' phase of the framing process, an analysis of the efforts made by, for example, the EU and domestic political parties and elites would be useful. This would shed light on the frame-building in its totality by assessing the choices made by journalists when choosing from the issue and discourse made available to them. This chapter dealt with the production side of news about European affairs. First the contours of the coverage were outlined by discussing the organization of the 'Europe beat', the challenges and constraints facing journalists and editors when reporting Europe, and the editorial approaches taken by the various news organizations. The investigation of news selection criteria served to make a link to the integrated process model of framing. In the next chapter, the focus changes to the actual news coverage, i.e. the outcome of the efforts and choices made about Europe in the newsroom.

CHAPTER 4

Europe in the News

Introduction

Citizens across Europe rely on the media for information about European affairs, the EU, and European integration.[1] More than two-thirds of EU citizens consistently name television as the most important source of information and a majority also identifies television as their preferred method for receiving news about the EU specifically (Eurobarometer, 56, 2002). There is therefore more than sufficient rationale for investigating the diet of information that news media across Europe make available to citizens. Yet we have only limited knowledge about the type of information that citizens receive about the EU and European integration. In an overview of the impact of Europeanization on political communication, we concluded that little is known about political communication from a comparative perspective and even less about how news differs cross-nationally in terms of the reporting of European political affairs (Semetko et al., 2000).

News coverage of foreign affairs has been found to influence public opinion more strongly than news about domestic affairs where citizens may have a larger contextual knowledge to draw on (Gavin, 1998; Page & Shapiro, 1992). A similar argument has been made with respect to the role of news for public opinion formation about European affairs (Norris, 2000), which provides another rationale for a systematic analysis of the diet of information available to European publics through the news. One purpose of this chapter is to provide an initial overview of the characteristics of television news coverage of European issues and events.

The content analysis has several aims. First, in line with the 'integrated process model of framing' outlined in Chapter 2, the content analysis investigates the way in which European affairs are framed in television news. This is linked with the findings from the interviews with newsmakers in the three countries (Chapter 3). The second aim of the content analysis is to identify key characteristics of the coverage of European affairs that serve as a baseline for understanding potential effects. That is to say, without knowing about the actual content, it makes little sense to speculate about the effects of this information. In practical terms this means that the content analysis serves to identify key features of the news coverage which are consequently used to design the stimulus material in the experiments (see Chapters 5 and 6).

The analysis consists of four components: [1] the January 1999 first-step introduction of the euro, [2] the June 1999 European Parliamentary (EP) election campaign, [3] key European Union council summits, and [4] a constructed "routine" period of news. The four components have been chosen because they represent a unique event (the introduction of the euro), an election campaign (EP), recurring key events (the EU summits) and a routine period. Based on previous research, we may expect to see specific content structures in the different periods. Campaign news coverage differs from traditional news coverage of daily politics (Patterson, 1993; Norris et al., 1999) and the specific EU news beat, as represented by the summits, has inherent particularities (Morgan, 1995). It is therefore important to investigate the periods separately and later address whether more general conclusions can be drawn about 'the' EU news coverage. Before outlining the components of the study, an introduction to extant research on the media depiction of European affairs is appropriate.

Europe in the news: The evidence from previous research

Previous research on the media coverage of European affairs is scattered. While the EU is covered on television in current affairs magazine style programs, the largest audiences turn to national news programs to learn about the economy and politics. In the news coverage of the EU, a distinction can be made between *news dealing exclusively with* EU *affairs* (such as summits, European elections, and European institutions) and *domestic political and economic news with a European dimension*. Within the first category, the most comprehensive study dates back to the 1979 European elections (Siune, 1983). A cross-national analysis of the television coverage in both the run-up and the actual election campaign showed that 'Europe' did not surface on the media agenda before the actual campaign started. With some cross-national variation it was found that economic topics, comments about the elections, and the "problems, strategies, and mechanics of waging the campaign" dominated the television programming in nearly every country (Siune, 1983, pp. 226-227).

In relation to subsequent European elections, a number of follow-up studies of the television news coverage of the campaign have been carried out. Generally, it is noted that while the first elections received some media coverage because of the novelty of the event, already from the second elections in 1984 and onwards, the campaign was 'nothing special' (Leroy and Siune, 1994, pp. 52-53). One comparative study of the role of television in Denmark and Belgium in the 1989 EP election campaign concluded that the elections were given low priority in the news and that most of the news coverage was of domestic nature, with only little reference to the European dimensions of the issues in question (Leroy and Siune, 1994).

The European Union provides two sources of information about media coverage of European affairs. One is a monitoring project of two newspapers from each EU country. The other includes monitoring of television in six EU countries. Both projects are attempts at gauging the volume of media attention devoted to 'Europe'. They give an overview of the focus of the media coverage and provide indicators for the slant of news about the EU. For the press, it was suggested that coverage of European Union affairs was focused on economic and financial affairs along with specific issues such as the 'mad cow disease', the enlargement of the EU, and social matters (Fundesco, 1997). In an analysis based on the television data from the period 1995 to 1997, it was found that European issues played a peripheral role on the news agenda in most countries (Norris, 2000). If the EU was covered, it was cyclical, peaking around EU summits. During routine periods the predominant topics were the economic and monetary union and the EU development. In addition, it was found that the television news coverage during that period was either neutral or with a modest, but consistent, negative slant (Norris, 2000).[2]

Beyond investigations of media attention to specific EU affairs, a number of studies emphasize the increasing importance of EU/Europe for domestic political and economic news reports. In Britain, for example, it was concluded that while coverage of the economy largely takes place within a 'national narrative', the British economy within the EU is also an important news story (Goddard, Corner, Gavin & Richardson, 1998, pp. 16-17). During two periods in 1996/97 and 1999 British television news carried, on average, more than eleven stories monthly about the single European currency and, on average, more than five stories per month with a link to the European economy. This means that 'Europe' accounted for about 18% of the economic news coverage on *BBC* and *ITN* (Gavin, 2000).

Similarly, studies of the news coverage of national elections suggest an increasing importance of Europe as a topic. While studies of national election campaigns in Britain, Denmark, and the Netherlands in the 1980s and early 1990s showed that 'Europe' was on the periphery, it became a more central issue of the political debate in recent elections.

In Britain, topics as 'Europe' and the European Union along with Britain's relations with foreign countries were much more visible in the news during the 1997 general election compared to 1992 (Norris et al., 1999). And by 2001, a central issue in the general election was the battle waged between Labour and the Conservatives over the euro. The Dutch national elections of 1998 also had a strong focus on Europe, in particular via the French-Dutch power play surrounding the nomination of Dutchman Wim Duisenberg as the first President of the European Central Bank which received extensive coverage (van Praag and Brants, 2000, pp. 70-71). In Denmark, during the 1998 and 2001 national elections, immigration and refugees were more prominent issues in the media coverage. These issues, however, were inherently 'Europe-related' as much of the debate on immigration was centered on the impact of the EU-based Schengen agreement (Andersen et al., 1999).

While the evidence from national election studies suggests an increase in the importance of European issues in national politics, one fundamental problem when examining the visibility of 'Europe' in the news is the lack of comparative perspective, both in terms of time and space. Little is known about how European issues are covered in the news in a longitudinal perspective and or about the ways in which news coverage may differ or share similarities between different European countries.

The European integration project is a continuous process with a number of key events and defining moments that signify Europe and receive the attention of news media. These include signing treaties, elections, and unique events such as the introduction of the common currency, and the inclusion of new member states. The empirical studies discussed above suggest that news about European affairs peaks around key events and is modestly visible in domestic economic coverage as well as during national election campaigns. The 'key events' are essential in shaping public opinion about European integration because they constitute some of the few moments where the EU is visible in mainstream news that attracts a large audience.[3]

Elements of the content analysis and research questions

The content analysis has several elements. All dimensions of the content analysis are investigated in a cross-national comparative perspective. Comparisons are made primarily between countries, but also between periods and types of European news, and between news coverage of European political and economic issues and news coverage of domestic political and economic issues.

VISIBILITY AND TOPICAL FOCUS. The first element establishes a baseline of the European news coverage. The study investigates [a] the visibility and priority, and [b] the topical agenda of European news on national television news. A previous study relying on secondary data analysis suggested that the EU is peripheral in national television news in Britain, Belgium, France, Italy, Germany and Spain, with occasional peaks (Norris, 2000).[4] Nothing is known, however, about the television news coverage of European affairs in Denmark and the Netherlands or whether the visibility of European news during different periods and events is similar.

Based on these consideration the first research question asks: How visible is European news compared to other political and economic news on the national television news agendas?

DOMESTIC OR EUROPEAN? The second element focuses on the extent to which European news is either *domestic* or *European* in focus. This is an important aspect that has only been investigated in a systematic and broader cross-national perspective in the 1979 European election campaign. Several scholars agree that news and information provide an important impetus for the emergence of European debates and a European public sphere (Hodess, 1997; Kevin, 2001; Kunelius & Sparks, 2001; Schlesinger, 1997). What is missing in this discussion, however, is an operationalization of the public sphere and an empirically based discussion of the role played by news media in this respect. One initial step was taken by Hodess (1997) in a comparative analysis of German and British news coverage of 'Europe' where it was concluded that news was more national in orientation in both countries. Kevin (2001), in an analysis of the national press coverage of the 1999 EP elections in eight countries, concluded that the media did not contribute to creating a common sphere outside the national sphere.

Looking from a domestic perspective, Gavin (2000), for example, found that the news coverage of economic issues in Britain was related to EU policies suggesting that Europeanness is not only a dimension of news taking place outside the national arena, but also an integral part of domestic political communication. In this study, the *focus* of news stories about the EU is investigated and compared to other political and economic news. An indication of the focus of European news is a prerequisite for any further advances in the discussions about the implications of news for, for example, a European public sphere. The second research question is: To what extent is news about European affairs focused domestically or on the EU-level?

FRAMES IN THE NEWS COVERAGE. The third element of the content analysis is an investigation of the 'framing of Europe' in the news. As discussed in Chapter 2 the analysis centers on an investigation of the *conflict* and the *economic consequences* frames. The conflict frame emphasizes tension, disagreement, and conflict between different entities, including individuals, groups, institutions, and countries (Neuman et al., 1992; Price et al., 1997; Semetko & Valkenburg, 2000). The economic consequences frame presents an event or issue in terms of the economic implications and ramifications that the event or issue may have for individuals, groups, institutions or countries (Neuman et al., 1992; Semetko & Valkenburg, 2000). In addition, indicators of *strategic* news coverage of European issues are explored. Strategic news has been defined as a focus on winning and losing, emphasis on language of war and games, focus on politicians and citizens as 'performers, critics and audiences', and focus on candidate style and perceptions (Jamieson, 1992).

The current study takes a *deductive* approach to the investigation of frames in the news (Tankard, 2001) and draws on multiple indicators for the investigating the presence of the frames discussed above. The operationalizations and measurement of the different frames are discussed elaborately in the Method section below. Based on the considerations here and in Chapter 2, the third block of research questions are:
- To what extent is news about European affairs framed in terms of conflict?
- To what extent is news about European affairs framed in terms of economic consequences?
- To what extent is news about European affairs presented in terms of strategy?

ACTORS AND TONE OF THE NEWS COVERAGE. The fourth element of the content analysis addresses the visibility and depiction of actors in the news. Actors are broadly understood as persons, organizations, institutions, political parties, candidates etc. The presence and depiction of EU actors is compared to the visibility and depiction of other actors in political and economic news. The visibility of political actors is a necessary condition for the functioning of political representation in a democracy. Several studies investigate the visibility and evaluation of actors in the news in national election campaigns (e.g., Kleinnijenhuis, Maurer, Kepplinger & Oegema, 2001; Kleinnijenhuis, Oegema, de Ridder & Ruigrok, 1998; Norris et al., 1999; Schönbach, de Ridder & Lauf, 2001; Wilke & Reinemann, 2001). However, we know little about the visibility of EU actors. There is no empirical evidence of how visible EU actors are or whether they are more or less visible than other (domestic) political actors (see Peter & de Vreese (2002) for an EU-wide analysis of the visibility of actors during the 1999 European elections). The presence of EU-level versus domestic actors is also an important indicator of the degree of Europeanness in the national television news coverage.

The *tone* of the news coverage of actors in the news is potentially crucial for the public evaluation of these actors. Evaluations of politicians have been investigated in content analyses of national politics (e.g., Caspari, Schönbach & Lauf, 1999; Herr, 2002; McCombs, Lopez-Escobar & Llamas, 2000; Kepplinger, 1998; Wilke & Reinemann, 2001). These studies suggest that the news coverage of candidates may significantly affect audiences' perceptions of these candidates (e.g., Kiousis, Bantimaroudis & Ban, 2001; McCombs et al., 2000) and under certain conditions even affect voting preferences and behavior (Herr, 2002). Evaluations are, when predominantly and permanently negative, considered to contribute to a decrease of citizens' participation in democratic processes (e.g., Kepplinger, 1998). To date, only one study has reported the directional bias of news about specific EU issues and a number of key European institutions (Norris, 2000). No study so far has focused specifically on the evaluation of EU representatives in news. It is therefore unclear whether EU representatives are depicted neutrally, whether they are evaluated positively or negatively, and how this compares to the evaluation of domestic political actors.

Based on these gaps in previous research the fourth block of research questions are:
- To what extent are European actors in national television news evaluated neutrally in comparison with other actors in the news?
- To what extent are European actors in national television news evaluated negatively in comparison with other actors in the news?

Method

The content analysis focuses on main evening television news of the public broadcaster and a private network in Britain, Denmark, and the Netherlands. During the time of the research, these programs were scheduled as follows:[5] *BBC Nine o'clock News* (21.00-21.30), *ITN* (18.30-18.50), *DRTV TV-Avisen* (21.00-21.30), *TV2 Nyhederne* (19.00-19.25), *NOS Journaal* (20.00-20.25), and *RTL4 Nieuws* (19.30-19.55). These news programs are the most widely watched evening news programs in all three countries.

All news programs were taped and coded manually. As recently demonstrated manual coding of news is preferred to utilizing computer assisted analyses of news archives for variables that go beyond, for example, simple word counts (Althaus et al., 2001).

PERIOD OF STUDY. *Introduction of the euro.* News was analyzed during a five-week period surrounding the first-step introduction of the euro on January 1, 1999 (from December 14, 1998 – January 17, 1999). This five-week period is analyzed to establish the visibility of the event in the news.[6] In addition, a sub-sample consisting of 10 days was selected for further analysis. This sample was divided into two periods: one event-period around the introduction of the euro (December 31, 1998 – January 4, 1999) and one constructed routine-period consisting of five days in January 1999.[7] This distinction was applied in order to compare the visibility of the euro introduction with other topics in the news between the two periods.

European elections. News was analyzed during a two-week campaign period (from May 28 – June 9, 1999) leading up to the European elections that were held in Britain, Denmark, and the Netherlands on June 10, 1999 and on June

13, 1999 in the remaining EU member states.[8] A two-week period has previously been defined as the 'hot phase' in a European election campaign (Leroy & Siune, 1994).

EU *summits*. News was analyzed around key EU Council summits in the period 1999-2000. The summits are held four times a year, twice during the spring and twice during the fall, and are hosted by individual EU member states holding the rotating EU presidency. The summits included in this study are Tampere (October 1999) and Helsinki (December 1999) during the Finnish presidency, Lisbon (March 2000) and Feira (June 2000) during the Portuguese presidency, and Biarritz (October 2000) and Nice (December 2000) during the French presidency. For each of the summits, news was collected during 8-10 day periods surrounding the summit and included both days before and after the summit. The exact periods are: October 12-18 and December 7-13, 1999, March 16-26 and June 19-25, 2000, and October 9-19 and December 4-14, 2000.[9]

Routine weeks. News was selected during several weeks in the period 1999 and 2000 to provide the opportunity to investigate news coverage of European affairs in a non-event setting. Though the selected weeks represent different months and years, the sample is not, strictly speaking, random (Riffe, Lacy & Fico, 1998). The sample includes a total of 63 days in the following periods: November 14-28, 1999, February 21-27, 2000, April 3-9, 2000, May 8-14, 2000, July 24-30, 2000, August 21-27, 2000, September 18-24, 2000, November 6-12, 2000.[10]

CODING PROCEDURE. An international team of coders, mostly MA students in the International MA program at the University of Amsterdam, who were native speakers of English, Danish, and Dutch, coded the news stories.[11] Coders were trained and supervised centrally at The Amsterdam School of Communications Research, University of Amsterdam by a team of principal investigators, including the author. The codebooks used in the studies were repeatedly pre-tested. During the coding process, coders were monitored closely and questions were resolved at regular meetings and in supervision of individual coders. For each country, the news stories were randomly assigned to the coders. Because in cross-national comparative content analyses, potential inter-country differences may result from insufficient coordination, the coder trainers were in almost daily contact to coordinate the coding in the groups and to resolve problems (Peter & Lauf, 2003). Overall, the reliability of the coding, based on inter-coder reliability tests discussed below, was satisfactory. More information about the procedure and the results of the tests are reported in the technical appendix (Appendix B).

Despite great efforts invested in the development and pre-testing of codebooks, the recruitment, training, and supervision of native speaking coders, and caution in the handling of the volume of data, cross-national content analyses are challenging and cumbersome. These cautionary remarks notwithstanding, the high level of attention to issues of reliability and coding procedures is an advancement compared to previous cross-national studies of, for example, election news coverage where these issues are not addressed (e.g., Blumler, 1983) or routine EU news coverage based on secondary analyses that did not allow for coding reliability assessment (e.g., Norris, 2000). Explication of methodological procedures and the provision of reliabilities are increasingly reported in content analyses in communication science (Riffe & Freitag, 1997). This information allows for assessment of the data quality and enhances the generation of theory based on content data.

The unit of analysis and of coding in all studies was the news story, defined as a semantic entity with at least one topic delimited from another story by a change of topic.[12] During each period, all news stories in the entire news bulletin were coded. A total of n=10,790 news stories, representing some 321 hours of broadcasting, were coded during the various periods.[13]

MEASURES. Content analysis has been criticized for a lack of systematic analysis and standardized, replicable categories as known from e.g. survey and experimental research (Shoemaker & Reese, 1996). The variables used in this study include variables previously applied in content analyses of news as well as new variables designed for the purpose of this study. In the subsequent sections, the key measures for each component of the study are described. Additional information about the variables is in the technical appendix.

EURO STUDY. *Topic.* In order to study the visibility of the euro launch and political and economic topics in the news compared with other news, all news stories were coded using a detailed topic list with nine main categories and several pertinent subcategories (see technical appendix). The same nine main categories are applied in all studies for reasons of comparability.[14] To assess the relative visibility of the different topics, the length of the news stories was measured. This is a more accurate measure of the visibility of topics than the number of news stories because the different programs are of varying length and some networks opt for only a few rather lengthy stories whereas others opt for more and shorter stories. The length-based measure is applied in all the components of the content analysis.

Focus. To investigate the focus of news a distinction was made between (1) news stories focusing on the country of the news outlet (domestically focused), (2) stories focused on the EU level, (3) stories with an international, but non-EU level focus. An additional residual category for news stories without a specific focus was also included. For example a story on Dutch television dealing with a topic that takes place in the Netherlands was coded as 1. A story on the British news about EU drug policies was coded as 2. A story on the Danish news about a meeting between the Israeli Prime Minister and the US president was coded as 3. A story about, for example fishing quotas in the Atlantic Ocean that has no ties to any specific location, was coded in the residual category. These four categories are applied in all studies in this book for reasons of comparability.

News frames. For the operationalization of the conflict and the economic consequences frames, measures developed by Semetko and Valkenburg (2000) were applied. Multiple-item scales are used to investigate the presence of the frames. The conflict frame scale was operationalized with four items, for example: "Does the news story reflect disagreement between parties/individuals/groups/countries?"[15] The economic consequences frame scale was measured with three items, for example: "Is there a mention of the costs/degree of expense involved?".[16]

The questions were answered with yes (1) or no (0) and were applied to all political and economic news stories. For each of the two frames, scales were formed by adding the scores of each item and dividing it by the number of items. Thus the values of each scale range from 0.00 (frame not present) to 1.00 (frame present). A high score on the conflict scale means that the story is presented in a fashion that emphasizes the disagreement between story actors and their reproaching one another. Typically, such a story referred to two or more sides of a problem, and/or stressed the achievement of one story actor versus another. A high score on the economic consequences scale indicate presentation of a story in terms of expenses, financial gains and losses, and general economic consequences of an action.

Actors. An actor was defined as an individual (or organization/ institution/ entity etc.) "who is an essential part of the content of the story [...] and who is mentioned or shown in the news story".[17] Up to six actors could be coded per story. Each actor was coded according to a detailed actor list. In the presentation of the results, the actors are recoded in to nine main categories. The main categories were: 'EU actors' (e.g, (members of) EU institutions and EU parliamentarians), 'Domestic government' (e.g., (prime) ministers, members of government parties), 'Domestic political actors' (e.g., members of opposition parties in national parliament), 'National institutions' (e.g., courts, army, and police), 'Organizations' (e.g., companies, trade unions, human right organizations), 'Non-organized actors' (e.g., individuals, pensioners, celebrities, experts, victims), 'Other EU-country actor' (e.g., British actors appearing in Danish news and Dutch actors on British news), 'International level actor' (e.g., US president, Russian president, and Middle East actors), and a residual 'Other' category. These categories are applied in all content studies reported in this book for reasons of comparability.

Actor evaluation. To investigate the tone of the news towards both EU actors and other actors, explicit judgments of story actors were coded. For each actor in the story it was coded whether this news story was either neutral (i.e. no evaluation), unfavorable, mixed, or favorable from the perspective of the actor. In the analysis a distinction is made between the share of neutral stories (i.e. stories in which no evaluations appear) and an *average tone* towards different actors. The average tone measure is computed per country. The measure is calculated by subtracting the number of negative evaluations from the number of positive evaluations and dividing this sum with total number of appearances of this actor group. The average tone therefore ranges for all groups of actors, irregardless of the number of appearances, from -1 to $+1$. If, for example, EU actors appear 50 times in a period, we may find that in 30 of these instances, the actor is not evaluated (i.e. 60% neutral). If the EU actors are evaluated favorably in 4 cases, mixed in 4, and unfavorably in 12, the average tone would be $((4 - 12) / 50)$ (number of positive evaluations minus number of negative evaluations divided by the total number of appearances) = $((-8)/50) = -.16$.[18] It should be noted in advance that the interpretation of the actor evaluation mean should be cautionary given the low number of cases in some analyses. This measure of actor evaluations is applied in all studies.

EUROPEAN ELECTION STUDY. Given the relative low visibility of the European elections in the national news programs and the limited number of stories (see Chapter 3 and the results below), the analysis of the European election campaign concentrates on the general news environment, the specific television news campaign agenda, as well as actors and their evaluations.[19]

Topic. To investigate the general news environment during the campaign, the topic of each news story was determined. For reasons of comparability, the topics were recoded into the same categories outlined above for the euro study (with the first category labeled 'News about the European elections' rather than 'News about the euro'). News about the elections was defined as stories mentioning the elections and/ or the campaign. Examples of such stories are stories dealing with candidate profiles, election strategies, polls, expected turnout, and party and candidate issue positions. In addition, a separate category for all news stories dealing with the Kosovo conflict was included. Because of the limited number of news stories dealing specifically with the elections, the topic of each news story about the elections was also registered by means of key words to provide a more detailed account of the campaign coverage.

Actors. To qualify as a story actor, a person, group, or institution had to be either depicted and mentioned at least once, or quoted and verbally mentioned, or mentioned verbally at least twice. Actors were then selected for coding in terms of their importance for the story (operationalized as amount of information given about a particular actor, frequency of being mentioned, visibility, and quotes by a particular actor).[20] Up to six actors could be coded per story, but the same actor was coded only once per story. The actors were recoded into broader categories identical to the ones outlined above for the euro study.

Actor evaluation. Evaluation of EU actors and other actors was assessed by coding explicit judgments of story actors. The coding categories were 0 (neutral), 1 (unfavorable), 2 (mixed), and 3 (favorable). An average tone was calculated using the same procedure as described above for the euro study.

SUMMIT AND ROUTINE STUDY. These two components of the content analysis were carried out simultaneously, using the same procedure, same team of coders, and an identical codebook. The measures are therefore discussed together and the reliabilities were assessed in the same inter-coder reliability test which included randomly selected stories from both the summit and the routine periods.

Topic. In order to study the visibility of European news compared with other types of news, all news stories were coded using a detailed topic list. The topic was recoded using the nine main categories outlined above and used in the euro and the election study. A screening question determining whether the story was about the EU, and/ or any of its policies or institutions was applied (see technical appendix).

Focus. The focus of the story was determined by assessing "where does the story or the actions it depicts (mainly) take place (in terms of prominence in the story or length)?" A detailed list of locations was recoded into the same categories used in the euro study. In the presentation of the data comparisons are made between the focus of EU stories versus other political stories. The definition of "other political stories" includes local, national and international politics.[21]

News frames. For the investigation of the framing of European news the measures discussed above (see euro study) were used.[22] Given the findings from the first study (the euro study, see Results section below), it was decided to focus the analysis on the framing of European news in terms of conflict because the economic consequences frames was found only to play a substantial role in the framing of the euro launch but not in other news stories. This also concurs with the findings from Chapter 3 in which newsmakers repeatedly identified the presence of conflict and disagreement as a key characteristic of an event or issue for it to be selected for the news. A multiple-item scale was formed by adding the scores of each item and dividing it by the number of relevant items. Thus the values of the conflict scale range from 0.00 (frame not present) to 1.00 (frame present).

Presence of strategy news. Two dichotomous indicators (coded as 0 (not present) or 1 (present) were used to investigate the presence of strategic news. The two items were derived from Cappella and Jamieson (1997):[23] "Does the story mention a person's, group's, institution's or organization's presentation and style of how, in which way, in which manner they handle an issue?" and "Does the story mention that an action of a person, group, institutions or organization was taken in order to stabilize, consolidate or enhance his/ hers/ its position, in order to make him/ her/ it look better in public opinion or in the political arena?".

Actors. To qualify as a story actor, a person, group, or institution had to be either mentioned and depicted and/ or quoted at least once, or (in news stories without film), mentioned twice. A main actor was then selected in terms of importance in the story (operationalized as amount of information given about a particular actor, frequency of being mentioned, visibility, and quotes by a particular actor). Remaining actors were coded in their order of appearance up to the maximum of six actors. The actors were recoded into broader categories identical to the ones outlined above for the euro and the election study.

Actor evaluation. Evaluation of EU actors and other actors was assessed by coding explicit judgments of story actors. The coding categories were 0 (neutral), 1 (unfavorable), 2 (mixed), and 3 (favorable). The percentage of neutral stories (i.e. with no explicit evaluation) and an average tone was calculated using the same procedure as described above for the euro and the election study.

Results

In the presentation of the results all research questions are dealt with for each of the components in the study. In the summary at the end of the chapter generalizations are made and specific aspects of the different types of event/ periods are discussed.

THE INTRODUCTION OF THE EURO: A SMOOTH OPERATION. The first-step introduction of the common European currency in January 1999 was a success. None of the scenarios of crashing stock markets or panic came through and the news during the period reflected this. The first research question deals with the visibility of the launch of the euro and the share of political and economic news compared to other news. An analysis of the general news environment during the time of the launch showed that during this five-week period, the introduction of the euro took up between 2% (*ITN*) and 7% (*DR*) of the news in terms of the amount of time. The share of political and economic news (euro launch, economy, and politics) was similar across all news outlets and varied between 43% (*RTL*) and 54% (*NOS*) with *BBC* (53%), *ITN* (45%), *DR* (48%), and *TV2* (52%) in between.

Figure 4.1 gives an impression of how the news about the launch of the euro was distributed during the five-week period. Figure 4.1 shows that the euro as a topic was virtually absent until a week before the introduction and vanished from the news within a week after the launch.

Figure 4.1. Percentage of news about the launch of the euro from December 14, 1998 thru January 17, 1999. The coverage of the euro peaks and vanishes.

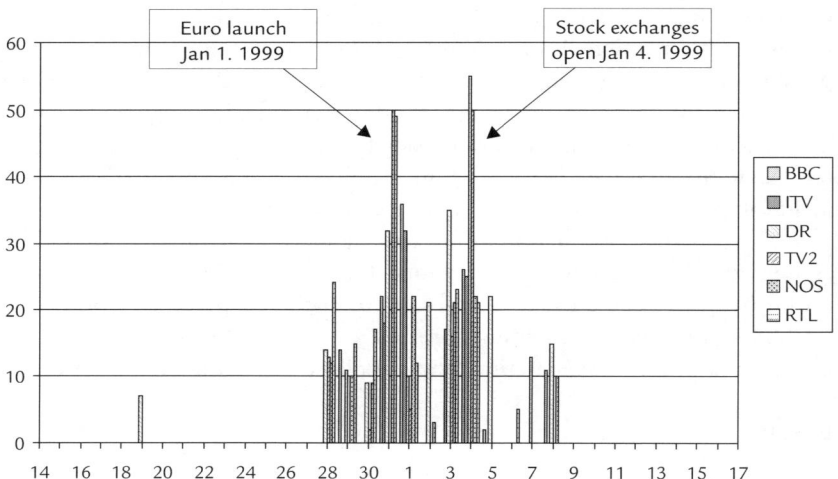

As described above, the remaining analyses focus on two five-day periods. One 'event period' around the introduction and one constructed 'routine period'. The amount of time news in each country devoted to different topics in the television news coverage during the routine news period and the period surrounding the launch of the euro (the event period) was compared. Table 4.1 shows that during the routine news period, the amount of time spent on political and economic topics ranged from a low of 49% of the news in Denmark to a high of 60% in the Netherlands, with Britain (56%) in between. Apart from political and economic news, societal stories (such as stories about crime, trials, poverty or sensations without political or economic implications) took up a considerable portion of time in the four countries. During the routine news period, this ranged from 18% in the Netherlands to 29% in Denmark with Britain (23%) in between.[24]

Table 4.1. Percentage of time devoted to different topics in British, Danish, and Dutch news during 'event' and 'routine' period surrounding the January 1999 euro launch

	Britain		Denmark		The Netherlands	
	Event: euro intro (n = 91)	Routine (n = 122)	Event: euro intro (n = 94)	Routine (n = 115)	Event: euro intro (n = 115)	Routine (n = 123)
Euro intro	20	1	26	5	23	2
Economy	3	5	2	10	5	10
Politics	31	51	10	34	23	48
Society	10	23	30	29	26	18
Social welfare/ education etc.	1	8	18	9	1	4
Agriculture/ environment etc.	1	2	6	3	2	1
Disasters	16	2	6	7	7	1
Sports/ Weather	17	8	3	7	13	13
Other	0	0	1	0	3	2
Tot percentage	99	100	102	101	102	99
Total time (sec)	7426	14408	10217	15010	9871	11277

Note. n refers to number of stories. Total percentages unequal 100% due to rounding. Table based on de Vreese et al. (2001).

In each country, during the event period (coinciding with the New Year celebrations), there was somewhat less political and economic coverage than during the routine period. During the event period, 38% of news in Denmark was devoted to political and economic topics, including the introduction of the euro, and this reached 51% in the Netherlands and 54% in Britain. A considerable portion of the political and economic news during the event period was devoted to the introduction of the euro, ranging from one-fifth in Britain (20%) to about one-fourth in Denmark (26%) and the Netherlands (23%). The major political and economic event did not increase the overall amount of time devoted to political and economic news in any of the countries studied. The coverage of the euro was entirely event driven and almost disappeared entirely in the immediate aftermath of the launch.

The next question deals with the focus of news about the euro launch compared to the focus of other political and economic stories.

Figure 4.2. Focus of news stories about the *euro launch* and *other political and economic news*. Euro launch stories have a predominant domestic focus but are more EU-focused than other political and economic news.

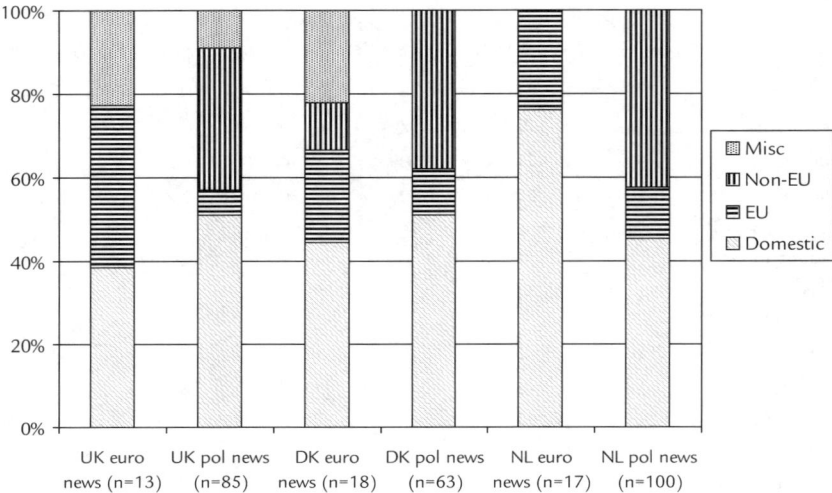

Figure 4.2 shows that news stories about the launch of the euro were more domestically focused than EU-focused. However, the stories about the launch of the euro were more EU-focused than other political and economic stories in the same period which was primarily of domestic nature.

The emphasis on conflict and economic consequences frames in political and economic news and news about the introduction of the euro was analyzed. Table 4.2 displays the mean visibility of the frames, distinguishing between all political/economic news stories and stories about the euro. Conflict was more prominent in political/ economic news stories in all three countries compared to economic consequences (with the visibility of the frame ranging from $M = .35$ ($SD = .33$) in the Netherlands, $M = .42$ ($SD = .30$) in Britain to $M = .43$ ($SD = .33$) in Denmark). When looking at stories about the introduction of the euro, the reverse is the case: conflict was less important than economic consequences in these stories.

Danish journalists put a stronger economic consequences spin on the coverage of all news than their British and Dutch counterparts. In Denmark economic consequences were most visible in the stories about the introduction of the euro $M = .37$ ($SD = .24$) and although less evident in political/economic stories $M = .24$ ($SD = .38$) they were nevertheless more visible than in Britain (where the comparable figures were $M = .15$ ($SD = .22$) for stories about the introduction of the euro and $M = .09$ ($SD = .22$) for political/economic stories).

Table 4.2. Presence of conflict and economic consequences frame in British, Danish, and Dutch news. The conflict frame dominated in political/economic stories while the economic consequences frame dominated in news about the euro launch.

	Conflict		Economic consequences	
	Political/ economic stories (n = 344)	Euro introduction stories (n = 66)	Political/ economic stories (n = 344)	Euro introduction stories (n = 66)
Britain	.42 (.30) (n=85)	.19 (.29) (n=13)	.09 (.22) (n=85)	.15 (.22) (n=13)
Denmark	.43 (.33) (n=63)	.19 (.30) (n=18)	.24 (.38) (n=63)	.37 (.24) (n=18)
The Netherlands	.35 (.33) (n=100)	.10 (.29) (n=17)	.17 (.24) (n=100)	.20 (.30) (n=17)

Note. Data entries are mean scores on the frame scales, figures in parentheses indicate standard deviations and number of cases. Table based on de Vreese et al. (2001).

In framing the introduction of the euro in terms of *economic consequences*, Danish news emphasized the implications of the launch for the domestic macro-economy and for individual businesses. Danish *TV-Avisen*, for example, opened its bulletin on January 4, 1999 with a story about a company whose competitive position was allegedly threatened by the introduction of the euro which would give international competitors an advantage in terms of currency stability and savings on money transfers. In Denmark, the euro was seen as a major market player and the introduction was watched with some anxiety and trepidation. One Danish journalist put it this way: "*The debut of the euro on the world stage marks one of the most important steps towards a United States of Europe.*" Leading politicians were openly in favor of joining the common currency as soon as possible and it was public opinion and opposition groups that, in the government's view, were holding the country back. The Danish Prime Minister was seen saying: "*We need to be in and the sooner the better.*" The Minister of Finance echoed this view: "*We do not want to have another referendum until public opinion says the answer will be 'yes'*".

Journalists in Britain and the Netherlands were less focused on economic consequences than their counterparts in Denmark, and this was evident in both political/ economic stories as well as stories about the introduction of the euro. Dutch news highlighted the conversion work in the financial sector, but was less concerned with the economic consequences of the euro for the Dutch economy. The only mention of economic consequences was the implications for businesses forced to do extra hours to complete conversion and software. *NOS* opened with the headline "*Spectacular introduction of the euro*" but the lead story began "*The most spectacular* (with a visual of champagne corks popping) *was that there was nothing spectacular at all*". The only emphasis on conflict in the Dutch news concerned the 'political disagreement' around the Wim Duisenberg 'issue'.[25] *NOS* described the problem this way: "*The Duisenberg issue is a typical example of the European Union. The economy is fine, but the political disagreement constantly threatens to disrupt.*" *RTL4 News* reported in a similar vein: "*The turbulence around Duisenberg does not say a lot about the stability of the new currency, but it does say a great deal about the political weaknesses in this cooperation. The big test will come when a country does not follow the agreements on finance policy, creates disputes, and threatens the euro.*"

Britain discussed the launch of the euro in terms of the potential economic repercussions for the British pound. Though economic consequences were not at the forefront of the coverage, reporters at both the *BBC* and *ITN* mentioned the future prospect of a diminished role for the British pound on the world market and noted that it may stand on the sidelines while future battles would be waged between the US dollar and the euro.

The final aspect of the investigation of television news during the time of the introduction of the euro deals with the visibility and evaluation of actors in the news. The analysis is based on the coding of actors in the news. In Table 4.3 a distinction is made between actors appearing in stories specifically about the launch of the euro and actors appearing in other political and economic news during that period.

Table 4.3 shows that in all countries there were more EU-level actors in stories about the euro than in other political and economic news. The analysis also showed that the majority of the actors in the euro stories in all three countries were either 'organizations', typically representing the financial sector, or 'non-organized actors', typically citizens on the street sharing their perception of the introduction or experts predicting the consequences of the introduction. These two categories taken together represented between 48% (Britain) and 68% (Denmark) of the actors. Only few domestic political actors (government or opposition) were present in the euro introduction stories, suggesting the rather a-political nature of the event.

In the other political and economic news, organizations and non-organized actors also dominated. Domestic political actors were more present in the other political and economic news as were international level actors who were typically US politicians appearing in news stories about the impeachment of US president Clinton which happened during the period of the study.

Turning to the evaluation of the different actors (Table 4.4) it can be seen that EU actors were most often not evaluated, i.e. were treated neutrally, in between 62% (Britain) to 79% (The Netherlands) of the cases. If EU actors were evaluated, this was mostly in a negative direction which leads to a modest average tone measure of -.08 in Britain, .00 in Denmark, and -.21 in the Netherlands.[26]

Table 4.4 also shows that domestic political actors, both government and opposition, were treated neutrally in between 54% and 94% of the cases. If domestic politicians were evaluated, this was (with the exception of non-governmental actors in the Netherlands) consistently in a moderate negative direction. The overall tone measure ranged from -.31 (Danish government) to -.08 (British government). Comparing the evaluation of EU as well as domestic political actors, two patterns emerge: first, the country differences are only negligible and do not appear to be systematic. Second, the pattern of evaluation (i.e. the percentage neutral and overall directional bias) is very similar between EU actors and domestic political actors suggesting that the two types of actors were not depicted systematically different in the news during the time of the launch of the euro.

Table 4.3. Percentage of actors in the euro launch period, in euro news and other political / economic news. EU level actors are more prominent in euro stories than in other political/ economic news. Organizations and non-organized actors (e.g., citizens) dominate the euro stories.

	Britain		Denmark		The Netherlands	
	Euro stories (n=21)	Other political stories (n=129)	Euro stories (n=37)	Other political stories (n=167)	Euro stories (n=37)	Other political stories (n=253)
EU level	24	6	8	3	11	11
Domestic government	5	18	8	6	11	4
Domestic political actor	10	10	5	8	0	7
National institutions	10	4	0	8	14	7
Organizations	48	17	11	17	54	28
Non-organized actors	0	21	57	35	5	19
Other EU country actor	10	0	5	3	0	4
International level	0	20	0	15	5	18
Other	5	4	5	6	0	3
Total	102	100	99	101	100	101

Note: The base for the percentages is the total number of actors in the different types of stories, e.g., 129 actors in 'other political stories' in Britain.

Table 4.4. Evaluation of actors in the news in the euro launch period. EU-actors are either evaluated neutrally or slightly negative and this is comparable to the evaluation of other actors.

	Britain (n=150)			Denmark (n=204)			The Netherlands (n=290)		
	n	Percentage neutral	Tone	n	Percentage neutral	Tone	n	Percentage neutral	Tone
EU level	13	62	-.08	8	73	0	33	79	-.21
Domestic government	24	63	-.08	13	54	-.31	15	87	-.13
Domestic political actor	13	77	-.15	15	93	-.07	17	94	+.06
National institutions	7	72	0	13	54	+.08	22	96	-.05
Organizations	32	66	-.34	32	66	+.09	90	70	-.09
Non-organized actors	27	85	+.15	80	50	+.13	49	67	-.18
Other EU country actor	2	100	0	7	57	-.67	9	67	-.22
International level	26	50	-.31	25	52	-.08	48	83	-.08
Generalizations	5			0			7		
Other	1			0			0		

Note: The base for the percentages is the total number of actors in all stories, e.g., 150 actors in Britain.

THE 1999 EUROPEAN ELECTIONS: VOTER APATHY AND FRAUD. Given the variation in editorial policies and application of news selection criteria in the newsroom of the different news programs (see Chapter 3), one would expect differences in the actual priority given to the campaign in the bulletins of the different networks. First, to provide a backdrop against which to understand the campaign coverage Table 4.5 is an overview of the news environment during the campaign.

The first observation is that the European elections took up between 1-2% (the Netherlands), 5-7% (Britain) and 11-17% (Denmark) of the news during the campaign (Table 4.5). Across all countries, the Kosovo conflict and the negotiated peace treaty dominated the news and took up between 24% and 56% of the total news. In the Netherlands, domestic politics was also strongly present given a government crisis during the campaign.

Table 4.5. News agenda during 1999 European election campaign (May 29 – June 9, 1999). The Kosovo conflict dominated the campaign and the visibility of the elections in the news ranged from 1-17%.

	Britain		Denmark		The Netherlands	
	BBC (n=132)	ITV (n=122)	DR (n=131)	TV2 (n=141)	NOS (n=90)	RTL (n=129)
European elections	7	5	17	11	2	1
Economy	3	3	3	3	5	3
Politics	10	9	13	11	28	30
Kosovo conflict	56	44	28	35	35	24
Society	5	15	20	22	19	17
Social welfare/ education etc.	1	2	4	4	2	1
Agriculture/ environment etc.	4	4	10	8	4	10
Disasters	1	2	3	2	6	3
Sports/ Weather	13	16	1	3	1	3
Other	1	0	0	1	0	6
Tot percentage	100	100	99	100	102	98
Total time (sec)	13,928	11,858	16,177	17,522	11,381	11,932

Note. n refers to the number of stories. Total percentages unequal 100% due to rounding errors.

In general, the visibility of the campaign was low to modest in all countries. This assessment, however, is relative. No comparable measures are available for television news in the previous European election campaigns. One indicator suggests that during the campaign for the 1979 European elections, between 40 (the Netherlands) and 100 (Britain and Denmark) minutes in the news bulletins of the public broadcasters were devoted to the European elections (Kelly & Siune, 1983). For the 1999 European elections, the public broadcasters devoted 15 (*BBC*), 4 (*NOS Journaal*), and 47 (*DR TV-Avisen*) minutes respectively. The proportion of election news as part of the total news varied from a high 17% at *DR* in Denmark to a low 1% at *RTL* in the Netherlands who, together with *NOS*, neglected the elections and both channels carried only one story on June 9, the day before the elections.[27]

Looking specifically at the news coverage of the elections, strong cross-national differences were found. Table 4.6 provides an overview of the issues covered in the news in all three countries. The Dutch news programs neglected the European elections and each channel carried only one obligatory story at the end of the news program reminding the electorate about the elections. Both of these Dutch stories emphasized the lack of voter interest and the anticipated low turnout.

Table 4.6. Overview of television news about European elections in Britain, Denmark, and the Netherlands

Date	Britain		Denmark		The Netherlands	
	BBC	ITN	DR	TV2	NOS	RTL
June 10	Polls close at 10. Turnout low (3, 0:25)	First proportional representation elections (5, 0:13)	Poll - who's in and who's out (2, 1:50) Danes stayed at home (3, 3:00) 'Mimi' lost the race (4, 2:00) Electorate stayed at home, only politicians out (5, 3:40)	One hour before closing: exit poll (3, 4:37)	-	-
June 9	Political leaders on final day of campaigning (3, 3:20) Proportional Representation and ballot papers (4, 2:00)	Turnout expected to go down; big ballots (8, 2:37)	Latest poll and analysis (2, 3:50) Party to return contribution (7, 7:23) Britain: Euro dominates elections (8, 3:05) DR-TVA apology to June Movement (9, 0:30)	Campaigning in empty rooms (4, 4:54)	European elections tomorrow - expected low turnout (10, 4:28)	Elections for European Parliament (11, 2:37)
June 8	Euro is election battleground. Britain to lead or leave Europe (5, 3:00)	-	EU is 'Roman Kingdom' of Committees (3, 3:32) Live debate in Jutland (5, 0:25) Fraud with salaries in EU (8, 4:01)	Italy wants strong EU defense (8, 2:48)	-	-
June 7	-	3 days away: persistent predictions of low turnout (8, 2:00)	Live: Nasar Kadar vs. Mogens Camre in Copenhagen (6, 3:36)	Commissioner Bjerregård 'interferes' in Danish campaign (7, 2:06)	-	-
June 6	-	-	June Movement to be halved (3, 02:30) Conservatives to loose (4, 2:58)	Mickey Mouse elections: Sport stars and actors dominate (7, 3:55)	-	-
June 5	-	-	-	EU elections (3, 4:39)	-	-
June 4	-	-	-	(Solana appointed) (4, 1:10)	(EU appoints Solana) (6, 0:32)	-
June 3	Conservative pressured to deny EU leaving policy (7, 1:57)	-	(Euro Suimmit Cologne) (4, 1:48)	(Euro Summit Cologne: Role EU in Kosovo, role DK in EU) (5, 3:50)	(Euro Summit Cologne: Role EU in Kosovo) (2, 3:14)	(Euro Summit Cologne: Role EU in Kosovo) (2, 2:17)
June 2	-	Campaign stepping up, fear for turnout (10, 2:01)	25% of EP administration 'moonlighting' (6, 4:20)	-	-	-
June 1	Hague calls for government to ban Euro (6, 2:45)	-	Danish PM supports EU defense cooperation (2, 2:35)	Europe-politicians don't show up at meetings (1, 4:56)	-	-

Note: Entries are "headlines" of television news. In brackets the story number in the news program and the length of story.

British news was primarily concerned with the euro, the Conservatives' 'no' policy on this issue, and the anticipated electoral apathy. *BBC* and *ITN* did not differ substantially in their perspective on the campaign, though *ITN* gave more room to the expected abstention rate whereas the *BBC* seemed to up-play the 'euro battleground'. A *BBC* senior political correspondent commented:

> "We ended up paying a lot of attention to the euro. Particularly we, but also the government, were driven by the agenda set by the Opposition. Because they were the ones campaigning most vigorously, they ended up setting the agenda for everybody else and they did very well. As a result, as they were the only people really setting an agenda, and the Government was choosing not to set an agenda, it was the Conservative agenda we followed."

In Denmark, the agendas of *DR* and *TV2* differed considerably. *TV2* dealt with expected low turnout, visited Italy, and addressed the fact that many 'celebrities', authors, and sport stars run for the European elections. *DR* visited Britain and Germany, covered two public debates about the elections, but paid the strongest attention to the fraud/ corruption issue. The Head of the Political Unit commented:

> "We responded to reality. Fact is, which perhaps is sad, that [1] there is hardly any interest for these elections, [2] the politicians have a very hard time selling anything with reference to the European Parliament, and [3] we know from other news and our own research that fraud and the lack of working discipline in the Parliament are the most important issues to the audience".

Turning to the actors in the election news stories and in other political and economic news during the campaign, there was, as a function of the cross-national variation in the number of stories, a very limited number of actors in election stories in the Netherlands (n=11) and Britain (n =45) and more in Denmark (n=108).

Table 4.7 shows that in Britain, election news was dominated by domestic political actors (78%) whereas in Denmark and the Netherlands EU-level actors dominated the news (68% and 64% respectively). However, almost three out of four of all EU-level actors in the Danish news were domestically based candidates for the European Parliament and could therefore also be considered as domestic actors. For the Netherlands, it is inappropriate to draw any conclusions given the low number of election stories.

In the remaining political and economic news during the campaign, international level actors dominated in all three countries. These were typically actors related to the Kosovo conflict, such as representative from NATO. EU level actors are virtually absent from stories that do not deal specifically with the European elections. In the Netherlands, a substantial amount of actors in the news were domestic politicians, both government and opposition, who featured frequently in relation to the Dutch governmental crisis.

The evaluation of EU actors (Table 4.8) during the election campaign was predominantly neutral, ranging from 63% stories without an evaluation of EU actors in the Netherlands to 86% in Britain. When evaluations were made, these varied from an overall tone measure of '.00' in the Netherlands to a modest positive directional bias in Britain (+.07) and a modest negative directional bias in Denmark (-.11).

International level actors, typically present in Kosovo-related stories, were mostly not evaluated (62-87%), but when evaluated this was with a modest, though consistently negative direction (ranging from -.06 to -.12). This pattern is very much the same for the evaluation of domestic governments. In Britain and Denmark these were not evaluated in 63% and 79% of the cases and received a modest overall negative coverage (-.11 and -.17). The Dutch government was evaluated in almost half of the news stories and received, overall, consistent negative evaluations (-.33). In sum, during the campaign for the European elections, EU actors, when featuring in the news, were evaluated in a fashion comparable to the pattern found for international as well as domestic political actors, or even marginally less negative.

Table 4.7. Percentage of actors in television news (election news and other political news) during the 1999 European election campaign.

	Britain		Denmark		The Netherlands	
	Election stories (n=45)	Other political stories (n=323)	Election stories (n=108)	Other political stories (n=386)	Election stories (n=11)	Other political stories (n=410)
EU level	4	4	68	3	64	3
Domestic government	9	5	6	16	0	28
Domestic political actor	78	8	4	11	9	11
National institutions	0	5	1	7	0	4
Organizations	4	14	7	17	9	10
Non-organized actors	4	16	8	6	18	5
Other EU country actor	0	12	3	12	0	6
International level	0	37	0	24	0	33
Other	0	0	0	0	0	0
Total	99	10	97	100	100	100

Note: The base for the percentages is the total number of actors in the different types of stories.

Table 4.8. Evaluation of actors in television news (election news and other political news) in the 1999 European election campaign.

	Britain (n=368)			Denmark (n=494)			The Netherlands (n=421)		
	n	Percentage neutral	Tone	n	Percentage neutral	Tone	N	Percentage neutral	Tone
EU level	14	86	+.07	103	77	-.11	19	63	0
Domestic government	19	63	-.11	70	79	-.17	113	57	-.33
Domestic political actor	61	56	-.02	45	84	-.11	46	78	-.15
National institutions	15	100	0	27	85	-.07	15	67	-.20
Organizations	48	60	-.13	72	83	-.13	42	82	-.14
Non-organized actors	54	87	-.04	34	100	0	23	100	0
Other EU country actor	39	77	-.13	50	88	-.02	26	73	-.27
International level	118	70	-.06	93	87	-.08	136	62	-.12
Generalizations	0			0			1		
Other	0			0			0		

Note: n refers to the number of actors in all news stories (election news and other political news).

SUMMITS: STRUCTURED ROWS ON A REGULAR BASIS. When the European Heads of Government meet twice every half year in the larger European cities for the EU Council meeting, a road-show of journalists follow their trail and in these periods, the EU becomes an issue on the national television news agendas. Table 4.9 provides an overview of the general news environment during the six EU Council summits held in the period October 1999 to December 2000.[28]

The table is primarily aimed at providing a baseline for the amount of coverage of the EU during the key moments of decision-making and negotiation as found during the summits. During the summit periods, the news programs devote, on average, about one-fourth to one-third of the time to political news, around 10% to economic news and about one-fourth to societal topics such as crime and court proceedings. Table 4.9 also shows that EU news takes up around 4% of the news in Britain, between 4-6% in the Netherlands, and between 8-12% in Denmark.[29] With the exception of Denmark, this finding concurs with a previous analysis of the visibility of the European Union in television news in a report to the European Commission in which EU-stories were found to peak around summits of the European council and represent about 4-6% of the coverage during the summits (Norris, 2000, pp. 188-89).

Table 4.9. News agenda during EU summit periods in 1999 and 2000. EU news (primarily about the summits) take up between 4-12% of the news.

	Britain		Denmark		The Netherlands	
	BBC (n=544)	ITV (n=536)	DR (n=694)	TV2 (n=663)	NOS (n=562)	RTL (n=566)
EU news	4	4	12	8	6	4
Economy	12	9	12	10	5	8
Politics	33	26	28	35	42	38
Society	21	28	24	27	23	24
Social welfare/ education etc.	11	5	7	6	4	5
Agriculture/ environment etc.	5	6	5	6	7	8
Disasters	7	9	4	4	2	3
Sports/Weather	8	13	7	4	9	7
Other	0	0	0	0	3	3
Tot percentage	101	100	99	100	101	100
Total time (sec)	65,534	57,834	76,323	65,960	64,976	49,849

Note. n refers to the number of stories. Total percentages unequal 100% due to rounding errors.

Looking at the coverage of the summits on a day-to-day basis it also becomes apparent that in all programs in the three countries, news about the EU and its summits enters the news agenda only during the days of the summit itself, with exceptions of one or two stories broadcast a day or two in advance of the summit. This pronounced and consistent pattern supports the suggestion that news about the EU is cyclical: it enters the news agenda and vanishes immediately after the end of a specific event.

The EU summits are recurring events that follow an almost identical format and usually last for two-three days. To get a notion of the issues addressed at the summits, the following table presents the most important issues of each summit, as defined by the news programs.

Table 4.10. Key issues during the EU summits

Finland Fall 1999		Portugal Spring 2000		France Fall 2000	
Tampere	Helsinki	Lisbon	Fiara	Biaritz	Nice
EU enlargement Membership Turkey		IT in the EU Employment issues in the EU		EU reorganization Negotiation of the Nice treaty	

During the period of analysis, one summit stands out as a particularly interesting case. The December 2000 summit hosted by France and held in Nice was longest Council summit in the history of the European Union and lasted for 1,5 days longer than scheduled. In the news coverage of the summit in Nice, all networks emphasised the crucial nature of the event for the future enlargement and development of the European Union.

The analysis of the Nice summit highlights a specific characteristic of the news coverage of EU summits. The summits take place in varying locations which implies that much of the news coverage is organized from these locations. Summit coverage is therefore inherently EU-focused in nature. Nonetheless, a substantial amount of the news coverage typically focuses on domestic reactions to the summit: both to the issues of the summits and in assessments of the negotiation success / failure of the national delegations.

Figure 4.3. Focus of news stories during the 1999-2000 summit periods. EU news during the summit periods is highly EU-focused. Other political/ economic news is mostly domestic.

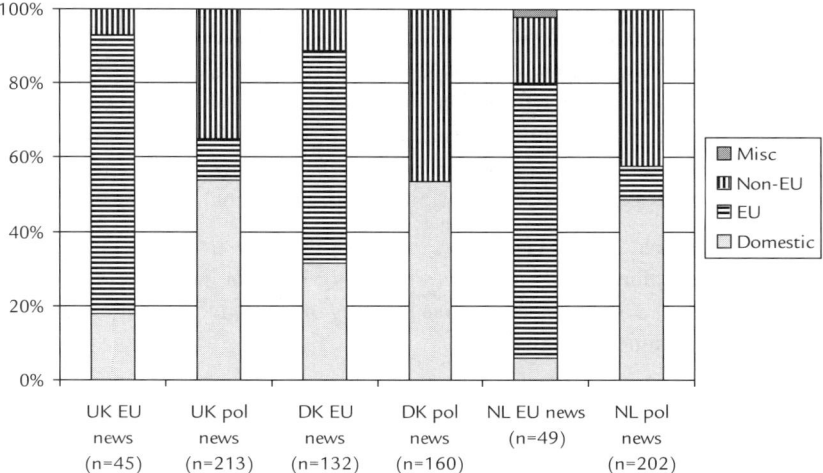

Note: n refers to number of stories

Figure 4.3 provides an overview of the focus of news stories during the summit periods. A distinction is made between EU stories (essentially the summit coverage) and other domestic political news during the summit periods. The figure shows that EU stories during summit periods have a strong EU-level focus (57% in Denmark and 73% in Britain and the Netherlands). Of the EU stories, between 31% (Denmark), 18% (Britain) and 6% (the Netherlands) have a domestic focus. In the remaining political and economic news, there is a domestic bias in the focus of the news. 54% of British, 48% of Dutch and 48% of Danish news stories are domestically focused. In these stories the EU level plays a less significant role (between 9-11%) and internationally focused stories constitute between 35-42% of the news.

The conflict frame was found to be consistently present in EU stories during the summit periods. The degree of presence, measured on the conflict frame scale from 0-1, ranged from $M = .48$ ($SD = .31$) in Denmark to $M = .51$ ($SD = .35$) in the Netherlands, and $M = .59$ ($SD = .34$) in Britain. The prime example of conflict driven news was the coverage of the Nice-summit in December 2000. The news was driven by the violent riots resulting from demonstrations in the streets of Nice and the controversy among the EU prime ministers. In Britain *BBC* and *ITN* both opened the coverage with focus on the tension:

> 'With riots on the outside and tension on the inside, European leaders are preparing themselves for a summit on the biggest rebuilt of the Union since Maastricht. [...] The differences in interpretation between French president Chirac and Tony Blair today was a teaching reminder of how difficult it is going to be to reach an agreement here' (*BBC* reporter, 7 December, 2000).

ITN echoed this by referring to '*Riots on the Riviera*' (7 December, 2000) and '*it is nice in Nice, but the summit is in troubled water. With power and national pride at stake, reaching agreement will be more than difficult*' (*ITN*, 10 December, 2000).

Danish news was not much different as *DR* (9 December, 2000) concluded that '*crisis unravels in Nice as compromise seem further away than ever*', and *TV2* (9 December, 2000) placed responsibility with the French hosts:

> 'Serious crisis in Nice as Germany and France enter row over power distribution in the Union. [...] The nice weather in Nice did not indicate a better climate inside the congress hall. Chirac is asking of all to give in a little, but refrains from doing so himself'.

Dutch television reported in a similar vein with *NOS* (7 December, 2000) highlighting '*tension in Nice as European leaders gather to reform the Union and redistribute the power*' and *RTL* (7 December, 2000) concluded succinctly that '*we will see a compromise to save the* EU, *but the summit so far has been bad for the image, bad for the enlargement, and bad for France*'.

An additional aspect of the study investigated the presence of strategic elements in the news. It was found that strategic news elements, measured as focus on, for example, politicians' presentation and handling of an issue or focus on interpreting an action as a consolidation in her/ his position, were hardly visible in the British news, somewhat visible in Dutch EU stories, and highly visible in Danish news.

Figure 4.4. Percentage of EU news stories containing strategy during the summit periods. Mixed evidence of presence of strategic news, with Danish news being the most strategically framed.

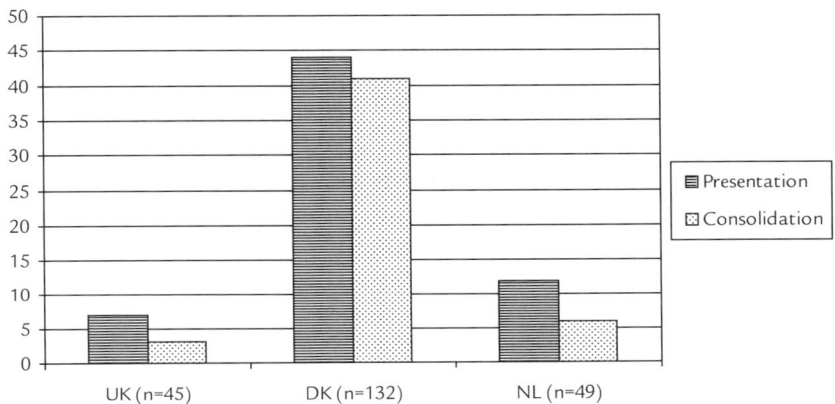

Note: n refers to number of stories

Danish news contained by far the most traces of strategic news (see Figure 4.4). One reason for this finding was the 2000 national referendum on the euro where political leaders fought in a close campaign (see also de Vreese & Semetko, 2002b; 2002c). This meant that news was focused on the position of politicians and their strategy both during the campaign and in the aftermath of the referendum.

Finally, the visibility of actors and their evaluation in the EU news stories during the summit periods was investigated. Table 4.11 shows that of the 200 actors in British news 34 (or 15%) were EU-level actors. In Denmark this was also 15% (n=62 of a total of 434 actors) and in the Netherlands 25% (38/165). In all three countries, the visibility of domestic political actors (government and opposition) was higher (35% in Britain (70/200) and Denmark (155/434) and 24% in the Netherlands (40/154)) than the visibility of EU actors.

The domestic political actors were primarily members of the national governments. Additionally, the analysis showed that in the EU stories during the summit periods there were also many actors from other EU-countries, typically representatives from the host country government, as well as prominent EU countries not in the sample, such as France and Germany, and Britain in the case of Denmark and the Netherlands.

The evaluation of the EU actors was predominantly neutral (ranging from 82% in Denmark to 87% in the Netherlands and 97% in Britain). When an evaluation was present, this was typically a negative evaluation resulting in a modest, but consistent negative bias (ranging from -.03 in Britain to -.08 in Denmark and -.13 in the Netherlands). The evaluation pattern of the domestic political actors as well as actors from other EU countries was very similar. In most cases these were not evaluated (i.e. neutral), but when evaluated this was modestly, though consistently negative.

As mentioned earlier, the key summit during the period of analysis was in Nice. During this summit EU-level actors and domestic government actors in all three countries were less often treated neutral and were more often evaluated negatively. In Denmark, the overall tone measure for the Nice summit was -.09 for EU actors and -.20 for domestic government actors. In Britain this was -.40 for EU actors and -.46 for domestic government actors and in the Netherlands -.26 and -.31 respectively.

Table 4.11. Presence and evaluation of actors in EU stories during summit periods.

	Britain (n=200)			Denmark (n=434)			The Netherlands (n=165)		
	n	Percentage neutral	Tone	n	Percentage neutral	Tone	n	Percentage neutral	Tone
EU level	34	97	-.03	62	82	-.08	38	87	-.13
Domestic government	67	72	-.04	85	88	-.05	39	97	+.02
Domestic political actor	3	100	0	70	91	-.09	1	100	0
National institutions	3	100	0	1	100	0	3	100	0
Organizations	6	100	0	29	93	-.07	6	100	0
Non-organized actors	2	100	0	19	100	0	2	100	0
Other EU country actor	72	90	-.10	117	93	-.05	47	85	-.13
International level	13	92	-.08	50	92	-.06	27	93	-.07
Generalizations	0			0			2		
Other	0			0			0		

Note: n is the number of actors in the EU stories during the summit periods. The percentage neutral is based on the n per actor category.

ROUTINE WEEKS: OCCASIONAL EUROPE HICK-UPS. As the final component of the analysis of Europe in the news, the characteristics of the coverage during a constructed routine period were investigated. The period consists of 63 days of news coverage collected in 1999 and 2000.

Turning to the first research question concerning the visibility of EU news, this study found that about 1-2% in the Netherlands and Britain and about 7-9% of the news in Denmark was about EU affairs (Table 4.12). The somewhat higher percentage in Denmark is largely due to the September 2000 national referendum on the introduction of the euro which received substantial media attention (de Vreese & Semetko, 2002a; 2002b). The share of the news devoted to European affairs in the Netherlands and Britain is comparable to an earlier study of non-summit coverage, where it was concluded that EU news takes up about 2-3% of the total television news (Norris, 2000, p. 189). In addition, the analysis revealed strong cross-national similarity in terms of the time devoted to different issues in the news. In all news programs in all countries, economic news took up about 10% of the news, politics somewhere between one-fourth and one-third of the time, and society news (such as crime and court proceedings) about 20%.

Table 4.12. News agenda during routine period. EU news takes up between 1-9% of the news.

	Britain		Denmark		The Netherlands	
	BBC (n=616)	ITV (n=621)	DR (n=838)	TV2 (n=818)	NOS (n=783)	RTL (n=736)
EU issues	1	1	9	7	2	1
Economy	11	10	10	9	10	11
Politics	35	25	31	30	33	27
Society	19	29	21	24	17	21
Social welfare/ education etc.	8	6	6	8	6	9
Agriculture/ environment etc.	7	6	9	9	8	8
Disasters	13	10	6	8	10	9
Sports/ Weather	6	14	6	4	10	9
Other	0	0	1	0	1	5
Tot percentage	100	101	99	99	97	100
Total time (sec)	73,726	69,521	90,463	83,878	80,608	66,247

Note. n refers to number of stories. Total percentages unequal 100% due to rounding errors.

Looking in greater detail at the news agenda for the EU stories during the routine weeks in 1999-2000, it was found that the topic of the euro dominated the television news EU agenda, in particular in Britain and Denmark where 48% and 36% of the EU stories respectively dealt with the euro issue (Table 4.13). In the Netherlands the euro accounted for 16% and formed, together with economic issues (24%) the two most important issues on the EU agenda. Again, these figures should be considered in the light of the limited number of cases in both Britain (n=11) and the Netherlands (n=25).

Table 4.13. News agenda EU stories during routine period (percentage of time devoted to different topics)

	Britain (n=11)	Denmark (n=126)	Netherlands (n=25)
Euro	36	48	16
Defense	27	7	8
Economy	0	6	24
EU development	9	5	8
EU institutions	10	1	12
Social issues	18	2	4
EU sanctions	0	10	12
Agriculture	0	3	4
Party conflict	0	6	0
Other	0	12	12
Total percentage	100	100	100

Note: The percentage is based on length of the stories, n refers to number of stories

Other important topics in the 'European news' during the routine weeks were defense, in particular EU's common defense competences and operations, EU development, mostly discussions of the future structure of the EU and its institutions following enlargement of the Union. Finally, Dutch (12%) and Danish (10%) news covered the sanctions implemented by the EU against Austria in 2000 following the election of the Haider government.

Turning to the geographical focus of the news coverage, it was found that British and Dutch EU stories tend to focus more on the EU level than on the domestic level whereas EU stories on Danish television are more domestically focused than concerned with the EU level (Figure 4.5). About half of the British and Dutch news deals with the EU level and about one third is focused domestically. In Denmark, 69% of the EU news is domestically focused with only 20% focused on the EU level. For other political and economic stories during the routine weeks, a strong and consistent domestic-focus bias emerges. 80% of the

Dutch, 88% of the British, and 94% of the Danish news is focused domestically. In the political and economic news stories, the EU-level plays a peripheral role.

Figure 4.5. Focus EU news and other political/ economic news during routine period

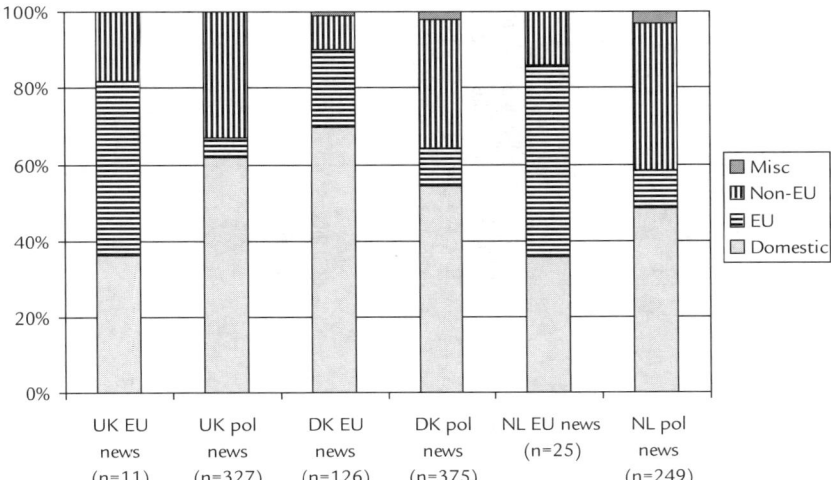

Note: n refers to the number of stories

In the framing of the EU news stories, the conflict frame was found to be consistently present in EU stories during the routine weeks. The presence, measured on the conflict frame scale from 0-1, ranged from $M = .42$ ($SD = .30$) in Britain to $M = .51$ ($SD = .38$) in the Netherlands and $M = .52$ ($SD = .32$) in Denmark. In the British news these conflicts were waged over, for example, the timing of a national referendum on the common currency with former Tory-leader William Hague clashing repeatedly with Labour-leader Tony Blair. In the Dutch news, conflicts included Dutch farmers being contrasted with farmers in the ascension countries over the issue of agricultural subsidies. In Danish news, conflicts were often in the context of the September 2000 referendum on the euro. Disagreement between the government promoting a 'yes' to the euro and the significant opposition parties and the popular movements advocating a 'no' dominated (see also de Vreese & Semetko, 2002b).

An additional aspect of the investigation was assessing the presence of strategic elements in the news. Based on the two indicators of news focusing on politicians' presentational style or interpreting their actions strategically, it was found that strategic news was hardly visible in British EU stories, somewhat visible in Dutch EU stories, and present in half of all Danish EU news stories (see Figure 4.6). Again, the Danish examples of strategic coverage come primarily from news related to the euro referendum.

Figure 4.6. Percentage of EU news stories containing strategy during routine period

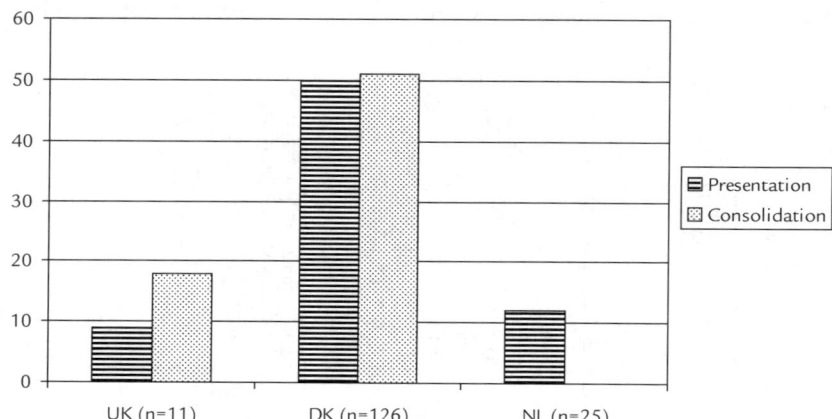

Note: n refers to number of stories

The final component of the content analysis of the routine weeks concerns the visibility of actors and their evaluation in the EU news stories. Table 4.14 shows that about 10% of the actors in British (n=4 of 41), 10% of the actors in Danish (n=41 of 438), and about 30% (n=28 of 93) of the actors in the Dutch EU-news stories were EU-level actors. In all three countries, the visibility of domestic political actors (government and opposition) was higher (Britain 39%, Denmark 47%, and the Netherlands 29%) than the visibility of EU actors. Additionally, the analysis showed that in the EU stories during the routine period on British and to some extent Dutch news there were also a fair share of actors from other EU-countries, typically representatives from prominent EU countries.

The evaluation of the EU actors was predominantly neutral (ranging from 83% to 100% of the cases). When an evaluation was present, this was typically a negative evaluation resulting in a modest, but consistent negative bias (ranging from .00 in Britain to -.07 in Denmark and -.11 in the Netherlands). The evaluation pattern of the domestic political actors as well as actors from other EU countries was very similar. In most cases domestic political actors were not evaluated (i.e., treated neutrally), but when evaluated this was modestly, though consistently negative, in particular the evaluation of the domestic governments.

Table 4.14. Presence and evaluation of actors in EU news during routine weeks.

	Britain (n=41)			Denmark (n=438)			The Netherlands (n=93)		
	n	Percentage neutral	Tone	n	Percentage neutral	Tone	n	Percentage neutral	Tone
EU level	4	100	0	41	88	-.07	28	83	-.11
Domestic government	10	80	0	95	66	-.23	16	81	-.19
Domestic political actor	6	83	-.16	109	82	-.14	11	100	0
National institutions	0			0			1	100	0
Organizations	3	100	0	61	90	-.02	9	100	0
Non-organized actors	1	100	0	60	100	0	6	100	0
Other EU country actor	14	86	-.14	39	95	+.02	15	87	-.13
International level	3	100	0	33	91	-.01	7	86	-.14
Generalizations	0			0			0		
Other	0			0			0		

Note: n refers to number of actors. The percentage neutral is based on the n per actor category.

Discussion

This chapter compared British, Danish, and Dutch television news coverage of European affairs in various contexts ranging from the launch of the euro, the 1999 European elections, EU Council summits and routine periods. Throughout the analyses a comparable set of content analytic variables were used to analyze in total more than 10,000 television news stories. In this concluding part of the chapter, the main points to emerge from each part of the study are summarized before addressing the broader question of whether there are recurring characteristics of EU news.

THE INTRODUCTION OF THE EURO: POSITIVE NEWS. In the analysis of the television news coverage of the 1999 introduction of the euro, it was found that approximately half of the television news time was devoted to political/economic topics in each country during the routine news period. In the three countries the launch of the euro occupied one-fifth to one-fourth of main evening news in the days leading up to and following the introduction of the euro.

The launch of the euro was primarily covered from a domestic perspective focusing on reactions in the country of the news outlet. Some stories were devoted to other EU reactions and happenings around the launch at, for example, the European Central Bank in Frankfurt. Reflecting this journalistic choice, most actors appearing in the news stories about the launch were domestic actors. That said, the euro stories more often included EU-actors than other political and economic news during the period.

Television journalists in all of the countries were more likely to emphasize conflict in the reporting of political/ economic news, but in the coverage of the event of the euro launch, journalists emphasized economic consequences more than conflict. Two issue- and context-specific factors may play a role here. First, the introduction of the euro was a success. None of the scenarios of crashing stock markets or panic scenarios came through. The launch was carefully prepared and staged and it went very smoothly. This of course did not provide the basis for a strong journalistic focus on conflict. Second, although the introduction of the euro was a much debated issue in Britain and Denmark, in the Netherlands the 'euro battles' had been fought years ago, and the actual introduction of the euro was simply the implementation of long-term planning. Even in Britain and Denmark, both currently outside the euro zone, the debates about the euro lacked the quality of conflict since the euro had already become a reality in much of continental Europe and the countries were not yet discussing a referendum on the euro. The discussion in Britain therefore centered upon the question what it meant not to belong to 'Euroland', and how the people and the country were affected by the euro in financial terms.

There appear to be interesting differences between European journalistic traditions, at least concerning the framing of news in terms of economic consequences. Framing news in terms of economic consequences emerged as more important in Denmark and the Netherlands. An emphasis on the domestic economic consequences of an event or issue is a 'translation' of the economic implication of a policy. From comparative research on journalistic cultures we know that British journalists perceive themselves as less interpretative and more often as mere transmitters of facts (see Chapter 3) which may explain the absence of economic consequences frame in British news.

The presence of the economic consequences frame in Danish stories on the euro dovetails with the findings from the 1999 European elections where it was found that Danish television news journalists took on a highly pro-active and interpretative role (see Chapter 3). Danish news not only devoted more time to the European elections, they also paid more attention to the consequences of different European issues. This is because Danish TV journalists in the European election campaign saw it as part of their role to explicate the consequences of advanced European integration and focus on the economy and financial fraud of European political institutions. Dutch journalists also focused on economic consequences though in the light of the conversion work in preparation of the launch, indicating their willingness to interpret and add analyses to the news (Deuze, 2002).

THE 1999 EUROPEAN ELECTIONS: A 'SECOND-ORDER' POLITICAL EVENT. The analysis of the television coverage of the 1999 European elections suggests that the elections received only limited coverage in Britain and the Netherlands. They were more visible in Denmark, but practically invisible on the main evening television news in the Netherlands. That said, there were other prime time programs in all countries that feature political discussions about the elections. Nevertheless, the low visibility of the European elections in the Dutch *news* is in line with observations made about the 1979 campaign. For the 1979 election, it was suggested that the Netherlands was the only country in which "neither broadcasters nor parties felt very concerned about promoting a European consciousness" through television which is one explanation for the absence in coverage (Noël-Aranda, 1983, p. 92). The argument put forward by Noël-Aranda (1983) suggests that news coverage of an issue on which there is widespread consensus will be only marginal. This seems like a plausible explanation and it is in line with other research that suggests that the presence of a viable anti-EU party contributes positively towards visibility of EP election campaigns on television (Banducci et al., 2002; Peter, 2002).

As discussed previously, the presence of conflict, often in the form of diverging views of political parties, is an important common criterion for selecting news (e.g. Eilders, 1997; McManus, 1994; Shoemaker & Reese, 1996; Staab, 1990). These conventions for journalism crystallized in the editorial policies of Dutch news – in the 'EU-consensus' context of the Netherlands – with both news programs evaluating the 1999 campaign against conventional journalistic criteria and thus neglecting the campaign as a consequence of the absence of conflict. Danish news – produced in the polarized Danish political climate – was much more attentive to the elections. The difference in approach to the elections between, for example, Danish and Dutch newsmakers and the differences in the amount of actual campaign coverage stresses the importance of cross-national comparisons. The findings from the Netherlands are in fact 'non-findings', but become interesting and better interpretable in a comparative perspective.

The topical focus of the news also revealed some cross-national differences. British news covered the euro as a main theme in the 1999 elections. Most notably, the Conservatives received extensive coverage and their "In Europe, not run by Europe"-slogan seemed influential. The Danish news coverage with the focus on the 'fraud' issue was the most significant and deviant editorial decision which materialized clearly in the coverage of *DR*. A shared feature across the countries was the frequent reference to expected low turnout and prevalent voter apathy. Critics suggested that the repeated predictions of abstention became a self-fulfilling prophecy that fuelled the low turnout.[30]

Most news programs reported the European elections as a domestic rather than a European event. Most stories were told from a domestic angle and most actors in the news were domestic political actors with the one noteworthy exception that candidates for the European parliament featured regularly in Danish news. The prominent domestic perspective found in the television news coverage dovetails with conclusions reached elsewhere about the press coverage of the 1999 European elections (Kevin, 2001; Kunelius & Sparks, 2001).

EU SUMMITS: PRESCHEDULED BATTLES. The analysis of the EU Council summits suggests that events of this magnitude propel the EU into relatively large and concentrated amounts of news coverage. All summits were, without exception, covered in all news programs and for certain summits, this coverage was considerable. The news coverage of EU summits was often European focused. That is to say that the news programs generally assigned correspondents to cover the summit and they often delivered live segments to the news programs from the summit host country. The news coverage often focused on the host country and featured several prominent EU actors as well as actors from the host country in addition to members of the national delegations.

Most summit coverage was dominated by a focus on conflict. The nature of the event obviously serves as an impetus for journalists to highlight conflict between member states and domestic disagreement about, for example, the tactics during negotiations. The most conflict-driven summit during the period of analysis was the December 2000 summit in Nice, France. *DR*'s generally proactive approach to covering EU affairs also then translated into a number of historically focused stories aired prior to the December 2000 Nice summit. Here, *DR* provided an introduction to contemporary French domestic politics (5 December, 2000) and to the historical German-French power play in Europe (8 December, 2000) in order to establish a context in which the agenda of the summit could be interpreted.

At the Nice summit, Dutch news played up the conflict with Belgium in the negotiations on the vote distribution in the Council. Danish news was focused on the attempt to keep a Danish Commissioner and speeding up the enlargement process as well as the question of the necessity for a national referendum to ratify the treaty. British news was centered on the defense issue and the veto right, which was interpreted with domestic politics as the backdrop.

At the end of the Nice summit, the *BBC* concluded (9 December, 2000) '*Had we given away on tax and social security, Tony Blair would have walked straight back to the Mother and Father of all rows in the House of Commons. At a point not far from an election this would have been a losing decision'*. Both *BBC* and *ITN* also provided domestic political reactions from ex-Tory leader William Hague on the result in Nice. This tendency towards evaluating international events in a context of national political competitions has been observed for both EU and other areas of foreign news coverage (e.g. Cohen, 1996; Hjarvard, 1999; Leroy and Siune, 1994) and it is in line with the 'cultural proximity' news value (Shoemaker and Reese, 1996).

ROUTINE WEEKS: IN SEARCH OF PATTERNS. During the 63 days of news sampled as a 'routine period' in which no major European events were scheduled, the visibility of EU news was low ranging from 1% to 9%. This finding concurs with findings from the press (Fundesco, 1997) and an investigation of television news from 1995 to 1997 (Norris, 2000). The EU news agenda appears, despite changing single-issues, to have certain elements of stability. Despite the great variance in the volume of EU stories (ranging from 126 stories in Denmark to 11 stories in Britain), most of the coverage seems to center around a handful of issues. In this study, conducted during 1999 and 2000, economic issues dominate, followed by EU development (evolution and enlargement) issues, and defense / foreign policy issues. In a previous study conducted between 1995 and 1997, foreign policy (20%), EU development (19%), EU institutions (16%) and economic issues (16%) dominated the television news agenda in Britain, Belgium, Italy, Germany, France and Spain (Norris, 2000, p. 193).[31]

The news stories were mixed in their focus with almost half of them, on average, reported from a domestic angle and the other half centered on a more general EU-level. The actors though were primarily domestic politicians from both the national governments and oppositions. The EU actors and domestic actors were both either treated neutrally or evaluated negatively. Concurrent with the other rounds of content analysis, the study suggested that the conflict frame was present in the news coverage in all three countries. The strategy frame was most prominent in Danish television news and hardly appeared in Dutch and British stories about the EU.

Conclusion

This chapter presented four distinct analyses of different events and issues. The results suggest that there are important differences in the news coverage European affairs when comparing an election campaign to regularly occurring key events (EU summits), to unique events (the introduction of the euro), and to general, routine news periods. The study also revealed significant cross-national differences in the coverage. The key question therefore is: what, if any, general conclusions can we draw about *the* television news coverage of European affairs in Britain, Denmark, and the Netherlands?

EU news can be characterized as hardly visible during routine periods and modestly visible during key events. *The* EU story is a primarily economic and technocratic news story, framed heavily in terms of conflict, more often domestically rather than EU focused, with a predominance of domestic political actors that are either treated neutrally or evaluated negatively. This summarizes some of the main features of the news coverage based on more than ten thousand news stories sampled from three countries over two years.

VISIBILITY: THE MORE THE BETTER? In terms of the *visibility* of news about European affairs it is difficult to conclude whether the documented coverage, which is best characterized as low to modest, is *too* peripheral or *too* invisible. Even though the glass appears to be half-empty, there are no criteria for evaluating adequacy in terms of the volume of coverage. The European Union itself has attempted, though allegedly not wholehearted (Meyer, 1999), to 'get their message across' more clearly (Tumber, 1995) which involves an increased visibility in national news outlets. From this perspective, the visibility found here is likely to be disappointing, especially given the poor score for the European elections and the inability to establish crucial issues such as the reorganization of the EU with regularity on the news agenda outside the periods of EU summits.

Proponents of the 'European public sphere' argument (see e.g., Kunelius & Sparks, 2001) are likely to consider the results poor, too. It is difficult to see how a healthy and continuous public debate over the future of Europe is to emerge from sporadic news coverage. However, the important question is whether the 'the more, the better' assumption can be sustained empirically. Other studies have suggested a relationship between negative slant in the news coverage of the EU and dissatisfaction with the EU on the aggregate level (Norris, 2000). But no study has investigated the effects of the mere volume of coverage. It may be that exposure to news about European affairs does not contribute positively to perceptions of the EU. In fact, exposure to news may activate certain stereotypes about the EU irregardless of the slant of the coverage, but as a result of its mere visibility. Along these lines, a negative relationship was found between exposure to news containing more EU actors, irrespective of the slant, and dissatisfaction with democracy in the EU (Peter & de Vreese, 2002). While the Peter and de Vreese (2002) study explores a relationship at the aggregate level only, it at least serves as a cautionary remark to the assumption in 'the more the better'-argument. Moreover, Peter (2002) finds that the effects of the volume of the coverage are contingent upon contextual factors such as the consonance of the media system. When modeling such contextual factors, it becomes clear that *more* coverage is not always either beneficial or disadvantageous, but depends on the specific context of the coverage.

EUROPE: FAR AWAY, CLOSE TO HOME. Directly related to the discussion of visibility are the observations concerning the focus of news about European affairs. By and large, the 'European story' is more a domestic story than a 'European' one, with the significant exception of the summit coverage. The 'domestic bias' is not only reflected in the location where the news takes place, but also in the journalists' selection of the actors who are more often domestic than EU-related actors.

NEWS FRAMES: ABUNDANCE OF CONFLICT. Turning to the framing of news about European integration, the study found compelling evidence for a strong presence of the conflict frame. With the exception of the introduction of the euro which was a unique success story largely framed in terms of economic consequences and financial repercussions, other European issues were presented in terms of conflict between countries, within political parties, and between EU institutions.

This allows for some tentative suggestions concerning the nature of a generic frame such as the conflict frame. The 'across-countries perspective' revealed similarities among the countries concerning the emphasis on conflict in the framing of political/ economic news. Explanations may be found in factors internal to journalism such as professional routines and news values (see Chapter 2). Moreover, the presence of the conflict frame in the news suggests that the considerations made by journalists when choosing events and issues for the news (see Chapter 3) are translated in to how these are presented in the news. Emphasizing the conflict-related aspects of an event or issue by framing it in terms of conflict may justify the publication of a news story above and beyond its news value and at the same time provides journalists with a clear conception of how to package and present the news. With respect to the conflict frame, the cross-nationally consistent pattern extends and specifies the finding of a more general convergence of journalistic traditions in western democracies (de Vreese et al., 2001; Weischenberg, Löffelholz & Scholl, 1994).

While the presence of a conflict frame in EU coverage was similar across all three countries, significant cross-national differences emerged in the use of the strategy frame. In sum it was found that in particular Danish journalists during the period of investigation came across as assertive and reported European affairs within a strategic frame far more often than their British and Dutch counterparts. Danish journalists were operating in the context of a referendum campaign during large parts of the period under study. This emphasis on strategy in Denmark may not appear overwhelming to American readers who may consider the strategic focus in Danish news negligible compared to the abundance found in US political reporting (Cappella & Jamieson, 1997).

SLANTED NEWS: ANTI-EU OR ANTI-POLITICS? Finally, the analysis suggested that EU-related actors in the news are most often not evaluated, but when they are evaluated the tone is consistently negative. This finding does not suggest that the evaluation of EU actors is any different from the evaluation that domestic politicians receive in the news (Kepplinger & Weissbecker, 1991). In fact, the data in this study did not find any discernable differences in the pattern of evaluation between domestic political actors and EU-actors in the periods under study.

A previous study reported in Norris (2000, pp. 197-198) concluded that the directional bias of television and newspapers is consistently negative and that "the coverage of the European Community in newspapers and on television news therefore often proved anti-Europe". This conclusion is, however, is based on aggregated data and there is no possibility to establish whether there are differences between the groups of actors. Norris (2000) found for the press that the Commission was consistently more negatively evaluated than for example the European Central Bank, but how this compares to the evaluation in television news or to other political and actors and institutions is not clear.

The present study suggests that there is no difference in the pattern of evaluation between EU and domestic political actors. The perhaps more appropriately conclusion is that news in general is either neutral or negative with a general *'anti-politics'*-bias more so than an *'anti-Europe'*-bias. To contrast the evaluation of different actors, Figure 4.7 the actors shows average tone towards EU-actors and domestic politicians (government and others). No structural differences are discernable, and EU actors are only more negatively evaluated than domestic actors in the summit periods.

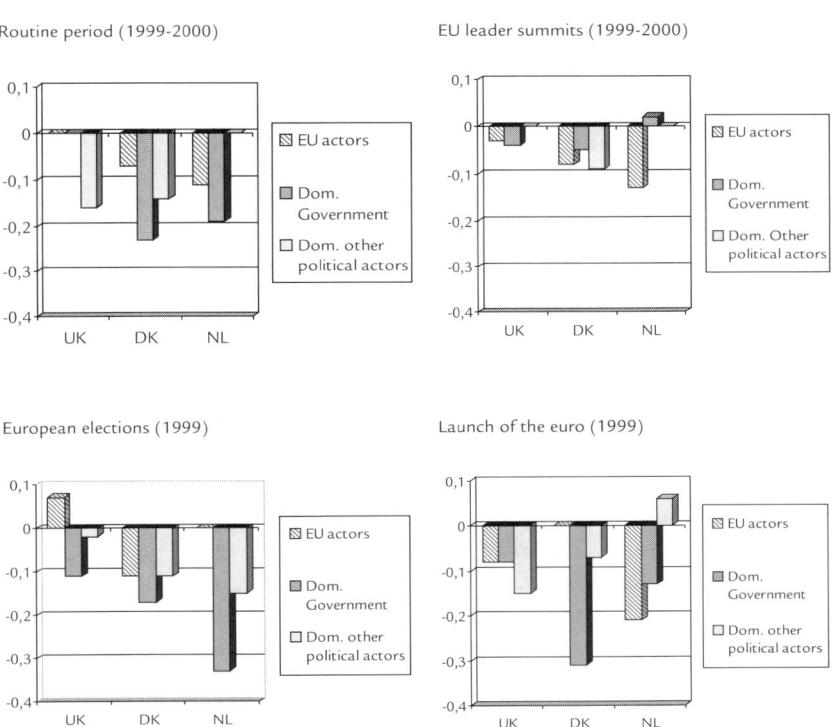

Figure 4.7. Comparison of the tone of coverage of EU actors, domestic government and other political actors during four different periods. EU actors and domestic political actors (both government and opposition) are evaluated similarly. Taken together they are either treated neutrally or evaluated slightly negatively.

LOOKING BACK, LOOKING AHEAD. The results above provide a baseline from which to consider political and economic news in Britain, Denmark, and the Netherlands, and the ways in which journalists emphasize different frames in the reporting of political and economic news. Theoretically, a lesson to be learned from this initial investigation of the news coverage of EU affairs is the important role played by media organizations in defining the *scope* and *content* of attention devoted to European affairs. The cross-national differences in terms of visibility and the composition of the news agenda are, at least for a certain part, the result of different editorial policies and varying degrees of effort invested in the coverage. Danish *DR*, for example, was found to take a more proactive and analytical approach than other news programs which was directly reflected in the coverage.

The chapter offers an exploratory investigation of the structure of news coverage of EU events in the initial phase of a research trajectory that is in need of further development. It is a largely descriptive enterprise which is limited in that it focuses on television only, looks at only a limited number of events and periods, and it is confined to three European countries.

These limitations notwithstanding, hopefully this content analytic study may serve as a baseline for future research on changes in the structure and characteristics of news about the EU. The question is of course if and how such coverage has an impact on public opinion formation about European affairs. We can only speculate about what the domestic focus does for the outlook of audiences in their understanding of European issues. And what does the framing of the news in terms of conflict do for the understanding and perception of Europe as a forum for national political leaders? What do the elements of strategic news coverage do to public perceptions of European politics? Though most EU actors are treated neutrally, how does the modest, but consistent negative evaluation of political leaders affect public perceptions of political candidates?

Given the embryonic stage of research on the effects of news about European affairs, these are all fundamental questions. In the next chapters, the focus is on the relationship between news and public opinion. To investigate media effects, knowledge about the actual coverage must be linked to observations of (changes in) public responses. To most compellingly study media effects, a research design must rely on either panel data with repeated measures or experiments (Cappella & Jamieson, 1997; Kosicki, 1993). The next chapters attempt to answer some of the questions about the impact of news about Europe and investigate the 'frame-setting' component of the integrated process model of framing.

CHAPTER 5

Europe in Public opinion

The effects of the conflict and economic consequences frames on issue interpretation, frame salience, and policy support

This chapter focuses on audience responses to news about European integration.[1] While the previous chapters mapped key features of the production process and how European affairs appear in the news, this chapter and the following one deal with the *effects* that such coverage may have. This is an investigation of the *frame-setting* component of the integrated process model of framing as discussed in Chapter 2.

Aggregate-level survey data show that public support for membership of the EU, satisfaction with democracy in the EU, and support for specific EU policies vary among the different member states and that the levels of support fluctuate over time. The assumption in this study is that the media matter in this process. In the studies discussed in this and the following chapter, the impact of news and information is considered at the individual level. In order to better understand aggregate-level fluctuations in public opinion, it is necessary to investigate if and when differences in news content may affect how citizens think about European issues.

EFFECTS OF FRAMES IN TELEVISION NEWS. Previous experimental investigations of the effects of news frames have suggested a range of individual-level effects from alterations in issue perception to cynical thinking about politics (see elaborate review of previous studies in Chapter 2). The premise of this line of research is that by means of activation of certain constructs, news can "encourage particular trains of thoughts about political phenomena" (Price et al., 1997, p. 483). This may lead citizens to make use of the considerations and beliefs emphasized by the news in subsequent judgments (Druckman, 2001b; Nelson et al., 1997).

The majority of studies investigating framing effects focus on *print media*, (e.g., Ball-Rokeach et al., 1990; Price et al., 1997; Shah et al., 1996; Tewksbury et al., 2000; Valkenburg et al., 1999). In terms of audience responses to frames in *television news*, we have limited knowledge though television is the main source of information for a majority of citizens in the US and Europe (e.g., Chaffee & Kanihan, 1997; Eurobarometer, 56, 2002).

FRAMING EFFECTS: CONFLICT AND ECONOMIC CONSEQUENCES. In framing effects research, the independent variable is typically the news frame. As an independent variable, news frames have been conceptualized and utilized differently in previous experimental studies. Some studies emphasize and document the validity and real-life occurrence of the frames that are investigated through either pre-defined news database word searches (e.g., Domke, et al., 1999) or literature reviews (e.g., McLeod & Detenber, 1999), or, more elaborately, via content analyses of news (e.g., Cappella & Jamieson, 1997; Iyengar, 1991). The justified argument has been made that a valid study of the effects of news frames must be preceded by systematically collected knowledge about the way events and issues are framed in the news. Along these lines, Cappella and Jamieson (1997) suggested that frames must have identifiable conceptual and linguistic characteristics and be commonly observed in journalistic practice.

The current study investigates the effects of two frames that have been found to be prevalent in political and economic news: the *conflict* frame and the *economic consequences* frame. The *conflict frame* comes from the observation that news about politics and the economy is often framed in terms of disagreement between, for example, individuals or political parties. In this way of framing the news, controversy and diverging aspects between conflicting parties are emphasized (Cappella & Jamieson, 1997; Patterson, 1993). The *economic consequences frame* reflects a "preoccupation with the 'bottom line', profit and loss" (Neuman et al., 1992, p. 63). The economic consequences of on an issue is a frequently observed strategy for packaging the news (Graber, 1988; McManus, 1994; Neuman et al., 1992) and news producers use the consequence frame to make an issue relevant to their audience (Gamson, 1992).

Conceptually, the notion of news frames employed in this study is indebted to a definition of a frame as "a central organizing idea or story line that provides meaning to an unfolding strip of events, weaving a connection among them. The frame suggests what the controversy is about, the essence of the issue" (Gamson & Modigliani, 1989). This definition is in line with a broader definition of frames (see Chapter 2) and the thoughts offered by political communication scholars (e.g., Cappella & Jamieson, 1997; Druckman, 2001a; Entman, 1993; Iyengar, 1991; Kinder & Sanders, 1996; Zaller, 1992). *Operationally*, the study is in line with Price et al. (1997) and Tankard's (2001) empirical approach to framing research. These studies suggest that a frame consists of specific elements in a news story which are detached from other information. This means that a news story can be divided into *frame-carrying* elements and *core parts* (Neuman et al., 1992; Price et al., 1997).

In acknowledgement of the potential limitations of previous research, the study has two goals. The first goal is to enhance the validity – both internal and external – of experimental framing research with television news by using realistic and professionally produced stimulus material to test the effects of news frames commonly identified in content analyses of news and journalistic practice. The second goal is to investigate whether frames in television news yield effects similar to what has previously been found for print news.

FRAMES OR FACTS: HOW AUDIENCES RELY ON THE NEWS FRAME. The two first goals of this study center upon gaps in previous research. In addition the study extends research on framing effects by investigating an aspect of the framing process that previous research has only alluded to but not addressed empirically. Though we know that frames in television news may, for example, generate negativity and cynicism about politics (Cappella & Jamieson, 1997) and affect the degree of tolerance extended towards political movements (McLeod & Detenber, 1999; Nelson et al., 1997); no study to date, however, has investigated how *salient*, relatively speaking, a news frame is for understanding an issue. Some studies address the salience of frames. These studies focus on the differential effects of frames according to the *weight* of a frame in the news and suggest that audiences are more susceptible to frames that are strongly present in the news (McLeod & Detenber, 1999; Tewksbury et al., 2000).

This research, however, does not assess the relative salience of the frame compared to other information elements in a news story. For example, if audience members respond to a news story about unemployment, how important are the core facts (e.g., employment rates, number of lay-offs etc.) compared to the frame in such a story?

No study to date has disaggregated a news story into different elements and subsequently assessed the salience of the different elements for understanding an issue. Tankard (2001) suggests that a news frame consists of specific elements, also called framing devices (e.g., the headlines, introductions, lead-outs etc.). This idea concurs with previous studies (e.g., Pan & Kosicki, 1993; Tewksbury et al., 2000). Conceptually, we may conceive these elements of a news story as the *frame* while other elements may be referred to as *core news facts* (e.g., answers to the questions of when, where, and who). Some studies explicitly define the news frame as distinct from other elements in the news (e.g., Neuman et al., 1992; Price et al., 1997). In fact, most other experimental framing studies implicitly apply this conceptual distinction in their operationalizations by keeping a core part constant and varying for example headlines, opening and closing paragraphs to constitute the framing manipulation (e.g., Cappella & Jamieson, 1997; Iyengar, 1991).

Based on previous research it remains an open question whether citizens pick up more of the news frame or the core facts when conceiving of an issue presented in the news. The third goal of this study is therefore to investigate the relative importance that citizens attach to information pertaining to the frame of a news story compared to the core part.

Hypotheses and Research Questions

The scheduled enlargement of the European Union is the backdrop to investigate the effects of the two frames. The issue of the enlargement of the EU was chosen because of its real world importance as a key issue in the future trajectory of European integration. In addition, only very limited work has been conducted on the relationship between news coverage and public perceptions of European affairs and this has not been investigated on the individual level in an experimental context.

Experimental studies of the effects of news frames in print media have suggested that frames such as the conflict and the economic consequences frame have the ability to direct readers' thoughts and define which aspects of an issue they consider particularly important (see Price et al., 1997; Tewksbury et al., 2000; Valkenburg et al., 1999). None of these studies have been able to test the effects of these frames in television news despite the importance of this medium for political information. However, given the consistency of the findings based on print news-based experiments, the first set of hypotheses can be formulated:
- Hypothesis 1a: Television news framed in terms of conflict stimulates and renders conflict related thoughts about an issue.
- Hypothesis 1b: Television news framed in terms of economic consequences stimulates and renders economic consequences related thoughts about an issue.

While studies of framing effects have assessed the impact of news frames on a variety of attitudinal, cognitive, and evaluative measures (see Chapter 2), no study to date has investigated the relative *salience* of a news frame for understanding a news story. As discussed above, there has been some work conducted on the differential effects of frames according to the weight of a frame in the news suggesting that audiences are more susceptible to frames that are strongly present in the news (McLeod & Detenber, 1999; Tewksbury et al., 2000). These studies, however, do not address the relative salience of the frame compared to other information in a news story. It therefore remains an open question whether viewers pick up more of the news frame than of the core news facts

when conceiving of an issue presented in the news. For an initial exploration of this, the following research question was formulated:
- Research question 1: What is the relative importance of the news frame compared to the core information/ news facts in a news story?

Finally, the study investigates the effects of framing of the enlargement issue on support for European integration. Nelson and Oxley (1999) contrasting an 'environmental' versus an 'economic' framing of a land development dispute found that participants exposed to the economic frame considered economic beliefs more important which led to endorsement of the land development plan. Conversely, participants exposed to the environmental frame considered environmental beliefs more important which led to an unfavorable evaluation of the plan. Tewksbury et al. (2000) found that news frames affected attitudes towards restricting hog farms. These studies contrast frames that emphasize either pros or cons of an issue. The economic consequences frame and the conflict frame do not have inherent valence and given the scarcity of research on the effects of frames on policy support, a research question was formulated:
- Research question 2: Does exposure to news framed in terms of conflict or economic consequences affect the level of support for European integration?

Method

EXPERIMENTAL RESEARCH ON THE EFFECTS OF TELEVISION NEWS FRAMES. To investigate the hypotheses and the research questions, an experiment was conducted. Experimental research is often criticized for low external validity, but is considered superior in an attempt to investigate effects of a key independent variable (Kinder & Palfrey, 1993). Paraphrasing Chapter 1, the following problems have been identified as pertinent to experimental research in communication science. First there is a problem of external validity in terms of not sufficiently concise operationalizations of the independent variable. Second there is the selection of messages to represent variance on one variable without controlling for other, unintended systematic differences which may endanger the internal validity of the experimental design. Third there is the problematic nature of single message stimuli where the effects of messages are tested without an appropriate context which increases the artificiality of the experimental situation (Reeves & Geiger, 1994; Slater, 1991).

An important goal of the present study is to address the potential shortcomings of previous research by fulfilling the requirements for conducting experimental research with television news. First, the independent variable explored in this study – the conflict and the economic consequences news frame – is theoretically grounded. The frames have been shown to occur through several content analyses of political and economic news. Second, the news stories used in this study are *produced* rather than *selected* as being representative of a particular frame. This ensures full control over the stimulus material, i.e. variation in the manipulation only and exclusion of other, unintended, variation in the material. In addition, it also ensures that participants in the study had not been exposed to the news story in advance of the study. Third, the experimentally manipulated news story is inserted into a simulated bulletin of a national main evening news program which addresses the challenge of using a single stimuli design.

SAMPLE. A sample of one hundred and forty-five (n=145) participants was randomly drawn from the database of the *NOS KLO* Audience Research Department.[2] Participants were recruited to reflect the composition of the adult Dutch population and to eliminate potential biases based on demographic differences as previous research has suggested that women, middle-aged, and less educated persons are less enthusiastic about European integration (e.g., Eurobarometer 48, 1998; Gabel, 1998). The sample is not representatives but is considered preferable to a homogeneous convenience sample. The sample consisted of 46% females, the age of the participants ranged from 16 to 65 ($M = 39.9$, $SD = 12.5$), and the education level varied from primary school (age 12 in the Netherlands) to university degree.

STIMULUS MATERIAL. Various scholars have stressed the necessity of utilizing realistic material in experimental research with television news (e.g., Brosius, Donsbach & Birk 1996; Graber, 1990; Reese, 1984). To improve the external validity of the study, the stimulus material used in the experiment was produced in cooperation with the national Dutch public broadcaster, *NOS Journaal*, which produces the most widely watched main evening news bulletin in the Netherlands. The assistance of *NOS* in terms of providing access to archival footage, editing facilities as well as assigning reporters and correspondents to participate in the production of stimulus material exclusively for this experiment cannot be underestimated.[3]

A news bulletin was produced with the characteristics of the regular 8 o'clock news [*8 uur Journaal*], including the nation-wide known anchorwoman, and according to common practices at *NOS Journaal* in terms of style of reporting and technical standards (see Figure 5.1). Within the bulletin, the experimentally manipulated news story was placed as story number two which is in line with editorial practices for the priority of routine political/ economic stories which are less likely to lead the bulletin. For the experiment, new footage was recorded, new interviews were held, and new stories were constructed.[4]

Figure 5.1. Experimental stimulus material

Anchor introduction

Member of Parliament (Labor Party)

Member of Parliament (LibDem)

President of the Dutch National Bank

The experimental news story dealt with the enlargement of the European Union. The focal point of the news story was the (simulated) publication of a report by the European Commission encouraging a fast entry of Poland into the European Union. The simulation of this plausible event ensured that all participants would be confronted with new information in a story that had not been broadcast previously. Two different versions of the experimental news story were produced. One contained a 'conflict frame', the other an 'economic consequences' frame. Both stories consisted of an identical core section and for each of the two experimental framing conditions, the final part of the news story was designed to establish one of the two frames. This design of the stimulus material, with a core section containing the news facts and a section in which the frame emerges, is consistent with earlier framing experiments (see e.g., Iyengar, 1991; Price et al., 1997).

First, the anchor introduced the story. The core part of the news story provided background information about the history of the European Union developing from a 1950s Steel and Coal Community to a 1990s Economic and Monetary Union. The core part also addressed the current plans of the EU to expand with a number of Eastern European countries, including Poland.

The story framed in terms of *conflict* then continued with a clash of opinion between two members of Parliament about the desirability of an accelerated ascension process. The two MPs, Weisglas (Liberal Party, VVD) and Timmermans (Labor Party, PvdA) from the two governing parties in the Netherlands in May 2000, stated opinions that are in line with the official party policies. However, their actual quotes had been scripted in advance specifically for the experiment.

The story framed in terms of *economic consequences* continued after the core part to address the potential economic and financial ramifications of an early entrance of Poland in the EU. The potential repercussions for Dutch taxpayers were emphasized. These effects were stated by Nout Wellink, the President of the Dutch Central Bank, who had also received a script with his quote formulated along the lines of the Bank's standpoint on this issue.

The experimental story had a domestic focus and included domestic actors which is in line with the findings of the content analysis of characteristics of Europe-news presented in Chapter 4. It is important to note that the core parts by far constitute the largest part of the story and that the framing manipulation pertains to specific elements only.

DESIGN. The experiment used a two x two factorial design. For both the conflict and the economic consequences story, two versions were made. One contained a traditional field report with visuals and an accompanying voice over, the other a live cross-talk between the anchor in the *NOS* studio and the Brussels-based EU-correspondent. The differences in format pertained to the visual side of the news stories only while the audio side (the script) was kept identical. One version was in the form of a speak accompanying visuals and short quotes (field report), the other in the form of a scripted live interview with the Brussels correspondent (cross-talk). The two versions were produced to investigate the impact of format differences on news learning and appreciation. The findings suggested that live cross-talks do not, contrary to common assumptions, enhance recall or appreciation of news. This, however, is not the focus of the present study and the format differences are reported and discussed in detail elsewhere (Snoeijer, de Vreese & Semetko, 2002).[5]

In the presentation of the results, the current study is treated as a single factorial design with framing condition as the factor. In all analyses, control for possible interaction effects between the experimental framing condition and format condition was completed. Format or the interaction between format and framing condition did not yield significant effects on the dependent measures in any of the analyses which is why it, for purposes of clarity in the data presentation, is appropriate to consider it a single factorial design.

PROCEDURE. Participants were invited to the headquarters of the Audience Research Department to participate in a study of television news. The experiment was conducted on four weeknights in May 2000. Participants were reimbursed for their travel costs and they received a gift voucher at the value of approximately 16 euro. As the participants arrived, they were randomly assigned to different conditions/ viewing rooms.[6] A control group was not included in this post-test only, between-subjects experimental design.[7] The viewing rooms were identical and participants watched the news bulletin in groups ranging in size from 8 - 12 persons. The experimental leaders were randomized between the different conditions and viewing locations. They had received extensive briefing and a manual in writing to eliminate any bias caused by the experimental leader.

The participants were informed that the study was about their "experience of television news". They were told that the study would involve them watching a proof taping of today's 8 o'clock News [*8 uur Journaal*], taped in the late afternoon of that day, and completing a questionnaire. An initial questionnaire addressed the participants' demographics, interest in news and current affairs, media use, political preference, and general political knowledge. A pre-test as such was not appropriate for this study as a pre-test could cue participants to watch the news in a specific manner. After viewing the experimental news bulletin, the participants received three questionnaires in numbered envelopes.[8] Each participant filled in one questionnaire at a time and left these in individually sealed envelopes immediately after filling them in. Given the small group size, the experimental leader easily monitored the participants' compliance with this guideline. Upon completion of the final questionnaire participants were debriefed.

MEASURES. *Issue interpretation.* To test the effect of the conflict and the economic consequences frames on viewers' cognitive responses, thought-listing procedures were used. The question wording was: "*We are interested to hear how you think about the issue of the enlargement of the European Union. You have just seen a news story in 'Het Journaal' about the enlargement. We are interested to hear all your thoughts and feelings about this issue. Please list all your thoughts about the enlargement*". This open procedure, known from social psychology, has successfully been employed in previous experimental research on the effects of frames in the news (e.g. Iyengar, 1991; Price et al., 1997; Valkenburg et al.,

1999) as well as in survey-based framing research (Sotirovic, 2000). The technique is preferred to tap interpretations and perceptions of issues above closed and pre-defined measures which have the inherent risk of reflecting the researchers' presuppositions and eliminating aspects provided in the responses that were not anticipated a priori (Shapiro, 1994).

To determine the extent to which the two news frames emerged in the responses provided by the participants, measures used in an earlier study of the effects of news frames in print media were adapted (see Valkenburg et al., 1999). The thoughts listed by the participants were analyzed by means of nine items, each designed to capture the presence of a dimension of a news frame. Examples of these questions are: "Does the answer reflect disagreement between parties/ individuals/ groups?" (conflict frame), "Does the answer mention the costs/ degree of expense involved?" (economic consequences frame).[9]

All questions were asked to the thoughts of each individual. The questions were coded as yes (1) or no (0). The coding was completed by a student, blind to the experimental condition. A second coder double-coded all the open-ended responses yielding a satisfactory inter-coder reliability with Cohen's κ ranging from .63 to .92 for the conflict items and .84 to .95 for the economic consequences items. Scales were created for each of the two frames by averaging the scores on the questions defining the frame. The value on the scales ranged from .00 (frame not present) to 1.00 (frame present). A high score indicated strong presence of that frame in the thoughts listed. Cronbach's α for the conflict frame scale was .56 and for the economic consequences scale .64.[10]

Salience of news frame. To measure the relative importance of the frame in the news compared to the core information, an open-ended free account procedure asking participants to retell the story to a person who has not seen the story him/herself was employed.[11] This procedure has been used successfully in previous studies to explore which aspects of a story a respondent considers most salient (e.g., Graber, 1990). The responses to this open, unaided account of the story were coded by means of a grading scheme through which each participant was assigned a score for *information pertaining to the frame* and a score for *information pertaining to the core facts* in the story. The text of each news story was divided into units containing the frame and the core news facts. Participants received 0.5 point for mentioning half of any unit and 1.0 point for mentioning the entire unit. For example, if a participant named three of the countries on the 'entry list' to the EU, the participant received 0.5 point whereas a participant listing all six countries in the first entry group would receive 1.0 point for that particular unit. Each participant was assigned a total score for the core part of the story and for the framed part of the story by averaging the number of points received. Each score consequently ranged between .00 and 1.00.

Support for European integration. To test the effect of the two frames on support for advanced European integration, three items forming a scale of 'EU support' was used. The three items, measured on a five-point Likert agree-disagree scale, tapped the degree of support for advanced European integration.[12] The three items formed a scale of support for European integration with α = .79.

Other variables. In addition to the effect of the news frame on the issue interpretation, other variables were expected to affect the nature of participants' cognitive responses. Specifically, political knowledge and the degree of issue elaboration was expected to influence the responses (Price et al., 1997; Rhee, 1997) as discussed in Chapter 2. Accordingly these variables were included in the analysis. Political knowledge was measured by eight factual questions, averaged to range from 0 to 1 (M = .61, SD = .28) (α = .78). As suggested by Rhee (1997), the participants' degree of elaboration on the issue was measured by verbosity, i.e. the number of words participants listed for the open-ended measure (M = 40.5, SD = 25.5). For the analysis of support for European integration, gender, age, education, political interest (one five-point scaled item), and political knowledge were included.

DATA ANALYSIS. To test the first set of hypotheses two separate ANOVAs with conflict versus economic consequences frame as main factor were carried out. To assess the influence of the control variables, two separate analyses of covariance (ANCOVA) were carried out with conflict versus economic consequences frame as main factor and political knowledge and issue elaboration as covariates. To investigate the first research question, two paired sample t-test were carried out because RQ1 addresses a within-condition effect. In addition, two ANCOVAs with conflict versus economic consequences frame as fixed factor and political knowledge and issue elaboration as covariates were used. To investigate the second research question, an ANCOVA with conflict versus economic consequences frame and gender as fixed factors and age, education, political interest, and political knowledge as covariates was used.

Moreover, to control for main effects of framing (conflict versus economic consequences), format (cross-talk versus field report) or interaction effects between format and framing on the dependent variables, MANOVAs were carried out. As mentioned above, these tests did not yield any effects of format or interaction between frame and format which is why the rest of the analyses are completed with a one factorial design.[13]

Results

THE EFFECT OF NEWS FRAMES ON ISSUE INTERPRETATION. The hypotheses suggested that the conflict and the economic consequences would influence participants' train of thoughts. To investigate the effects of the news frames on participants' thoughts, the thought-listing procedure was utilized. Table 5.1 shows that participants in the conflict condition ($M = .26$) used more conflict related thoughts than economic consequences thoughts ($M = .05$) ($F(1, 144) = 48.65$, $\eta^2 = .25$, $p < .001$). Similarly, participants in the economic consequences condition reflected the experimentally induced frame in their thoughts ($M = .39$) and hardly used any thoughts related to conflict or disagreement ($M = .05$) ($F(1, 144) = 87.79$, $\eta^2 = .38$, $p < .001$).

Table 5.1. Use of frames in thoughts by experimental condition

	Experimental condition	
	Conflict (n=73)	Economic consequences (n=72)
Use of conflict related thoughts	.26$_a$ (.24)	.05$_b$ (.12)
Use of economic consequences related thoughts	.05$_b$ (.08)	.39$_a$ (.29)

Note. Cell entries are means, entries in parentheses are standard deviations. Means with different subscript are significantly different ($p < .001$).

Figure 5.1. Interpretation of enlargement issue by experimental condition

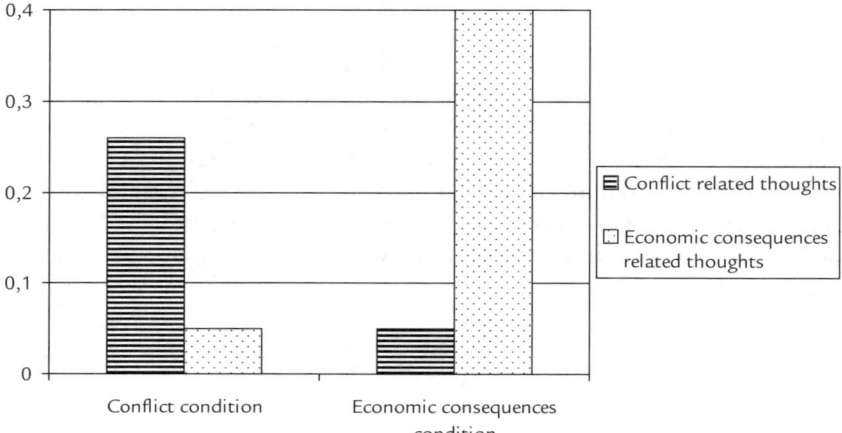

Figure 5.1 shows these findings graphically. Participants in the conflict condition displayed much more of the conflict frame in their thoughts than economic consequences considerations. Conversely, participants in the economic consequences condition displayed much more of the economic consequences frame in their thoughts than conflict-related considerations.

Covariates. Introducing the covariates did not significantly alter the results of in any of the conditions. Table 5.2 shows that the effect of exposure to conflict framed news remained significant ($F(1, 144) = 72.95$, partial $\eta^2 = .34$, $p < .001$) as did exposure to economic consequences framed news ($F(1, 144) = 82.59$, partial $\eta^2 = .37$, $p < .001$) after adjustments for the covariates. Political knowledge was a positive covariate but did not significantly alter the results in either of the conditions. The number of words used by participants positively affected the dependent measure for both the conflict ($\beta = .03$, $t(144) = 5.78$, $p < .001$) and the economic consequences condition ($\beta = .03$, $t(144) = 3.36$, $p < .01$).

Table 5.2. ANCOVA of conflict and economic consequences interpretations of EU enlargement

		Conflict interpretation		Economic consequences interpretation	
	df	F	Partial eta²	F	Partial eta²
Covariate					
Number of words	1	34.43 ***	.19	11.27 ***	.07
Political knowledge	1	2.25	.02	0.95	.00
Main effect					
Frame	1	72.95 ***	.34	82.59 ***	.37
Error	141	(0.26)		(0.48)	

Note: N = 145 (conflict = 73; economic consequences = 72). Numbers in parentheses are mean square errors. *** p < .001.

THE SALIENCE OF NEWS FRAMES VERSUS OTHER INFORMATION IN THE NEWS. The first research question addressed the relative importance of the news frame compared to other information in the news story. To investigate this, the free account procedure was employed and the responses were coded for presence of information pertaining to either the frame or the core parts of the story. Table 5.3 presents the mean scores for presence of information pertaining to the core part and information pertaining to the news frame by condition (ranging from 0 to 1).

Because the research question deals with a within-condition effect, namely the presence of information pertaining to the news frame compared to information pertaining to the core news facts, two paired sample t-tests were conducted. No significant difference was found in the level of presence of information pertaining to the frame and information pertaining to the news facts, neither for the comparison within the conflict condition ($t(72) = -.63$, $p = .53$) nor for the comparison within the economic consequences condition ($t(71) = -1.50$, $p = .14$). In other words, as Table 5.3 shows, to the participants, the news frame was as important as the news facts presented in the core part when retelling the news story in their own words.[14]

Table 5.3. Reference to information pertaining to news frame versus other information by experimental condition

	Experimental condition	
	Conflict (n=73)	Economic consequences (n=72)
Reference to core news facts	.38 (.35)	.47 (.43)
Reference to news frame	.42 (.47)	.47 (.39)

Note. Cell entries are means, entries in parentheses are standard deviations.

Covariates. In addition, as shown in Table 5.4, an ANCOVA revealed no main effect of framing condition for referring to core elements ($F(1, 144) = 1.44$, partial $\eta^2 = .01$, $p = .19$) suggesting that the two conditions elicited a similar amount of references to information from the core part of the news story (conflict condition $M = .38$ and economic consequences condition $M = .47$). Verbosity ($F(1, 144) = 7.46$, partial $\eta^2 = .05$, $p < .05$) and political knowledge ($F(1, 144) = 40.08$, partial $\eta^2 = .22$, $p < .001$) contributed positively to making reference to the core information in the news story. For making reference to the frame elements, two ANCOVAs revealed a main effect of framing condition.[15] Introducing the covariates did not alter this relationship, but suggested in addition that the more politically knowledgeable and participants offering greater issue elaboration were more likely to make use of the news frame. This finding was statistically significant in the conflict condition.[16]

Table 5.4. ANCOVA of salience of core information and news frame

	Salience core information			Salience news frame			
				Conflict		Economic consequences	
	df	F	Partial eta²	F	Partial eta²	F	Partial eta²
Covariate							
Number of words	1	7.46 **	.05	3.75 *	.03	2.20	.02
Political knowledge	1	40.08 ***	.22	2.82 #	.02	.65	.00
Main effect							
Frame	1	1.44	.01	59.92 ***	.30	96.82 ***	.41
Error	141	(.11)		(.11)		(.08)	

Note: N = 145 (conflict = 73; economic consequences = 72). Numbers in parentheses are mean square errors. # p < .10, * p < .05. ** p < .01. *** p < .001.

THE EFFECT OF NEWS FRAMES ON SUPPORT FOR EUROPEAN INTEGRATION. The second research question addressed the impact of the two news frames on support for European integration. Participants in the conflict condition ($M = 3.3$, $SD = .96$) and participants in the economic consequences condition ($M = 3.2$, $SD = .96$) did not differ in their support for European integration.[17] Inclusion of the covariates yielded a significant effect of political interest on support for European integration ($F(1, 137) = 4.41$, partial $\eta^2 = .04$, $p < .05$).

Discussion

The study showed that frames in television news have the ability to direct the thoughts of viewers when conceiving of a contemporary political issue. It was found that participants exposed to a news story inserted in a bulletin of the national evening news and framed in terms of conflict or economic consequences expressed thoughts about the issue that reflected how the news was framed. Participants who watched a story framed in terms of the potential economic consequences of the enlargement of the European Union displayed thoughts in which this specific spin on the issue was present. The thoughts addressed costs, benefits, and financial implications of the enlargement of the European Union. Participants who watched the story framed in terms of a party conflict over the enlargement issue displayed thoughts referring to the public and political friction over the issue, often including more and opposing points of views in their thoughts.

In addition, the study showed that participants who elaborated in their interpretation of the issue were more likely to reflect the frame presented to them in the news in their responses. In other words, verbose persons, who reflect more elaborately on an issue, were more likely to use the frame as a resource. Political knowledge was also a positive, albeit not statistically significant covariate suggesting that political knowledge contributes to making use of the news frame in the interpretation of issues. These findings emphasize the importance of considering individual characteristics in understanding the process of framing effects (e.g., Neuman et al., 1992; Pan & Kosicki, 1993; Price & Tewksbury, 1997; Rhee, 1997).

The effects of the news frames found in this study of television news are supportive of previous studies of the impact of conflict and economic consequences frames in print news (Price et al., 1997; Valkenburg et al., 1999). Taken together these studies point towards a certain robustness in the effects of the conflict and economic consequences frames. The effects have been found in different national contexts, for both television (this study) and the press (Price et al., 1997; Valkenburg et al., 1999), in relation to high salience issues (such as increasing tuition fees for a student sample), and with respect to the less personally obtrusive political-economic issue of the enlargement of the European Union.

The first research question addressed the relative importance of a news frame compared to other information in a news story and found that the news frame is equally important to core facts in the news. Moreover, the study suggested that the more politically knowledgeable and the participants offering greater issue elaboration were more likely to make reference to *both* the core information *and* the news frame than less knowledgeable and less elaborate participants. These findings also stress the importance of individual-level differences for understanding framing effects and specifically the results suggest – in line previous research (e.g., Hsu & Price, 1993; Rhee & Cappella, 1997) – that knowledge facilitates a deeper and more sophisticated information processing.

While the relative importance of a news frame had not yet been investigated, this study suggests that the *salience* of news frames is an area in need of further research. Extant media effects literature has discussed salience as a dependent variable (e.g., agenda-setting research assessing the salience of audiences' issues) or salience as an independent variable (e.g., priming research where the salience of certain considerations drive evaluations of political leaders). Scheufele (2000, p. 309) concludes that agenda-setting and priming rely on the same mechanisms whereby the media "increase the salience of issues or the ease with which these considerations can be retrieved from memory [...] to make political judgments about political actors". Framing, he argues, is inherently different and affects how audiences think about an issue "not by making aspects of the issue more salient" (Scheufele, 2000, p. 309).

However, other framing researchers argue that "framing essentially involves selection and salience. To frame is to select some aspects of a perceived reality and make them more salient" (Entman, 1993, p. 52). Scheufele's (2000) argument that salience per se makes an agenda-setting or priming study and that attribution is the theoretical premise of framing challenges existing research where these terms are used interchangeably. In framing research, Nelson et al. (1997) and Druckman (2001a) have demonstrated how frames make certain considerations more salient for subsequent judgments. News frames affect attitudes by stressing specific values, facts or other considerations and endowing them with greater relevance to an issue than under an alternative frame. Tewksbury et al. (2000) found evidence that the degree of presence – the weight or salience – given to a frame in the news affected the relative emphasis given to this frame in readers' interpretation of a local policy issue. Previous research, as well as this study, suggests that *salience* is a concept relevant to framing research. Given the terminological inconsistencies in extant research, however, Scheufele's (2000) call for precision and the need to specify and explicate not only antecedents of, but also the labeling of the dependent variables remains eminent.

A question for future research is what roles *news facts* and the *news frame* play when new information about the same issue is processed. Information processing theory suggests that retrieval of information depends on what is accessible which in turn is influenced by the recency and frequency of activation (Price & Tewksbury, 1997). The effects of news frames may in fact emerge more strongly and with more implications in later processes of retrieving information when the frame is activated and certain inferences about an issue or event are encouraged.

The second research question asked whether the two news frames elicit different levels of support for future European integration. The study showed no difference in the policy support between the two conditions. Previous research has demonstrated significant effects of different frames on, for example, political tolerance (McLeod & Detenber, 1999; Nelson et al., 1997) and support for local political issues (Nelson & Oxley, 1999; Tewksbury et al., 2000). A plausible explanation for the lack of effect on support for European integration in comparison with these aforementioned studies could be the nature of the issue under study. Previous research has focused on controversial rather than routine political and economic issues. Issues such as social protests and local politics might be more personally obtrusive and controversial in the news than the enlargement of the European Union. This explanation dovetails with Vallone, Ross, and Lepper (1985) who in a study of media bias perception found effects only for a controversial, evocative issue and not for a routine political issue. This explanation, however, is of course tentative.

Beyond the implications for framing research the current study also addresses issues important to scholars, news practitioners, and politicians. First, a focal point for all previous studies of framing effects is the focus on short-term effects. Future research should address the effects of news frames on public opinion in a temporal perspective. This would require a more elaborate non-experimental research design or a delayed post-test with repeated dependent measures. One attempt at investigating the longevity of effects is discussed in Chapter 6. Second, the experimental bulletin used in this study points to the potential fruitful cooperation between practitioners from news organizations and academia. Third, the study suggests that news frames are influential in shaping an individuals' direction of thoughts on a political issue. Previous research has demonstrated that public opinion about European issues is highly volatile and that support can be changed by simple wording differences in questionnaires (Saris, 1997). With television news consistently listed as the most important source of information for citizens across Europe when receiving information about European issues (Eurobarometer 56, 2002), the framing of news about 'Europe' plays an important role in contributing to public opinion formation over issues such as the enlargement of the European Union.

In the next chapter the relationship between exposure to news coverage about European issues and public opinion is explored further.

CHAPTER 6

The effects of strategic news on political cynicism, issue evaluations and policy support: A two-wave experiment

Introduction

Content analyses of political news in the US suggest that the balance of news coverage changed from *issue-based* stories to *strategic coverage* that emphasizes the horse race and tactics of politics (Jamieson, 1992; Patterson, 1993).[1] Indicators of *strategic coverage* have been defined as coverage of candidate motivations and personalities, focus on disagreement between parties, candidates or voters, and the presence and emphasis on polls in the news (Cappella & Jamieson, 1997; Crigler, Just & Belt, 2002; Jamieson, 1992). In the same vein, *game news* has been defined as the game providing the plot of a news story about politics while focusing on polls, and positioning the electorate as spectators and candidates as performers (Patterson, 1993). The argument has been put forward that this type of news coverage is not only found during election campaigns and that the strategic frame is also found in the coverage of public policy issues (Cappella & Jamieson, 1997; Lawrence, 2000).

In the content analysis of European news (discussed in Chapter 4), mixed evidence of presence of the strategy frame in political reporting was found. The content analysis suggested that there was significantly more strategic framing of European issues in Denmark which was related to the national referendum on the euro in 2000 (see also de Vreese and Semetko (2002b)). However, the assessment of the prevalence of the strategy frame is without reference point, because we do not have any studies in Europe that investigate the use of the strategy frame comparatively (neither cross-nationally nor over time) that may serve as benchmarks for this study. Other studies in Europe have addressed the focus on the horse race in the news coverage of elections (e.g., Brants & van Kempen, 2002; van Praag & Brants, 2000), but they have not specifically investigated the strategy frame. Whether or not the strategic focus in news about European affairs is limited or substantial it remains important to investigate the effects this mode of news coverage have. This chapter studies the effects of strategic news in a European context.

STRATEGIC NEWS AND POLITICAL CYNICISM. The significance for democracy of understanding antecedents and effects of political cynicism is widely acknowledged (e.g., Cappella & Jamieson, 1997; Hetherington, 1998; 2001). Decreasing trust in political institutions and increasing public cynicism about politics have led scholars to search for explanations in terms of social and cultural changes and developments in political parties and partisanship (e.g., Abramson & Aldrich, 1982; Miller, 1974; Nye et al., 1997). The contents of political communication and political campaigning styles have been blamed for driving some of these trends. Beginning with the 'video-malaise' thesis (Robinson, 1976), several studies focused on the role played by the media in undermining political trust and producing political cynicism (e.g., Hart, 1994).

Scholars have claimed that the media – through which most citizens experience politics – contribute to increases in political cynicism on the one hand and decreases in political efficacy, confidence in political institutions, and public sentiments to participate in elections on the other (Bennett & Entman, 2001; Entman 1989; Fallows, 1996; Nye et al., 1997; Patterson, 1993). Specifically, previous research has suggested that news about politics framed in terms of strategy, that is news emphasizing the game aspects of politics and stressing politicians' motivations for their actions, may evoke political cynicism and negative perceptions of political campaigns (e.g., Cappella & Jamieson, 1997; Crigler et al., 2002; Rhee, 1997; Valentino et al., 2001a, 2001b).

Most evidence of the effects of strategic news coverage on political cynicism stems from experimental studies in the U.S. (Cappella & Jamieson, 1997; Rhee, 1997; Valentino et al., 2001, 2001b). These studies have contributed with important empirical evidence to the general claims made about the negative impact of (news) media on politics (Fallows, 1996; Hart, 1994; Lichter & Noyes, 1996; Patterson, 1993; Robinson, 1976). To date, the majority of these studies has focused on the effects of strategic news coverage on political cynicism in the context of election campaigns (Cappella & Jamieson, 1997; Valentino et al., 2001a).[2] Given the bias towards studying the effects of strategic news in the context of election campaigns, the first goal of this chapter is to investigate the effects of the strategic news frame in relation to a policy discussion of a routine political/ economic topic, outside the context of an election campaign.

NEGATIVE AND STRATEGIC COMMUNICATION AND MOBILIZATION. Studies investigating behavioral effects of negative campaign communication on mobilization and turnout have, for the most part, focused on the effects of negativity found in political advertising and commercials. Ansolabehere et al. (1994; 1999) challenged the notion that campaigns boost citizens' involvement (in terms of interest, awareness, and sense of importance) as suggested in classical voting behavior studies (e.g., Berelson, Lazarsfeld & McPhee, 1954). They found that exposure to negative advertising dropped intentions to vote by five percentage points and concluded "the demobilizing effects of negative campaigns are accompanied by a weakened sense of political efficacy. Voters who watch negative advertisements become more cynical about the responsiveness of public officials and the electoral process" (Ansolabehere et al., 1999, p. 829).

Drawing on aggregate level survey data and content indicators for political ads, they additionally demonstrated that electoral turnout was lower in states with a higher presence of negative ads (Ansolabehere et al., 1999). A later review of experimental and survey data boldly concluded "negative advertising demobilized voters" (Ansolabehere et al., 1999, p. 901). Another study also found that strong attack advertising demobilizes the electorate while 'balanced' or contrasted ads have a mobilizing effect (Romer, Jamieson & Cappella, 2000). The evidence is by no means conclusive, however. Finkel and Geer (1998), for example, draw on content analysis of presidential ads and panel survey data and found no demobilizing effects of negative ads. Freedman and Goldstein (1999) actually found that exposure to negative ads increased likelihood of voting. And Wattenberg and Brians (1999) questioned the demobilizing effects of negative campaigns and attack advertising by arguing that the intent of these campaign messages is to change voters' minds and voting *preferences* rather than to demobilize the electorate and depress *turnout*. These studies and others suggest that the evidence on the effects of negative advertising with respect to turnout in US elections is mixed (see also Lau, Sigelman, Heldman & Babbitt, 1999).

These studies all focus on advertisements, but news is a more important and credible source of information about politics (Chaffee & Kanihan, 1997; Zhao & Chaffee, 1995). It remains an open question whether negative political coverage, in the form of strategic news, affects the electoral process in a negative direction and depresses turnout. The second goal of the study is therefore to investigate the relationship between exposure to strategic news and electoral mobilization.

AMERICAN EXCEPTIONALISM? While the discussion of the role of (news) media in political processes has received attention both within the U.S. and in Europe, the evidence is not conclusive as to whether exposure to news contributes in a negative or positive direction towards, for example, political cynicism, trust, and electoral mobilization. Studies in the U.S. suggest that media disengage citizens, fuel cynicism, and erode social capital (Bennett et al., 1999; Cappella & Jamieson, 1997; Patterson, 1993; Putnam 1995; 2000). This perspective is challenged by studies drawing on data from both the U.S. and Europe suggesting that attention to news media is associated with higher levels of trust, knowledge, and political mobilization (Norris, 2000). Others suggest that effects, either virtuous or vicious, are not omni-present but contingent upon, for example, the type of media use, political sophistication, and education (Aarts & Semetko, 2003; Moy & Pfau, 2001; Moy & Scheufele, 2000). In this vein, Brants and van Kempen (2002) found that audiences exposed to commercial news were more cynical about politics than audiences exposed to public broadcasting news.[3]

The claim that strategic news coverage fuels political cynicism is largely based on evidence from the American political context. While news in other countries is also framed in terms of strategy and focuses on, for example, aspects of candidate motivations and campaign conduct during elections (e.g., Norris et al., 1999), no study has investigated the effects of strategic news. There are no indicators as to whether previous evidence of the effects of strategic news may in fact generalize across countries and political systems or whether our current knowledge is biased by single country data (Gurevitch & Blumler, 1990).

ALL PEOPLE EQUAL: THE EFFECTS OF POLITICAL KNOWLEDGE AND POLITICAL EFFICACY. Previous research is inconclusive about the contribution of political knowledge to the frame-setting process. For example, Kinder and Sanders (1990) found that persons with lower levels of political information were more susceptible to framing effects and Valentino et al. (2001a) found exposure to strategic news to be associated with lower levels of turnout intention for participants with lower levels of education, which they called political sophistication. Along these lines, Crigler et al. (2002) found strategic news to affect undecided voters more than voters with a strong political preference. However, Nelson et al. (1997) found persons with higher levels of political information to be more susceptible to framing effects and Rhee (1997) found political knowledge to significantly bolster readers' use of an experimentally induced frame in their interpretation of an election campaign. Cappella and Jamieson (1997) in one of their field experiments found 'political sophistication' to be a significant positive predictor for political cynicism, but this was not a consistent finding across all their experiments. Finally, Price et al. (1997) found that political knowledge contributed to more elaborate responses to news, but did not find evidence that knowledge either enhances or depresses susceptibility to news frames. Given the inconclusive nature of previous research, this study investigated the potentially intervening role of political knowledge in the frame-setting process.

The current study investigates the effects of strategic news with political cynicism as the dependent variable. Recent studies suggest that political efficacy, that is citizens' feeling of making a difference in the political process, is an important factor for understanding political cynicism. One study found a negative relationship between efficacy and cynicism suggesting that efficacious citizens were less likely to be cynical about politics (Pinkleton & Austin, 2001). In an additional study, the negative relationship between efficacy and cynicism was confirmed and it was additionally concluded that cynicism was a key predictor of negativism towards both political campaigns and the media (Pinkleton & Austin, 2002). Based on this evidence the current study also considers the impact of political efficacy in the frame-setting process. The effect of efficacy on political cynicism is assessed simultaneously with the effect of political knowledge, which Pinkleton and Austin (2001; 2002) did not use in their studies.

CYNICAL TODAY, CYNICAL TOMORROW? Previous studies have focused in detail on a variety of effects of strategic news coverage. Strategic news has been found to activate attention to personality traits and motivations of politicians which in turn produce negative campaign evaluations and cynicism about politics (Cappella & Jamieson, 1997). Strategic news predisposes viewers to attend to and process less substantive information more actively and it produces lower levels of information retention (Cappella & Jamieson, 1997; Valentino et al., 2001b). Finally strategic news produces more negative reactions towards politics than sincere/ issue-based news (Valentino et al., 2001b) and strategic news impedes feelings of civic duty and trust in government for less educated segments of the electorate (Valentino et al., 2001a).

The effects on these dependent variables have all been established in post-tests held immediately after exposure to experimentally manipulated news. In studies investigating effects of other frames in television news, such as, for example, effects on the degree of tolerance extended towards political movements (McLeod & Detenber, 1999; Nelson et al., 1997) and the assignment of responsibility for social and political problems (Iyengar, 1991) effects were also documented as immediate short-term responses to the manipulated stimulus material. It remains an open question, however, whether the effects of strategic news coverage persist over time, whether they diminish or whether they disappear entirely.

Most experimental designs in political communication research do not include a temporal component.[4] Iyengar and Kinder's (1987) experimental studies of the agenda-setting process are exceptions. In two experiments they included a delayed post-test one week after participants had been exposed to an experimentally manipulated television news program. In both studies they found support that the agenda-setting effect was maintained over the one week period in between the immediate and delayed post-test. A potential shortcoming of their design was the lack of knowledge about what information participants encountered during the period between the post-tests. In the investigation of the persistency of agenda-setting, they did not control for participants' media use and attention. It is very well possible that participants were exposed to additional news about, for example, unemployment or education which could cue participants to consider these problems salient. It is therefore difficult to confidently ascribe the effect entirely to the experimental manipulation.[5]

While some work has been conducted on the persistence of agenda-setting effects, this is virtually absent in the framing literature. Most experimental framing studies investigating *change* have utilized pre- and post-tests in the design, but these studies still focus on immediate responses to stimuli (and compare how exposure affected initial pre-test responses). The series of experiments by Cappella and Jamieson (1997) was conducted during five consecutive days, but the design did not include delayed or repeated post-tests. In one field experiment, participants were interviewed two to three days after exposure, but this time lag was not the focus of the investigation (Cappella & Jamieson, 1997, p. 105). The persistence of effects of news frames over time therefore remains unclear. Cumulative effects of repeated exposure to specific types of content can be investigated in panel studies. However, such designs are often less successful in identifying the effects of a single independent variable, exposure to strategic news, which is the essence of experimentation (Brown & Melamed, 1990; Kinder & Palfrey, 1993).

The literature on framing effects suggests that the impact of certain news frames may be persistent, but little prior research has investigated the longevity and robustness of these effects. One notable exception investigated the effects of an advocate news frames, that is a frame advocating an interest group's perspective on a local farming issue (Tewksbury et al., 2000). The presence of the frame was manipulated to vary in different news stories to which students were exposed. A retest three weeks after the initial exposure revealed significant, though muted effects of the news frame which is a first indication that framing effects might be persistent. However, previous studies specifically investigating the effects of the *strategic* news frames have not been able to address the longevity of such effects.

Hypotheses and Research Questions

Based on the considerations outlined above, an experiment exploring the effects of strategic news on political cynicism, issue evaluations, policy support, and electoral participation was designed. The study focuses on the enlargement of the European Union.

As discussed in the preceding pages, previous research has centered on the effects of the strategy frame in election campaigns or in relation to high salience issues such as health care (Cappella & Jamieson, 1997; Crigler et al., 2002; Valentino et al., 2001a). The current study investigates the effects in the context of the enlargement of the European Union and investigates the effects of the strategy frame in television news. Recent advances in the field have focused on

the press only, while the investigators themselves acknowledge that television news is a potentially more powerful medium (e.g., Valentino et al., 2001a). Based on the findings by Cappella and Jamieson (1997), which were partly replicated by Valentino et al. (2001a), it is hypothesized that exposure to strategic news induces political cynicism compared to issue-based news.
– Hypothesis 1: Exposure to news framed in terms of strategy produces a higher level of political cynicism relative to exposure to issue-based news.

Exposure to strategy-based news has also been found to activate negative evaluations of a policy issue (Rhee, 1997; Valentino et al., 2001b). Previous studies have demonstrated this effect for print news and based on these findings it was expected that exposure to strategic television news activates negative issue evaluations and depresses positive issue evaluations.
– Hypothesis 2a: Exposure to news framed in terms of strategy renders more negative thoughts about political issues relative to exposure to issue-based news.
– Hypothesis 2b: Exposure to news framed in terms of issue coverage renders more positive thoughts about political issues relative to exposure to news framed in terms of strategy.

The effects of strategic news on support for European enlargement are also investigated. As argued in the previous chapter, there is some evidence to suggest that news frames alter support for a political issue, such as, for example, support for social protests and local farming issues (McLeod & Detenber, 1999; Tewksbury et al., 2000) so a hypothesis was cautiously formulated.
– Hypothesis 3: Exposure to news framed in terms of strategy suppresses policy support relative to exposure to issue-based news.

The effects of exposure to strategic news on electoral mobilization are also investigated. The expectation is that strategic framed news suppresses vote intention (Valentino et al., 2001a).
– Hypothesis 4: Exposure to news framed in terms of strategy suppresses, relative to exposure to issue-based news, voting intention.

Finally, to investigate the duration of effects of strategic news two research questions are posed:
– Research question 1: Do effects of exposure to news framed in terms of strategy on political cynicism persist over time?
– Research question 2: Do effects of exposure to news framed in terms of strategy on policy support persist over time?

Method

DESIGN. To investigate the effects of strategic versus issue-based news coverage, a two-wave experiment with immediate and delayed post-tests with repeated measures was conducted. Despite criticisms of impeded external validity, experimental research is superior in an attempt to investigate effects of a key independent variable (Kinder & Palfrey, 1993). This study focuses on television because television is repeatedly identified as the most important source of political information (Eurobarometer, 56, 2002; Zhao & Chaffee, 1995). To address potential shortcomings in previous experimental studies of television news (see below), an entire version of the main national evening 8 o'clock news broadcast in the Netherlands was produced in co-operation with *NOS Journaal*. Inserted into this bulletin was a news story on the enlargement of the European Union. Two versions of this story were produced for this post-test only, between-subjects experimental design.[6] One version of this story was framed in terms of strategy and the other was focused on substantive aspects of the issue.

The study was designed to investigate the longevity of the effects of exposure to strategic news. In a delayed post-test one week after the experiment, participants were re-interviews drawing on repeated measures. To control for any confounding influence of information obtained about the EU between the immediate and the delayed post-test, the participants' news media exposure and attention to news during the week between the immediate and the delayed posttest was mapped. In addition, a content analysis of all television news and current affairs programs as well as print media (newspapers and magazines) during that week was conducted to explore whether exposure to additional news about the enlargement issue affected responses.

PROCEDURE. The experimental design consisted of three distinct stages. First, participants were sampled and invited to come to the headquarters of the *NOS KLO* Audience Research Department to participate in a television study. The study took place on three weeknights in October 2001. Upon arrival, participants were randomly assigned to the two conditions.[7] The news programs were watched in different viewing rooms with a maximum of 12 participants per room. Coffee/tea, soft drinks, and cakes were available in all rooms, and participants were encouraged to help themselves. The experimental leaders were randomly assigned to the different viewing rooms/ conditions.

First, participants filled out a background questionnaire containing demographics, measures of media use, an assessment of political knowledge, and feeling of political efficacy. Second, participants watched the experimental bulletin. They were informed that they would watch a proof taping of today's 8 o'clock News [*8 uur Journaal*], taped in the late afternoon of that day.[8] A post-test was taken immediately after watching the news. Upon completion of the post-test, participants were reimbursed for their travel costs and they received a gift voucher at the value of approximately 16 euro. A second post-test was conducted by telephone one week after the experiment took place. This design allows investigating in how far the experimentally induced effects remain stable or diminish over time. Following this delayed post-test participants were debriefed.

SAMPLE. Participants were recruited by the *NOS KLO* to ensure variation in terms of gender, age, and level of education as these demographic indicators have proven to be important for understanding support for European integration (Eurobarometer, 49, 1998; Gabel, 1998). A total of 83 participants (60% males, age 15-67 (M = 43.8, SD = 15.2), with varying levels of education) completed all steps in the study. This sample is not representative but superior to student samples generally used in framing experiments given the nature of the issue.

STIMULUS MATERIAL. As discussed in Chapters 1 and 5, previous research on the effects of frames in television news has a number of potential shortcomings in design and external validity. First, insufficient control over the stimulus material, i.e. lack of ability to specifically manipulate the independent variable which may jeopardize the experimental design (Reeves & Geiger, 1994; Slater, 1991). Second, minimal discussion of the validity of the frames whose effects are investigated (Cappella & Jamieson, 1997). Third, single message stimuli-designs where the effects of messages are tested without an appropriate context which increases the artificiality of the experimental situation (Slater, 1991).

The frame explored in this study – the strategy frame – is theoretically grounded, observed in daily journalistic practices, and its presence has been documented in content analyses of political news. Second, the news stories used are *produced* rather than *selected* as being representative of a particular frame. This ensures full control over the stimulus material, i.e. variation in the manipulation only and exclusion of other, unintended, variation in the material. Third, the experimentally manipulated news story is inserted into a bulletin of the national main evening news, thus not utilizing a criticized single-stimuli design.

To improve the external validity of the study, the stimulus material used in the experiment was produced in cooperation with the Dutch public broadcaster, *NOS*. A bulletin with the characteristics of the regular 8 o'clock news [*8 uur Journaal*], including a nation-wide known anchorman, was produced. This bulletin, with the experimentally manipulated story as the second story, was made according to common journalistic practices and technical standards at *NOS Journaal* (see Figure 6.1).

Figure 6.1. Still-shots of the manipulated television news story about the enlargement of the European Union

NOS Journaal introduction

NOS Journaal anchor

Secretary of State D. Benschop

Treaty of Rome, the launch of the ECSC

Map of Europe with ascension countries

European Union flag in front of the European Parliament

The focal point of the experimentally manipulated news story was a (simulated) publication of a report by the European Commission encouraging a fast entry of Poland into the European Union. The story was introduced by the anchor. It then contained a brief summary of the report's conclusions. Following this, Dick Benschop, at that time Secretary of State for European Affairs, provided a quote which was scripted in advance. The news story then provided brief background information about the history of the European Union developing from a 1950s Steel and Coal Community to a 1990s Economic and Monetary Union. A second quote was then delivered by the Secretary of State before a closing statement about public support for the enlargement in other EU countries. The stimulus material was produced to reflect characteristics of the coverage as identified in the content analysis in Chapter 4. For example, the story had a primarily domestic focus and featured domestic politicians. Figure 6.1 illustrates the stimulus material.

One version of the news story contained a strategy frame and the other an issue frame. With the exception of three sentences the two stories were identical in each of the experimental conditions (the full text of both stories is included in Appendix C). The experimental manipulation consisted of one sentence in the opening section of the story. In one version the journalist here referred to a 'charm campaign' and a 'strategic plan' (strategy version) rather than 'concrete policies' (issue version). Second, the Secretary of State referred to a 'battle' (strategy) as opposed to a 'signal' (issue) in his quote. Finally, the closing sentence referred to mobilizing public support (strategy) versus focusing on policies (issue).

Strategic news is defined in the literature as [1] emphasis of performance, style, and perception of the candidate, [2] analysis of candidate actions as part of a consolidation of positions, [3] language of wars, games, and competitions, and [4] focus on polls (Cappella & Jamieson, 1997). It was specifically chosen to vary the focus on motivations for political actions (to gain public support versus focusing on concrete policies) and the use of war language to create the issue and strategy versions of the news story. Varying all elements of strategic news leaves too much uncertainty about which of the elements may cause variation in cynical responses.

MEASURES. *Political cynicism.* Four items were derived from Cappella & Jamieson (1997) to tap perceptions of politicians' motivations, their character, and confidence in the substance of policy debates:[9] (a) Politicians are too superficial when dealing with enlargement, (b) Politicians are too concerned with public opinion about enlargement, (c) The debate about enlargement is more about strategy then content, and (d) Politicians are clear and honest in their arguments about enlargement (reverse coded). The items formed a scale of political cynicism (wave 1 $M = 3.89$, $SD = .79$, $\alpha = .64$; wave 2 $M = 3.44$, $SD = .73$, $\alpha = .67$).

Issue evaluation. The second hypothesis predicted that strategy news activates and renders negative associations about a target, in this case the issue of enlargement, while issue framed news activates and renders positive associations. To measure the volume of negative versus positive reactions to the issue of enlargement of the European Union, an open-ended thought-listing item was used. The question wording was: "*We are interested to hear how you think about the issue of the enlargement of the European Union. One of the news stories in the 'Journaal' was about the enlargement of the EU. Please list your thoughts and feelings about the EU enlargement*".

This procedure has successfully been employed in previous experimental research on the effects of frames in the news (e.g. Iyengar, 1991; Price et al., 1997; Tewksbury et al, 2000; Valentino et al., 2001a; 2001b; Valkenburg et al., 1999). Each respondent, on average, listed about three thoughts ($M = 2.87$, $SD\ 1.48$). The affective tone of each thought was assessed as 'positive' towards enlargement, 'negative' or 'neutral'. The thoughts were coded by two coders blind to the experimental condition. The inter-coder agreement on the classification of thoughts ranged from $r\ .91$ to $r = .95$.

Policy support. To test the effect of the two frames on support for advanced European integration in the form of enlargement of the European Union, five items were used. The items (measured on five-point Likert agree-disagree scales) included positively and negatively framed statements: (a) The enlargement of the EU has more disadvantages than advantages, (b) The enlargement of the EU should happen faster than it is currently happening, (c) I would be willing to sacrifice to help a less strong country in Europe, (d) The EU should be enlarged with former East-bloc countries such as Poland and Lithuania, and (e) The EU should be enlarged with South European countries such as Cyprus and Turkey. The responses to the statements were recoded and averaged to form a scale of 'enlargement support' ranging from 1 to 5 (wave 1 $M = 3.06$, $SD = .80$, $\alpha = .83$; wave 2 $M = 3.04$, $SD = .79$, $\alpha = .76$).

Vote intention. The study also investigated whether the strategic news frame suppressed electoral mobilization. Given that no election was waged on the issue of EU enlargement, but that discussions took place as to whether more of future EU decisions should be determined in national referendums, the (hypothetical) question to what extent participants considered it likely that they would vote in such a referendum was posed. Participants were asked to assess the likelihood of them turning out to vote if a referendum on the enlargement issue would be held. It is acknowledged that a self-reported turnout approximation based on a potential election is susceptible to numerous biases. Because the likelihood of over-reporting the intention out to vote is likely to be randomly distributed across the conditions and because the study does not make any inferences about the relative level of turnout intention this measure is still appropriate to assess the effects of differences in the news reporting (strategy versus issue) on turnout intention. The answers to this question were dichotomized into 'intends to vote' and 'does not intend to vote'.

Other variables. In addition to the effect of the news frame on issue evaluation, other variables were expected to affect the nature of participants' cognitive responses. Specifically, political knowledge and the degree of issue elaboration (Price et al., 1997; Rhee, 1997) were expected to influence the responses. Accordingly these were included in the analysis. Political knowledge was measured by six factual questions, averaged to range from 0 to 1 ($M = .67$, $SD = .28$) ($\alpha = .63$). Issue elaboration was measured by verbosity, i.e. the number of words participants listed for the open-ended measure ($M = 32.3$, $SD = 21.7$).

For the analysis of political cynicism, a measure of internal political efficacy was included (Pinkleton & Austin, 2001; 2002). Political efficacy was measured by three standard items and averaged to form a scale from 1 to 7 ($M = 3.53$, $SD = 1.43$) ($\alpha = .61$).[10] For the analysis of support for European integration (H3), gender, age, education, and political knowledge were included in the analysis.

CONTENT ANALYSIS. In the week between the experiment and the delayed post-test, a content analysis was carried out of the major news outlets in the Netherlands. The main evening television news programs, the main weekly current affairs magazines, and the front page of daily newspapers were monitored to identify news about the EU.[11] For a news story to be included in the analysis, the EU had to be mentioned at least in two independent sentences. The news stories were coded for topic and indicators of strategic news framing (see above). The content analysis showed that two news programs in the week between the immediate and the delayed post-test contained news about the EU.[12] Three front pages of the daily newspapers contained news about the EU, these were however unrelated to the topic of enlargement.[13] No stories were found in the magazines included in the sample. The content analysis was carried out during the week between the experiment and the delayed post-test to inform the exposure measures used in the second post-test.

DELAYED POST-TEST. In the delayed post-test, the measures of political cynicism and EU enlargement support were repeated. The measures were part of a battery of attitude questions about current political news to avoid undesired panel test effects in the repeated measures. Prior to the delayed post-test, the content analysis (see above) revealed in which outlets at which days, news about European affairs had been included.

Exposure to news about the EU was tapped by specifically asking the respondents if they had seen either of any of the two news programs that contained EU news in the week between the immediate and the delayed post-test.[14] Exposure to the newspaper stories about EU was tapped from the pre-test questionnaire of media use. Most respondents reported reading only one daily newspaper. An additional attention measure asked respondents to report how much *attention* they had paid to different topics in the news. One item (ranging from 1 ('no attention') to 4 ('a lot of attention')) dealt with 'attention to news about the EU' specifically ($M = 1.85$, $SD = .73$).

DATA ANALYSIS. To analyze the difference between the conditions in the immediate post-test analyses of variance with covariates (ANCOVA) were used. The experimental condition was the fixed factor and political knowledge, verbosity, and political efficacy were used as covariates. To analyze the difference within each condition over time (between the immediate and the delayed post-test), paired sample t-tests were used.

Results

THE EFFECT OF STRATEGIC NEWS ON POLITICAL CYNICISM. The first hypothesis suggested that exposure to news framed in terms of strategy produces a higher level of political cynicism compared to exposure to news based on issue-coverage. The first research question additionally asked if such an effect would persist or diminish over time.

Table 6.1. Political cynicism by experimental condition, immediate post-test and delayed post-test

	Immediate posttest		Delayed posttest	
	Issue (n=42)	Strategy (n=41)	Issue (n=42)	Strategy (n=41)
Political Cynicism	3.67_{ax} (.88)	4.11_{bx} (.60)	3.43_y (.67)	3.45_y (.78)

Note: Cell entries are mean scores of cynicism on a 5-point scale, standard deviations in parentheses. Different a, b subscripts indicate significant between-condition difference with $p < .01$. Different x, y subscripts indicate significant within-condition over-time difference with $p < .05$. Entries with no subscript do not differ significantly.

Table 6.1 displays the means of political cynicism in the two conditions in the immediate and delayed post-test. The first hypothesis is supported as participants in the strategy condition ($M = 4.11$) displayed a significantly higher level of political cynicism compared to participants in the issue condition ($M = 3.67$) in the immediate post-test ($F(1, 82) = 6.89$, $\eta^2 = .08$, $p = .01$). In the delayed post-test, participants in the strategy condition ($M = 3.45$) did not differ from participants in the issue condition ($M = 3.43$) in their level of cynicism ($F(1, 82) = 0.17$, $\eta^2 = .00$, $p = .90$).

Table 6.1 also shows that the difference found between the two conditions in the immediate post-test does not persist in the delayed post-test conducted one week later. The level of cynicism decreased for participants in the strategy condition (from $M = 4.11$ in immediate post-test to $M = 3.45$ in the delayed post-test). Figure 6.1 illustrates the level of political cynicism in both conditions in the immediate and the delayed post-test:

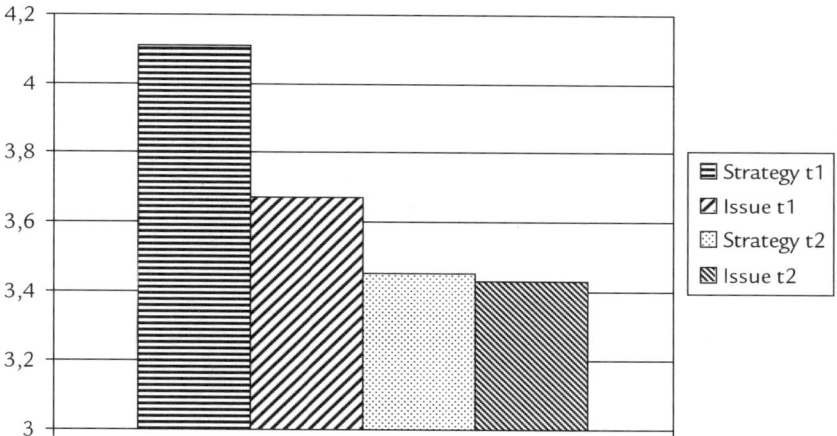

Figure 6.1. Political cynicism by experimental condition, immediate post-test and delayed post-test

Note: Entries are mean scores of cynicism on a 5-point scale.

Introducing political knowledge and political efficacy as covariates did not affect the impact of exposure to the strategy frame on political cynicism. The effect of exposure to strategy news was still significant in the immediate post-test after adjustment for the covariates ($F(1, 82) = 12.92$, partial $\eta^2 = .14$, $p = .001$) (see Table 6.2). Political knowledge significantly covaried with political cynicism ($\beta = .89$, $t(82) = 3.05$, $p < .01$) while political efficacy was a significant negative covariate for political cynicism ($\beta = -.09$, $t(82) = -1.67$, $p = .08$). This suggests that the more politically knowledgeable and the participants feeling less efficacious were more likely to express higher levels of political cynicism.[15]

Table 6.2. ANCOVA of political cynicism

	df	Immediate post-test Political cynicism		Delayed post-test Political cynicism	
		F	Partial eta^2	F	Partial eta^2
Covariate					
Efficacy	1	3.16 #	.04	.12	.00
Political knowledge	1	9.33 **	.11	.00	.00
Main effect					
Strategy frame	1	12.92 ***	.14	.06	.00
Error	77	(.48)		(.55)	

Note: N = 81 (strategy = 40, issue= 41). Numbers in parentheses are mean square errors. # $p < .10$. ** $p < .01$. *** $p < .001$.

In the analysis of political cynicism in the delayed post-test, *exposure to strategic news* in the period between the immediate and the delayed post-test was not formally modeled. This is because of the virtual absence of news about European affairs and the low number of participants reporting being exposed to and paying attention to this news.[16] Essentially this means that the delayed post-test was conducted after a week in which the participants were not exposed to any additional information about the EU. The implications of this are addressed further in the discussion.

THE EFFECT OF STRATEGIC NEWS ON ISSUE EVALUATION. The second set of hypotheses predicted that in comparison with exposure to news with an issue-focus, exposure to news framed in terms of strategy activates and renders negative evaluations of the enlargement issue.

Table 6.3. Positive, neutral and negative issue evaluations by experimental condition

	Issue frame condition (n=42)	Strategy frame condition (n=41)
Number of positive comments	.79x	.44y
	(1.00)	(.74)
Number of neutral comments	1.10	.90
	(1.25)	(1.07)
Number of negative comments	.95a	1.54b
	(1.27)	(1.25)

Note: Cell entries are means with standard deviations in parentheses. Different subscripts indicate significant between-condition differences a,b $p < .05$, x,y $p < .10$.

Table 6.3 shows the valence – positive, neutral, and negative – of the thoughts participants reported in each of the conditions. As predicted in Hypothesis 2, the number of positive thoughts differed significantly between the two conditions with participants in the strategy condition ($M = .44$) listing fewer positive thoughts than participants in the issue condition ($M = .79$) ($F(1, 82) = 3.20$, $\eta^2 = .04$, $p = .07$). Conversely, participants in the strategy condition ($M = 1.54$) listed more negative thoughts than participants in the issue condition ($M = .95$) ($F(1, 82) = 4.47$, $\eta^2 = .01$, $p < .05$). The volume of neutral thoughts was not affected by the experimental condition so that participants in both conditions listed, on average, a comparable amount of neutral thoughts ($F(1, 82) = .56$, $\eta^2 = .01$, $p = .46$). In sum, the frame significantly influenced the likelihood that participants reacted with valenced – both positive and negative – responses. Figure 6.2 illustrates the level of political cynicism in both conditions in the immediate and the delayed post-test:

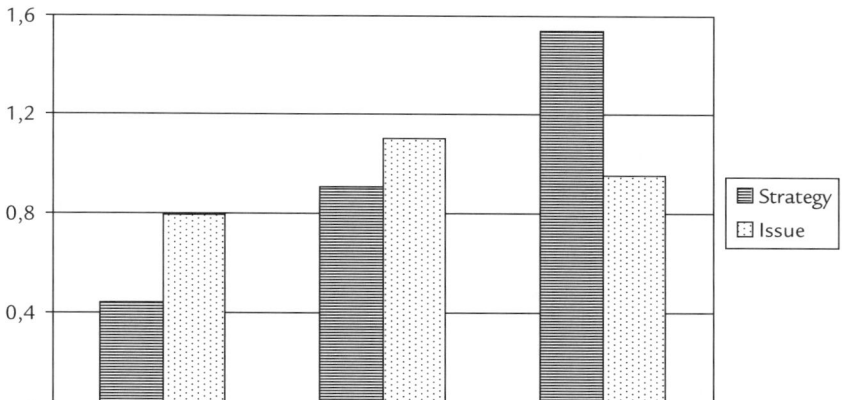

Figure 6.2. Positive, neutral and negative issue evaluations by experimental condition

Introducing political knowledge and issue elaboration (i.e., verbosity) as covariates did not alter the results. Exposure to strategy news still had a significant negative effect on listing positive thoughts ($F(1, 82) = 4.13$, partial $\eta^2 = .04$, $p = .08$) and a positive significant effect on listing negative thoughts ($F(1, 82) = 9.40$, partial $\eta^2 = .11$, $p < .01$) after adjustment for the covariates (see Table 6.4).

Verbosity was a positive predictor of the number of neutral thoughts ($\beta = .74$, $t(82) = 3.05$, $p = .01$). Political knowledge ($\beta = .94$, $t(82) = 2.11$, $p < .05$) and verbosity ($\beta = .03$, $t(82) = 4.30$, $p < .001$) were both significant positive covariates for the number of negative thoughts. This suggests that the more politically knowledgeable, and participants elaborating more on the issue, more often provided negative comments. None of the covariates were significant for predicting the number of positive thoughts.[17]

Table 6.4. ANCOVA of issue evaluation by experimental condition

	df	Neutral		Positive		Negative	
		F	Partial eta²	F	Partial eta²	F	Partial eta²
Covariate							
Number of words	1	9.03 **	.10	1.54	.04	18.75 ***	.11
Political knowledge	1	.46	.00	.43	.01	4.46 *	.05
Main effect							
Strategy frame	1	.44	.01	4.13 #	.04	9.40 ***	.11
Error	79	(1.26)		(.77)		(1.17)	

Note: N = 81 (strategy = 40, issue= 41). Numbers in parentheses are mean square errors.
# p < .10. * p < .05. ** p < .01. *** p < .001.

THE EFFECT OF STRATEGIC NEWS ON POLICY SUPPORT. Hypothesis 3 suggested that exposure to news framed in terms of strategy suppresses policy support. Table 6.5 presents the index of 'EU enlargement support'.

Table 6.5. Support by experimental condition, immediate and delayed posttest

	Immediate posttest		Delayed posttest	
	Issue condition (n=42)	Strategy condition (n=41)	Issue condition (n=42)	Strategy condition (n=41)
EU enlargement support	3.10 (.80)	3.08 (.79)	3.10 (.80)	2.98 (.79)

Note: Cell entries are means with standard deviations in parentheses. The means do not differ significantly from each other.

Table 6.5 shows that there was no significant difference in the level of support for future enlargement of the EU between participants in the strategy and the issue condition. Political knowledge was a positive covariate in both post-tests and this was statistically significant in the immediate post-test ($F(1, 82) = 5.41$, partial $\eta^2 = .07$, $p < .05$) ($\beta = .80$, $t(82) = 2.33$, $p < .05$). The findings suggest that more politically knowledgeable individuals are more supportive of the EU enlargement plans and that exposure to strategic news coverage does not affect policy support.

THE EFFECT OF STRATEGIC NEWS ON TURNOUT. The final aspect of this study was an investigation of the effect of exposure to strategic news on political mobilization. The findings suggest that the intention to turn out to vote in a potential referendum on the enlargement issue did not differ significantly between the two conditions. Thirty-eight percent of the participants in the strategy condition reported being likely to turn out to vote compared to 39% of the participants in the issue condition.

Discussion

The study was designed to investigate the effects of strategic news coverage of politics on a number of dependent variables and to explore whether any effects induced by exposure to news framed in terms of strategy were persistent or would diminish over time. The evidence is supportive of the claim that exposure to strategic news encourages political cynicism (Cappella & Jamieson, 1997; Valentino et al., 2001a). This evidence is found outside the US in the context of a routine political news topic in a non-election period.

The effect of strategy news on cynicism was not persistent and disappeared over time. The data do not provide empirical support for claims inferred from previous studies of the long-term effects of strategic news coverage. However, this study is merely a first exploration of effects of strategic news in a temporal perspective. Therefore only tentative conclusions about the longevity and robustness of effects on cynicism are appropriate. We may for example find that repeated exposure to news framed in terms of strategy produces a cumulative effect. Such a phenomenon would be in line with arguments advanced by Zaller (1992; 2002) suggesting that media effects are likely to be of modest magnitude and most prominent in cases of extensive coverage with consistent directional bias.

The study was designed to control for the effect of repeated exposure to news about the EU framed in terms of strategy. In the delayed post-test, the individual participants' news media exposure and attention was mapped during the week between the immediate and the delayed posttest. A content analysis of all television news and current affairs programs as well as print media (newspapers and magazines) during that week was conducted to explore whether exposure to additional news about the enlargement issue might alter responses. This dimension of the research is not formally modeled in the analysis because the EU enlargement was almost entirely absent from the news during that week.[18]

On the one hand, this is an asset for the design because it is possible to quite confidently rule out that participants were exposed to additional information about the enlargement issue during the week between the immediate and the delayed post-test. This control makes the experiment quite unique in a real life setting. On the other hand, an experimental design with a temporal dimension in combination with individual-level news exposure and attention measures in addition to a content analysis of these news outlets would provide an interesting and compelling design. Such a design is a worthwhile path to pursue in the quest to disentangle the robustness and persistency of effects of strategic news on political cynicism.

Participants' feelings of political efficacy and their political knowledge also affected the level of political cynicism. Politically efficacious individuals were less likely to express cynicism. This finding is an experimentally based corroboration of Pinkleton and Austin's (2002) survey-based evidence of the negative relationship between cynicism and efficacy. In addition, the study suggested that political knowledge contributed to political cynicism. This finding is in line with Cappella and Jamieson's (1997) findings. However, whereas Cappella and Jamieson (1997) found political knowledge (or 'political sophistication' as they call it) to be a stronger predictor of political cynicism than exposure to news containing the strategy frame in a multivariate analysis, this study suggests that exposure to the strategy frame drives political cynicism more than political knowledge. Both contribute to political cynicism, but knowledge is a weaker predictor compared to exposure to the strategic news frame.

The study also suggests that strategic news activates negative evaluations of a policy issue compared to issue-based news that renders more positive issue evaluations. Participants in the issue condition produced significantly more positive thoughts and comments about EU enlargement compared to participants in the strategy condition. In addition, participants who were exposed to strategy-framed news listed significantly more negative thoughts and comments about EU enlargement compared to participants in the issue condition. The degree of issue elaboration and political knowledge were both positive covariates for expressing negative comments suggesting that persons with a higher level of political knowledge and individuals offering a more elaborate evaluation of the issue were more likely to express negative evaluations.

This effect of strategic news on the affective responses by participants exposed to strategic news is supportive of previous studies that found the strategy frame to produce negative campaign evaluations (Valentino et al., 2001b). However, the Valentino et al. (2001b) study was not able to assess their findings in terms of the impact of individual characteristics on the framing effects process and therefore the specific role of political knowledge and issue elaboration in the framing process was not investigated. Previously, Rhee (1997) concluded that more knowledgeable and verbose persons made more use of the strategy frame in their issue evaluations. The current study supports Rhee's (1997) conclusions, but whereas his findings suggested that the degree of issue elaboration was *more* important than exposure to the strategy frame for participants' issue interpretation, this study finds the strategy frame to be the strongest predictor for negative issue interpretation.

The current study found effects of the strategy frame in television news. In this sense the study contradicts Rhee (1997, p. 42) who only found effects of the strategy frame for print news and not broadcast news. He ascribes this finding to television's lack of ability to transfer "prepositional systems" because of the multi-model presentation of information including both visuals and text. This study does not support this conclusion and instead lends support to Graber's (1990; 2001) argument, that the combination of text and visuals leads not to a more shallow issue interpretation, but rather a deeper and more sophisticated level of information processing.

The third expectation in the current study was that strategic news also would have an impact on policy support, but this hypothesis was not supported. The type of frame does not affect the level of support for EU enlargement. A similar level of approval for future enlargement of the European Union was found in the two conditions both immediately after exposure to the news bulletin containing a story about the enlargement and in the delayed post-test. Thus it is cautiously concluded that strategic news does not affect policy support. The study also does *not* provide any evidence to suggest that the strategic mode of news reporting depresses citizens' intention to vote.

The overall conclusion of the study is that news media may indeed contribute to political cynicism and negative associations with political and economic issues. However, these effects diminish over time and it is possible to quite confidently rule out that this was the effect of exposure to new information since most participants were in an 'information-vacuum' between the immediate and the delayed post-test. The study suggests that knowledgeable citizens were both more likely to express political cynicism and to evaluate the enlargement issue negatively, but they were at the same time more supportive of EU enlargement plans.

These findings are an addition to the 'spiral of cynicism' argument. Knowledgeable citizens appear to be more sophisticated in their information processing and to reflect at greater length about an issue. This leads to relying more on a frame provided in the news when expressing reactions to an issue, but does not imply that a strong attitudinal change takes place. The evidence from earlier studies in the priming tradition suggesting that 'novices are more susceptible' to media effects (e.g., Krosnick & Kinder, 1990) cannot be sustained by this study. The current findings, however, corroborate with recent advancements in priming research that suggest that political 'experts' perhaps *choose* to rely on a source – for example the news – when thinking about and expressing reactions to an issue in the news (Miller & Krosnick, 2000).[19]

For the process of advanced European integration, the experiment reported here suggests that news coverage may be a very important though often neglected intermediary for understanding public opinion about European issues. Strategic news about the EU evokes political cynicism and activates negative associations with its policies, but this does not automatically affect the level of support for EU policies.

CHAPTER 7

Discussion and Conclusion

Introduction

Television news plays an important role in providing information about political and economic European integration. Citizens across Europe repeatedly identify television as the most important way of receiving information about European issues. Extant research explored antecedents of public opinion about European affairs, but has, by and large, neglected the role of media in the process of opinion formation. However, all contextual variables and individual-level pre-dispositions and characteristics not withstanding, this study shows that the information provided by television news is a key resource for public thinking about European integration.

The current project was designed to investigate the production, contents, and effects of the television news coverage of European affairs. The project takes a cross-national comparative perspective and focuses on Britain, Denmark, and the Netherlands. The research was carried out at a key point in the European integration process and includes events such as the first-step introduction of the euro, the 1999 European elections as well as priority agenda issues such as the enlargement of the EU. The design is multi-methodological and draws on interviews with newsmakers, content analyses of news coverage, and experiments testing the effects of television news. The production of news about European affairs was investigated through interviews with journalists and editors in Britain, Denmark, and the Netherlands. The characteristics of the television news coverage of European political and economic issues were analyzed in four rounds of content analyses involving more than 10,000 news stories. The effects of news on audiences' thinking about and attitudes towards European integration were investigated in two experiments conducted in cooperation with a national news program to improve the quality and validity of the studies.

In this final chapter the theoretical issues introduced at the outset, the methodological considerations discussed throughout, and the empirical data gathered on the production, contents, and effects of news about European integration are pulled together. First, the key findings of the project are summarized. Second, the merits and shortcomings of the study are discussed and the findings are positioned within the context of the political communication literature. Third, the implications of the study with reference to three general questions are discussed: What did we learn in terms of theory building? What did we learn about journalism and European integration? What did we learn about politicians, media, and European integration?

The findings

PRODUCTION: EUROPE IN THE NEWSROOM. Based on interviews with journalists, editors, and Editors-in-Chief of the main evening television news programs in Britain, Denmark, and the Netherlands, the organization of the coverage of European affairs, the perceived constraints and challenges in covering 'Europe', the editorial approach, and the application of news selection criteria when selecting European events and issues for coverage were investigated.

The coverage of European affairs is organized in a very similar triadic structure in the three countries. The central headquarters (in London, Hilversum, and Copenhagen respectively) coordinate and facilitate the coverage in cooperation with the parliamentary units (based in Westminster, London, Christiansborg, Copenhagen, and in The Hague) and the news programs' Brussels-bureaus. While there is a high degree of similarity in the organization of the European news coverage, there are differences in the degree of perceived autonomy of the journalists and correspondents which amount to internal friction over for example the volume of EU-related news (see below).

The most important constraints and challenges perceived by journalists and editors when covering European affairs fall into four areas. The first, 'distance and time', refers to the EU-decision making procedure in which key decisions are taken in EU power centers such as Brussels, Luxembourg, and Strasbourg. Despite the relative geographical proximity of these locations to Denmark, Britain, and the Netherlands, this was repeatedly identified as a barrier. In addition, the time span in which decisions are taken at the EU-level is considered a problem in terms of news reporting with issues put on the agenda and decisions taken months or years later. Time was also considered a challenge with regard to the length of television news. European affairs are perceived to be abstract and complex and these characteristics are difficult to reconcile with the television news format where 'long' stories generally have a maximum of three minutes.

The second challenge perceived by newsmakers in the three countries, labeled 'access and terminology', relates to the institutions of the EU. These institutions are considered closed and bureaucratic. The terminology used by the Union is perceived as complex and inaccessible. In addition, journalists, especially from the 'smaller' countries (Denmark and the Netherlands) considered the access to top officials and politicians cumbersome and restricted in comparison with access to key members of the domestic administration, including for example, ministers.

The third challenge was identified within the news organizations and is labeled 'internal disagreement'. Journalists assigned to 'European' stories experienced editors in the central newsrooms to be critical and difficult to approach with ideas for European stories. This view was reflected in the interviews with editors, who acknowledged being restrictive with regard to the volume of EU-stories.

The fourth and final challenge emerged from a (perceived) lack of audience knowledge about and interest in European affairs. Editors and journalists alike expressed concern over the difficulty of providing 'intelligent' news coverage with in-depth information about a topic where the audience competences are considerably lower than in the case of domestic politics. The comparison was made with domestic political news coverage which too is complex and abstract. However, audiences generally have some notion about the key stakeholders and political authorities, which is oftentimes absent in the European case leaving journalists with the need to explain and provide additional information so that news stories may become too 'information dense'.

In sum, the perceived complexity of the issue, the lack of interest from peers and editors internally and the audience externally, as well of the lack of background knowledge were considered the key challenges.

Although the editorial policy of the different news programs varied, the approach of all programs was rather 'pragmatic', 'conventionally journalistic', and 'analytical' in Blumler et al.'s terminology (1989). A pragmatic approach implies that politics (including political campaigns) are not considered newsworthy *per se* but that political events and issues compete against other topics in the allocation of time in the news. The 'conventionally journalistic' and 'analytical' approaches refer to selecting events "laced with drama, conflict, novelty, movement, and anomaly" (Blumler et al., 1989, p. 163) and a role for political journalists in which they analyze and interpret in order to provide coherence in the individual news stories. These approaches are theoretically contrasted with a 'sacerdotal' approach in which political processes are considered crucial to democracy and therefore newsworthy *per se*. The attitude to politics is cautious and respectful and the role of the journalist is minimal, guided by the agendas of political parties and candidates.

Though this study is not designed to investigate changes over time in the approach to European politics and the role assumed by journalists, by bringing together what we know from previous research, we can expect that a systematic investigation would reveal that the approach taken by television journalists in the coverage of European affairs has changed considerably over time. Noël-Aranda (1983) concluded that broadcasters during the 1979 European election campaign were 'cautious' and adhered largely to the agenda put forwards by politicians. This is no longer an appropriate description when assessing the approach taken by broadcasters in the 1999 elections based on the interviews. In 1999 all the news programs were pragmatic, but this took different forms. Some news programs chose to (1) neglect the elections due to an editorial assessment of the event as non-newsworthy (e.g., *NOS Journaal* and *RTL Nieuws*), or (2) to set their own agenda without paying attention to the political party agenda (e.g., *DR TV-Avisen*) or (3) to make the anticipated voter apathy a key theme in the coverage (e.g., *BBC, ITN, TV2*).

It remains an open question whether the findings presented in this study represent recent changes or a continuation of long-term evolving developments. In this sense, the findings are limited to the 1999 election only. Previous studies concluded that political journalism and the approach of broadcasters was rather 'sacerdotal', which meant that political campaigns were covered extensively and with only minimal and respectful intervention by journalists (Blumler & Gurevitch, 2001). However, the findings in the current study dovetail with studies of political journalism during national elections that also suggest that 'sacerdotal' approaches have been replaced by more 'pragmatic' considerations and more selective editorial strategies (Blumler & Gurevitch, 2001). One might even speculate that journalists and editors exert even more discretion in their coverage of European elections than when dealing with national elections. European elections are low-key events which provide more leeway for exerting discretion in terms of defining and implementing editorial policies.

The cross-national perspective showed that differences, such as those between the Danish and the Dutch broadcasters during the 1999 European elections, are rendered visible and interpretable by virtue of comparison. The Dutch news programs displayed their pragmatic approach towards the elections by means of a highly selective editorial policy whereby they only covered the European elections in one news story on the day prior to the elections. Danish news programs, however, were pragmatic in their deliberate and proactive editorial strategy in which the issue of fraud and mismanagement was brought to the fore.

According to the newsmakers, with respect to the application of news selection criteria, conflict and tension between elites as well as events with significant domestic consequences were among the key qualities that European events and issues should have to get in to the news. Despite this common ground, the different news programs applied news selection criteria very differently in relation to the 1999 European elections in terms of the sheer amount of news. The political event was not considered to have sufficient intrinsic importance or interest to yield coverage *per se*, but in the Netherlands this meant almost no news whereas in Denmark and Britain this meant covering the campaign but paying only marginal attention to the issues put forward by the political parties and candidates. The European Parliament was evaluated critically by journalists in all three countries though for most part news was neutral. In general, the elections were not 'up-graded' and events in the campaign were mostly evaluated according to normal news selection criteria.

The pragmatic approach and choice to opt for the application of conventional news selection criteria did not detract from the aim that television should remain balanced and impartial. Despite the selective and at times assertive journalistic style, editors and reporters at all programs were still concerned with balance in terms of letting the various parties and political perspective on the EU be heard.

CONTENT: EUROPE IN THE NEWS. The analyses of the news coverage of European affairs included four distinct periods and more than 10,000 television news stories in Britain, Denmark, and the Netherlands. The results suggest important differences in the news coverage of European affairs between an election campaign, regularly occurring events (such the EU summits), unique events (such as the introduction of the euro) and 'routine' news periods sampled throughout a 15-month period. The content analysis shows that news about European affairs is modestly visible in the three countries. EU news often deals with economic topics and it is heavily framed in terms of conflict. It has a primarily domestic focus with a predominance of domestic political actors who are either treated neutrally or evaluated negatively.

The analysis suggests that the 'European' news story is essentially a *domestic* story. Not only is the majority of actors in 'European news' from the country in which the news is broadcast, most of the news is also covered from a domestic angle and focuses on implications of EU issues in the country of the news program. The absence of a 'European perspective' in the news coverage of integration issues is striking, but is theoretically in line with news selection criteria such as *proximity* (Shoemaker & Reese, 1996).

The current study suggests that certain news selection criteria not only influence the choice of topics in the news, but also provide a template for organizing and structuring news stories. In this vein, the study shows that when European issues are covered in the news this often happens with a strong emphasis on *conflict*. This presence of the conflict frame suggests that the considerations made by journalists when choosing events and issues for the news (see Chapter 3) are translated into how these are presented in the news. Emphasizing the conflict-related aspects of an event or issue by framing it in terms of conflict may justify the publication of a news story above and beyond its news value and at the same time provides journalists with a clear conception of how to package and present the news.

The investigation of the *visibility* of European affairs in national television news shows that news organizations vary considerably in the volume of attention given to European affairs. This pattern is determined, on the one hand, by factors internal to the news organizations such as the editorial policies and resources investigated in covering European events. On the other hand, systemic characteristics affect the volume of the coverage. For example, studies looking at all EU countries in the 1999 European elections found the presence of a viable anti-EU party and political debates on European issues to be contextual-level factors that contributed positively to the amount of coverage (Banducci, Karp & Lauf, 2000; Peter, 2002). Putting these observations to a test in Britain, Denmark, and the Netherlands, the proposed positive relationship between presence of anti-EU-sentiments (a polarized political climate) and visibility of the campaign on television news is supported. The relationship, however, does not appear to be linear or uni-dimensional so that the "the stronger the polarization, the more coverage". In Denmark, for example, the election campaign was more visible than in Britain even though the British Conservative Party is a strong and significant anti-EU party, whereas in Denmark, the opposition to European integration comes most strongly from smaller political movements that are successful at getting media attention. In sum, the volume of coverage appears to be influenced by a combination of factors including both contextual factors and factors internal to news organizations.

Finally, the analysis suggests that EU-related actors in the news are *most often not evaluated*, but if evaluated this is consistently *negative*. This finding suggests that the evaluation of EU actors is not different from but indeed rather comparable to the evaluation that national politicians receive in the news (Kepplinger & Weissbecker, 1991). In fact, this study did not find any discernable differences in the pattern of evaluation between domestic political actors and EU-actors. The conclusion from previous research that EU news is modestly negatively slanted (Norris, 2000) is sustained, but the important perspective is added that this 'bias' is not structural towards EU actors as an exception, but applies to the evaluation of political actors in the news in general.

It is of course important to note that this observation pertains only to the three countries examined in this study. However, a study examining the coverage of EU actors in television news in all EU member countries during the 1999 European elections provided supportive evidence of the pattern found in these countries (Peter & de Vreese, 2002). The 15-country study also found that EU actors were evaluated negatively, but that this was similar to the evaluation of other political actors. In countries where the overall evaluation of EU actors was, on average, positive, the evaluation of other actors was still modestly negative. These findings support the conclusion that though EU actors may be evaluated negatively, if evaluated at all, this does not deviate from the evaluation of other political actors, neither in countries traditionally skeptical towards integration (such as Denmark or Sweden) nor in traditionally pro-integration countries (such as Spain and Italy).[1]

EFFECTS: EUROPE IN PUBLIC OPINION. Survey-based research indicates that the level of support for the EU and its policies fluctuates (e.g., Eurobarometer, 56, 2002). A key question in the current study was to investigate the effects of frames in television news on public opinion and attitudes towards European integration. Previous research has, by and large, neglected the role of the media when discussing influences on public opinion about Europe (see Gabel (1998) for an overview). Other studies have tentatively concluded that the media matter in the process of opinion formation about Europe (e.g., Norris, 2000). A study of the 1999 EP elections examined the aggregate-level relationship between the evaluation of EU actors in the news and citizens' satisfaction with democracy in the EU (Peter & de Vreese, 2002). The study showed that satisfaction with democracy in the EU was lower in countries with more coverage of EU representatives or when EU representatives were negatively evaluated. Moreover, the effects of evaluations of EU representatives on satisfaction with democracy in the EU were conditional on the amount of coverage. Taken together, these studies suggest that research pay more attention to the media when studying public opinion about European integration. However, these studies are not able to address issues of causality when discussing the impact of, for example, news media.

In the current study experiments were used to address questions about the effects of television news frames. Experimentation is generally superior to other research methods when trying to establish the effect of a variable (e.g., exposure to a certain news frame) on another variable (e.g., interpretation and evaluation of an issue) (Brown & Melamed, 1990). To address shortcomings in research involving television news, the experiments in this study were conducted in cooperation with a national news program in order to make use of realistic and professional stimulus material and to be able to embed the experimentally manipulated news story in the natural context of an evening news bulletin. In addition, the studies do not rely on student samples. Instead participants in the experiments included a broad array of audience members with variation in terms of gender, age, and education which have previously been identified as predictors of public opinion about European affairs (Gabel, 1998).

EFFECTS OF THE CONFLICT AND ECONOMIC CONSEQUENCES FRAMES. Based on an extensive literature review and findings from the content analyses, the first study investigated the effects of the conflict and economic consequences frame. The results from the first experiment showed that frames in television news have the ability to direct the thoughts of viewers when conceiving of contemporary political issues, such as the enlargement of the EU. Participants exposed to a news story framed in terms of conflict or economic consequences expressed thoughts about the enlargement that reflected how the news was framed. For example, participants who watched a story framed in terms of the potential economic consequences of the enlargement of the European Union addressed costs, benefits, and financial implications of the enlargement of the European Union.

The main effect of exposure to the conflict and economic consequences frame was significant after adjustment for the influence of individual-level characteristics such as verbosity and political knowledge. This is supportive of previous studies of the impact of conflict and economic consequences frames for print news (Price et al., 1997; Valkenburg et al., 1999). Taken together these studies provide empirical robustness to the effects of the conflict and economic consequences frames. The effects have been found in different national contexts, for both television (this study) and the press (Price et al., 1997; Valkenburg et al., 1999), in relation to high salience issues (such as increasing tuition fees for a student sample), and with respect to the less personally obtrusive political-economic issues of enlargement of the European Union.

The study was also designed to address a gap in previous framing effects research. A news frame can be conceived of as particular elements (frame-carrying devices) in a news text (e.g., Tankard, 2001). These parts of the news story are distinct from the core news facts which, naturally, are also the result of a selection process, but can be conceived of as independent and different from the news frame (see e.g., Price et al., 1997). In previous studies, the degree of presence of a news frame has been manipulated to investigate whether a frame strongly present in a news story elicits stronger effects than a news frame only marginally present (e.g., McLeod & Detenber, 1999; Tewksbury et al., 2000). These studies are roundly supportive of the notion that the degree of presence of a news frame affects the extent to which audiences make use of the frame. However, no study to date had investigated the *relative importance* of the news frame compared to the core facts in a news story. The current study found that a news frame plays an equally important role as core facts when individuals recap a news story in their own words. This implies that a news frame, often present in specific textual elements, and often less prominent compared to factual information, carries great importance for the public understanding of political issues.

EFFECTS OF STRATEGY NEWS. Given trends in journalism emphasizing *strategy* in political reporting and the fact that this type of framing was found (in varying amounts) in the content analyses reported here, the second experiment investigated the effects of strategic news coverage of European politics.

Specifically, strategy framed news was expected to influence political cynicism, issue evaluation, policy support, and mobilization. In addition, the study explored whether any effects induced by exposure to news framed in terms of strategy were persistent or whether they diminished over time.

The study suggested that exposure to strategic news encourages political cynicism. Participants who watched a news story framed in terms of strategy were significantly more cynical in their responses compared to participants who watched a news story with an issue-focus. As suggested in previous research, political efficacy and political knowledge also affected the level of political cynicism. Politically efficacious individuals were less likely to express cynicism. This finding is an experimentally based corroboration of Pinkleton and Austin's (2002) survey-based evidence of the negative relationship between cynicism and efficacy. In addition, the study suggested that political knowledge contributed to political cynicism which is in line with Cappella and Jamieson (1997).

The study also suggested that the effects of the strategic frame were not persistent and that the effects on cynicism disappeared over time. The study was designed to control for any additional information that participants might have received in the period between the immediate and the delayed post-test. Given the historical timing of the study (in the aftermath of September 11, 2001), the virtual absence of news about European integration in the period makes the control compelling. It is therefore possible to rule out, with great confidence, that the changes in political cynicism emerged as a result of exposure to new information. However, this experiment is merely a first exploration of effects of strategic news in a temporal perspective and any firm conclusions about the longevity and robustness of effects on cynicism would require an elaborate research design.

The second set of hypotheses predicted that strategic news activates negative evaluations of a policy issue compared to issue-based news that renders more positive issue evaluations. The study supported these hypotheses as participants who were exposed to the strategy-framed news story listed significantly more negative thoughts and comments about EU enlargement compared to participants in the issue condition. Conversely, participants in the issue condition produced significantly more positive thoughts and comments about EU enlargement compared to participants in the strategy condition.

The third and fourth expectations were that strategic news would reduce policy support and depress voter mobilization. The findings suggested that exposure to either strategic or issue-framed news neither affected the level of support for EU enlargement nor the intention to vote. A similar level of approval of future enlargement of the European Union was found in the two conditions both immediately after exposure to the news bulletin containing a story about the enlargement and in the delayed post-test. Additionally, participants in the two conditions did not differ in their intention to vote.

Taken together, the findings of the second experiment suggest that news media may indeed contribute to political cynicism and negative associations with political and economic issues. However, these effects diminish over time in a situation where audiences are not exposed to any new information, strategic or not. The study does *not* provide any evidence to suggest that the strategic mode of news reporting influences public support for policies on a routine political topic or that it depresses citizens' intention to vote. The study suggests that knowledgeable citizens were both more likely to express political cynicism and to evaluate the enlargement issue negatively, but they were at the same time more supportive of EU enlargement plans.

These findings may be seen as an addition to the 'spiral of cynicism' argument. Knowledgeable citizens appear to be more sophisticated in their information processing and to reflect at greater length about an issue. They rely more on a frame provided in the news when expressing reactions to an issue. However, this does not imply that a strong attitudinal change takes place. As argued in Chapter 6 these findings corroborate recent advancements in *priming* research that suggest that political 'experts' perhaps *choose* to rely on, for example, news when thinking about political issues (Miller & Krosnick, 2000).

CYNICAL AND ENGAGED? The experimental evidence can be used to make a more developed 'spiral of cynicism' argument. Citizens exposed to strategic news may become more cynical, but this cynicism cannot be equated with large shifts in policy support or depressed mobilization. The conclusion from this experiment dovetails with a study of the 2000 Danish national referendum campaign on introducing the euro. The referendum study draws on panel survey data with a nationally representative sample and content analysis of all major news outlets during the campaign. In the Danish campaign, the level of political cynicism about political candidates was fairly high one month prior to referendum day, the beginning of the 'hot phase' of the campaign. The 'hot phase' of the campaign produced an increase in the level of political cynicism and an increase in negative campaign evaluations. The news media contributed to this increase in cynicism so that persons who were exposed the most to strategic news about the campaign, even when controlling for a number of other influences, displayed the strongest increases in cynicism and negative evaluations of the campaign (de Vreese & Semetko, 2002b).

The referendum study also suggests that the strategic news coverage – and the cynicism and negativity that it fuelled – did not appear to have any detrimental influence on turnout or mobilization, as has been suggested in previous US studies of the effects of negative campaigning (e.g., Ansolabehere & Iyengar,

1994; Ansolabehere et al., 1999). What might explain these cross-national differences? One explanation seems to be the conditions under which the Danish referendum campaign took place. The Danish political tradition is fundamentally different from the US, one in which voters are generally engaged, and where participation in national elections is high (more than 80 percent of the eligible voters usually vote in national election and this is almost comparable in national referendums). Actual turnout in Denmark in the referendum remained high despite the presence of strategic news and its contribution to political cynicism.

All this is meant to suggest that in a context in which most citizens were aware of the issues at stake, strategic or negative news while increasing cynicism and negative campaign evaluations may have played little or no role in mobilizing electors to go to the polls or in encouraging them to stay home. It also may very well be the case that (European) voters have the capacity to distinguish between their cynical views of politics and the importance of participating in an election. Earlier research suggests that there is a difference between cynicism about political candidates on the one hand and political institutions on the other (Erber & Lau, 1990). Voters may be dissatisfied, cynical, and negative, but still mobilized and sufficiently engaged to turn out to vote. Such an explanation finds resonance in recent work in political science trying to make sense of the Clinton era in American politics. Popular wisdom during the Clinton presidency and later studies suggested that citizens were stunningly capable of distinguishing their rating and evaluation of Clinton as a person, on which he scored poorly, and as a president, for which he received high ratings (see e.g., Shah et al., 2001; Zaller, 1998).

Some scholars argue that cynicism is little more than an indicator of 'healthy skepticism' which is a characteristic of a democratic political culture (Miller, 1974) with 'critical citizens' (Norris, 1999). Indeed, the fact that political news framed in terms of strategy fuels political cynicism and renders negative thoughts about individual politicians' motivations is perhaps less detrimental to democratic processes than assumed in the literature (Cappella & Jamieson, 1997). Taken together, the experimental evidence reported here corroborates the evidence found in a study relying on panel survey data and content analytic measures. Both studies suggest that the findings from previous research arguing that individuals are influenced by strategic news not only so that cynicism and negative evaluations increase, but also so that support for policy issues and vote intention decrease, cannot be substantiated. In speculative terms, it may very well be the case that voters have the capacity to distinguish between their cynical views of politics and the importance of participating in democratic processes.

Limitations of the study

The study aimed at investigating the 'framing of Europe' in national television news in Britain, Denmark, and the Netherlands by means of an integrated process model to framing. The design included interviews with newsmakers at key news programs in the three countries, various rounds of content analyses of the television news coverage of European affairs at different points in time, and finally individual-level studies of the effects of news about European affairs on the public's issue interpretations, evaluations, political cynicism, and policy support. The project resides in the initial phase of an emerging research trajectory focusing on the interface between the politics and economics of European integration, the media, and public opinion. The study may ideally serve as a baseline from which further to develop this line of research. A number of limitations pertain to the current study. The findings must therefore be interpreted as tentative, marking the first steps in the direction of more sophisticated studies of this dynamic under the specific conditions of European integration.

Cross-national perspective. The study is designed with a cross-national component which was useful for understanding and interpreting differences in for example editorial policies and structures in the news. However, the study focused on only three current member states of the EU. Even though Britain, Denmark, and the Netherlands represent a broad spectrum in terms of aggregate level public opinion towards European integration, the country sample has a strong north-European bias. Extending future research with countries such as Italy or Spain and even countries currently outside the EU would not only enrich the understanding of the dynamic, but would also potentially recast the findings in a different light.

Medium sample. A second limitation stems from the selection of medium. Though television is repeatedly identified as the key source of political information and information about European affairs (Eurobarometer, 56, 2002) and though most other studies neglect the influence of television and discuss the impact of the press only (e.g., Hewstone, 1986; Kevin, 2001), the focus on television news only undoubtedly affects the findings and limits the scope of the conclusions. While television may reach the largest audiences, is perceived as the most important source of information, and has the ability to direct attention to issues, newspapers provide more political and economic news and studies suggest that newspapers are processed more intensively and are a stronger predictor of, for example, political knowledge than television (e.g., McLeod, Scheufele & Moy, 1999). Future research may consider not only mainstream evening news and key national newspapers, but also include, for example, current affairs television programs, local press, and weekly magazines. In addition, interactive, on-line sources as well as interpersonal communication would be useful additions to obtain a more detailed image of the news and information environment made available to European citizens.

Content analysis. The study covered the period 1999-2000. The sample does not allow for any historical comparisons or conclusions. Future research should aim at producing content analyses that replicate key variables so that comparisons over time become possible (Shoemaker & Reese, 1996). In addition, cross-national studies should aim at advancing the link between content analytic indicators and contextual variables. In analyses of news in more than one setting, it is important to identify and specify which factors influence and shape the volume and content of the news coverage (see Peter, 2002). In the analysis of the EP election campaign, it was not appropriate to formally model such relationships given the limited coverage (and the low number of cases) in the three countries.

Public opinion expression. The current study relies on experimentation as the method for understanding public opinion formation and change. The unique qualities and assets of experimentation in terms of internal validity, systematic observation, and causality guided the choice of experiments, but the endangered external validity in experiments is acknowledged. Future research should aim at designing studies that draw on truly multi-methodological designs in which, for example, experimentally established evidence is tested in a survey setting. Such designs should aim at integrating media exposure and attention measures with content analytic indicators (Riffe et al., 1998; Scheufele, 2000).

Frame-building. Theoretically, the current study would be enhanced by a more elaborate design in which the output from the political arena were integrated in an investigation of how and to what extent media pick up on this elite framing of issues. (see Terkildsen, Schnell & Ling (1998) for a discussion of an interactive model of public policy debate formation). Assessing for example the efforts of the European Parliament, as suggested by Meyer (1999), and comparing information from content analyses of, for example, party manifestos and press releases with interviews, observations as well as news media coverage, would make it possible to investigate the frame-building process in greater detail.

With these general limitations in mind, some theoretical and practical lessons can be drawn and paths for future research can be suggested.

Theoretical lessons
Framing theory: the next steps

Studies of framing to date have posed as many questions as they have answered. Research has offered too little in terms of structured theoretical and operational coherence which the "fractured paradigm" (Entman, 1993) of framing research requires. This study proposed an integrated process model to framing that involves investigations of the production process (frame-building), content (news frames), and framing effects (frame-setting). This theoretical model can inform and guide the investigation of a communicative process in its entirety. Entman (1993) and later McLeod et al. (2002) suggested that the true potential of the framing concept lies in its ability to link research domains that are often treated as separate and disconnected while in fact interrelated and interdependent. The reciprocal process of production, content, and effects is one such example. Previous studies of framing have more often than not focused on *either* production (e.g., Liebes, 2000), content (e.g., Lawrence, 2000; Norris, 1995) *or* effects (e.g., Domke et al., 1999; McLeod & Detenber, 1999). Few notable exceptions link content and effects (e.g., Cappella & Jamieson, 1997; Iyengar, 1991; Semetko & Valkenburg, 2000 / Valkenburg et al., 1999). Thus far no study has addressed the framing process in its totality. The potential virtue of applying an integrated process definition of the framing concept, as suggested in this study, lies in the coherence it offers for understanding the *process*.

This is not meant to suggest that *theoretical parsimony* in general is inherently and unconditionally preferable to specific approaches. The integrated process model is not meant to be *prescriptive* for future research. However, the approach is meant to suggest that findings pertaining to both the production process, the content, and potential effects are more easily understood when conceived in a broader perspective.

Throughout the research project, a number of issues have arisen that are in need of attention in the further explication and application of the framing concept. Three aspects deserve particular attention at this point: (1) the relationship between framing research and agenda-setting and priming research, (2) the psychological antecedents of framing effects, and (3) the moderators and mediators of framing effects.

SECOND LEVEL AGENDA-SETTING OR FRAMING? A contentious issue in recent political communication scholarship is the relationship between different cognitive media effects: agenda-setting, priming, and framing. While the discussion is not novel (see Price and Tewksbury, 1997), recent scholarly attention has fuelled the debate (Kiousis et al., 1999; Lopez-Escobar et al., 1998; McCombs et al., 1997b; McCombs et al., 2000, Scheufele, 1999; 2000; Weaver, 1998). The question at stake is whether framing is considered a distinct media effect or a 'second level agenda-setting effect'. Two perspectives are emerging but both suffer from lack of precision and terminological inconsistency. Furthermore, the research field is not yet sufficiently mature to classify framing as *one* particular kind of effect. Any attempt at doing this would entail a research program specifically designed to explore the antecedents and consequences of either second-level agenda-setting or framing (Scheufele, 2000). The current study was not designed to reconcile or support either of the two perspectives, and it remains an unsolved question.

Proponents of the *second level agenda-setting approach* lend credibility and empirical support from one of the most widely cited theories concerning media's role in the process of public opinion formation: agenda-setting.[2] The link between agenda-setting and framing was succinctly summarized almost a decade ago: "Framing analysis expands beyond agenda-setting research into *what* people talk or think about by examining *how* they think and talk about issues in the news" (Pan & Kosicki, 1993, p. 70). The question is whether framing adds a new dimension (a second level) and is best conceptualized as a second level agenda-setting effect (e.g., McCombs et al., 1997a; Weaver, 1998) or whether framing is a distinct concept building on specific premises and should be treated accordingly (Scheufele, 2000).

SALIENCE AND ATTRIBUTIONS: TERMINOLOGICAL INCONSISTENCIES. The thrust of the second-level agenda-setting argument is that in addition to setting the agenda of issues, the media may also set the agenda in terms of which elements within these issues are emphasized (McCombs et al., 2000). Experimental evidence suggests that emphasis on candidate attributes (personality and qualifications traits) in news is mirrored by readers in different experimental conditions (Kiousis et al., 1999). In studies of elections in Spain it was found that attributes of candidates emphasized by the news media correlated with candidate attributes salient to audiences for these media (Lopez-Escobar et al., 1998; McCombs et al., 2000).

Although these studies position framing as a second-level agenda-setting effect, neither offer any theoretical arguments or propositions as to why framing effects are best seen as a form of agenda-setting. McCombs et al. (2000, p. 90) conclude that agenda-setting has converged with framing and applaud the theoretical parsimony emerging. This conclusion is based on an argument of conviction rather than theoretical advancements or empirical data.

The strongest and most explicit plea for considering framing as different from agenda-setting comes from Scheufele (2000). Framing, it is argued, draws on other cognitive processing mechanisms than agenda-setting and priming that follow a model of attitude accessibility and a memory-based model of information processing. Agenda-setting has issue salience as the dependent variable and priming has issue salience as an independent variable for making evaluations of political leaders. Framing, Scheufele (2000, p. 309) argues, is based on the concept of prospect theory and on the assumption that "subtle changes in the wording of a description might affect how audiences think about this situation". Moreover, it is stated that framing is *not* making some "aspects of an issue more salient, but invoking interpretative schemas that influence the interpretation of incoming information".

As outlined above, Scheufele's (2000) argument that salience *per se* makes an agenda-setting or priming study challenges extant research where these terms are used interchangeably. In framing research, Nelson et al. (1997) and Druckman (2001a) have demonstrated how frames make certain considerations more salient for subsequent judgments. News frames affect attitudes by stressing specific values, facts or other considerations and endowing them with greater relevance to an issue than under an alternative frame. Moreover, Tewksbury et al. (2000) found evidence that the degree of presence – the weight or salience – given to a frame in the news affected the relative emphasis given to this frame in readers' interpretation of a local policy issue. These studies in addition to the current study suggest that salience is a concept relevant to framing research.

McCombs et al. (2000, p. 90) argue that the "question of which of these conceptualizations or their intellectual descendents is the more productive will be settled by the accumulation of research. In the meantime, this variety of perspectives provides a rich research environment". While the settlement of an intellectual dispute may find solution in the magnitude of research, the core of the dispute appears to remain unsettled. The ultimate test, as suggested by Scheufele (2000), is to explicate *if* and *how* framing differs from agenda-setting and priming in terms of its antecedents and outcomes.

Future studies need to empirically address this issue and provide compelling evidence of whether there is a link between first- and second-level agenda-setting. Are second-level agenda-setting effects conditional upon first-level effects? In other words must first-level agenda-setting occur before second-level agenda setting? If the news media 'fail' to set an issue on the public agenda, but the way this issue is framed still affects public perceptions of the issue, despite the low salience on the public and media agendas, is it still appropriate to speak of agenda-setting effects? If framing effects are second-level agenda-setting effects, what effects of the mass media are then not second or even third-level agenda-setting effects? Answers to these questions go beyond the scope of this current study. Initial answers should be empirically grounded, which is not always the case in the current debate.

THE PSYCHOLOGICAL ANTECEDENTS OF FRAMING. A second issue that deserves attention in future framing research is the explication and identification of psychological antecedents of framing effects. Reviewing the existing literature, two strands of research addressing the effects of frames can be distinguished: *framing as an accessibility effect* and *framing as a consideration salience effect*.

Early empirical studies of framing effects conceive of the framing process almost entirely as an *accessibility* effect (Iyengar, 1991). Given the key role of news media for the provision of information about politics, news is a key determinant of accessibility. Television news, for example, makes information accessible or retrievable from memory, and easily retrieved or accessed information then dominates "judgments, opinions, and decisions" (Iyengar, 1991, p. 131). Iyengar (1991) makes no distinction in the psychological processes underlying agenda-setting, priming, and framing effects. They all amount to making certain characteristics more or less accessible in memory.

Cappella and Jamieson (1997) review considerable literature in psychology to develop a mental model of framing effects. What news frames essentially accomplish, according to Cappella and Jamieson, is to activate knowledge and invite inferences by making certain beliefs more accessible for use in evaluations and interpretations of issues. Knowledge is defined as organized as nodes, concepts and constructs in more or less associative networks. Information provided by, for example, a frame in the news stimulates access to certain information in memory, making it more accessible. Cappella and Jamieson (1997) point out how the strategic news frame, by virtue of its focus on the behavior of politicians, for example, make salient self-interest, negative character attributions, and cue stock stories in memory about "politics as usual" which then in turn foster and reinforce political cynicism.

Cappella and Jamieson (1997) thereby also introduce framing as an accessibility effect. However, they elaborate this model by arguing that political judgments, as a result of framing, are based on a combination of memory-based (such as accessibility) and on-line activities.[3] Frames, upon activation of nodes, work either through memory, making certain considerations more accessible for use in subsequent judgments and/ or through immediate, on-line evaluation of these nodes which are then anchored or adjusted and used in subsequent judgments without necessarily accessing memory.

That framing effects might go beyond mere accessibility effects is a perspective that is gaining support in both theoretical arguments (e.g., Scheufele, 2000) and in several empirically based studies of framing effects (Druckman, 2001a; Nelson et al., 1997, Nelson & Oxley, 1999; Price & Tewksbury, 1997; Price et al., 1997).

Price and Tewksbury (1997) develop an elaborate model of the ways in which knowledge is activated and used in consequent political judgments and evaluations. This model is empirically tested in Price et al. (1997). They distinguish *applicability* and *accessibility* effects. Framing is seen as an applicability effect whereas priming is seen as an accessibility effect. Framing effects are immediate effects occurring during the initial message processing and the interpretation and reaction to specific news stories. Salient attributes of a message affect the applicability of particular thoughts which result in their activation and use in evaluations (Price & Tewksbury, 1997). Priming effects by contrast are second-order effects with a temporal component which they illustrate with the following example: "First, a media message renders one or another construct applicable, and that construct – say, unemployment – is activated. By virtue of its activation [...] that construct remains temporarily accessible. Subsequently, when a person is asked to evaluate the performance of the president, unemployment is likely to be activated" (Price & Tewksbury, 1997, p. 197).

Most radically opposing the *accessibility* interpretation of framing effects is the work by Nelson and colleagues (Druckman, 2001a; 2001b; Nelson et al., 1997, Nelson & Oxley, 1999). The accessibility model is criticized for its dependency of memory for formulating attitudes (e.g., Nelson & Kinder, 1996). To put the accessibility theory to a test, participants in an experiment completed a reaction time task measuring the cognitive accessibility of concepts induced in the experimental news stories (Nelson et al., 1997). If framing effects are mediated by accessibility, the authors argue, then "participants should respond swiftly to words most consonant with the frame they viewed" (Nelson et al., 1997, p. 573). No effect of framing condition was found on participants' reaction time which is the empirical base to discard the accessibility explanation.

Framing effects stem from the *weight* and *importance* that citizens attach to certain considerations when making political judgments. News frames have impact on opinions and attitudes, not by mere accessibility, but by stressing specific values, facts or other considerations, endowing them with greater relevance to an issue than under an alternative frame. Selectively enhancing the psychological importance and relevance or weight to specific beliefs can be accomplished without accessibility of these concepts in memory (Nelson & Kinder, 1996). Nelson and Oxley (1999) find that salience attached to beliefs, activated by a news frame, is a strong predictor of political attitudes such as tolerance. One path to pursue in future research is to develop tasks including measures of reaction time to investigate whether responses occur on-line or whether they are memory-based (see Cameron & Frieske, 1994).

MODERATORS AND MEDIATORS OF FRAMING EFFECTS. A third aspect which framing research needs to focus on to advance the current knowledge is the area of *moderators* and *mediators* of framing effects. These have been subject of some discussion in the framing effects literature. Since the early studies of framing, there has been agreement on the importance of individual characteristics and context in the processing of information and in the susceptibility to frames provided by, for example, the news (e.g., Gamson, 1992; Graber, 1988; Neuman et al., 1992; Price et al., 1997). With the observation in mind that framing effects are not universal, it is intriguing that only few studies have explicated moderators of framing effects. In particular within the 'cognitive paradigm' in framing research (as discussed in Chapter 2), there has been a strong focus on how audiences respond to and mirror frames in the news, but only limited attention has been paid to moderators and mediators of these effects.

In the media effects literature, political knowledge (oftentimes referred to as 'political sophistication' and 'political awareness') is a key variable, but there is only limited exploration of this in the framing effects literature. Price et al., (1997) found that political knowledge contributed to more elaborate responses to news, but did not find evidence that knowledge either enhances or depresses susceptibility to news frames. Rhee (1997) found political knowledge to significantly bolster readers' use of an experimentally induced frame in their interpretation of an election campaign. Cappella and Jamieson (1997) found greater 'political sophistication' (measured as high political knowledge) to be a significant positive predictor for political cynicism.

Given the inconclusive nature of previous research, this study investigated the role of political knowledge in the frame-setting process and found political knowledge to be a positive predictor for audiences to rely on a frame presented to them in the news. More sophisticated individuals tend to process new information (for example in the form of news frames) deeper and more actively. They may draw more on this resource of information in their subsequent interpretation and evaluation of the issue, but may not necessarily display attitude change.

More work is needed to explicate and model direct effects of individual characteristics as well as mediators and moderators. Future research should aim at identifying these influences and hypothesizing about directional effects so as to explore, for example, differences between how moderators behave in relation to high and low involvement issues.

Covering Europe: lessons for journalism

For journalists covering 'Europe', the 'traditional' constraints and challenges related to covering, for example, domestic political and economic issues, are somewhat magnified. While political reporting in general is challenged by the complexity of issues, potential lack of audience interest and knowledge, and internal tensions in the newsroom about the priority of political news, these challenges apply to the coverage of European affairs in manifold: European-level governance has a different pace from domestic local and national politics, the competence and organization of the institutions is different from domestic politics, the issues at stake involve the opinions and preferences of (at least) 15 countries, the audience oftentimes is better able to identify national politicians than EU-level politicians, domestic tax issues mean more to more viewers than, for example, corporate tax harmonization in the EU, and journalistic colleagues are generally as skeptical towards EU news as they believe their audiences are.

Why worry about these challenges? The evidence in this study suggests that the choices made by journalists when covering Europe have significant implications for how the public perceives and evaluates European issues. To consider and explicate these challenges is therefore also a first step in considering the effects that these choices have.

What might be done to meet the challenge? The challenges are far from easy to meet. One solution lies in the field of education, not only for the audience, but also for journalists and editors. In a recent overview of developments and needs in journalism training, the issue of European integration emerged as a key area in need of attention (Bierhoff, Deuze & de Vreese, 2001).[4] Journalism training in this field should be two-fold. There is a need for training in 'bringing home the European story', that is to make the complex political issues accessible and relevant to audiences without reducing the inherent complexity to simplicity. Refining the skills and tools to frame and find a peg in international political news in order to make it relevant to national audiences without compromising the inherently international nature of the issue is one area in need of attention.

The second area in need of attention in terms of education is 'Sachwissen', i.e. factual and procedural knowledge about the European integration processes, their historical and political antecedents, and future implications. The need for education in this respect is only likely to grow as the competences and authority of the Union expand to new areas. Many journalists covering EU affairs have perhaps too limited or outdated knowledge about the socio-political contours of the European continent which in the midst of the integration process help to explain and understand diverging national interest at the EU negotiation scene.

BLAMING THE MESSENGER: THE FAULT OF TELEVISION JOURNALISM? Given the effects of television news demonstrated in this study, does this mean that journalists are responsible for fuelling political cynicism about Europe? No. It is not a journalistic responsibility as such to promote integration in Europe. European integration is but *one* of several concurring political, economic, and social developments that compete for attention in the news. Journalists are obliged to cover the key issues of the political arena, but only if politicians are convincingly engaged in a topic, the discussion of *how* journalists choose to cover this issue emerges. And still, it is journalism's responsibility to act as a watchdog and hold politicians accountable, even though this may be at stake with politicians' interests.

However, it *is* a journalistic and editorial responsibility to reflect upon the choices made in the 'Europe-coverage'. One conclusion from this study is that 'Europe is a choice'. While television news programs were all pragmatic, that is selective and critical in their choice of stories, the cross-national design showed that this may lead journalists to either, by and large, neglect the European story (such as in the Netherlands) or pro-actively set an agenda, independent from the politicians' agenda (such as in Denmark).

Journalists are and should be aware of their role and the effects it has when covering, for example, European politics as a strategic game. As the Editor-in-Chief of *ITN* said: "It certainly gives the viewer the information they need to make their own judgment, but it may make politics appear quite arcane and quite marketing oriented and further removed from ordinary people's worries."

Not only the choice of whether or not to cover an event or issue, but also the framing of that event matters for the public understanding of the European integration process. The current study demonstrated the effects of journalistic framing of European affairs in terms of, for example, conflict, economic consequences or strategy. The study showed that the spin given to a story was equally important as key news facts when audiences processed the news. Other research has focused on the effects of advantageous and disadvantageous coverage of the enlargement issue. In one experimental study, participants who watched a story that focused on the historical rationales for EU enlargement and portrayed the enlargement as advantageous, led to higher levels of general EU support and higher levels of support for the enlargement plans in particular (Boomgaarden & de Vreese, 2002). Conversely, a disadvantageous focus and non-historical context led to lower levels of support. The conclusion is not that television news stories should always contain either positive interpretations or a broader historical context, but merely to say that *if* they do, this appears to have an effect. Therefore, the choices made by journalists and editors in the production process should be informed and conscious ones.

Creating Europe: lessons for the political arena

Almost two decades ago, Inglehart (1984, p. 20) suggested that the European Community was at a key moment in history in its decision whether or not to develop the *community* into a *union*:

> "Probably, only a bold new departure can recapture the imagination and support of the most dynamic segments of the European public. If it is pursued vigorously, the proposed European Union might rekindle a European spirit, and provide a sense of purpose that is palpably lacking. Bringing about a European Union would not be easy: it will unquestionably give rise to opposition and could even split the Community, in a worst-case scenario. But the gamble is worth taking: if the Community allows itself to stagnate further, as it has during the past decade, it seems likely to become a moribund and largely meaningless institution".

Much of the skepticism and call for rigorous change voiced by Inglehart is applicable today. National and EU politicians would most likely argue that the European Union has become a reality, that monetary unity has been created by virtue of the common currency, and that the 'European spirit' is developing with the planned inclusion of former East European countries. It is hard to disagree with these points, but the question is whether these very 'real' changes matter.

Different scholars have demonstrated and alluded to the fact that public perceptions of political and economic issues such as European integration can be completely independent from factual indicators (Gabel, 1998; Hetherington, 1998). Public support is a key condition for a successful future integration trajectory. With public support for EU membership at best stable and support for crucial issues such as the enlargement declining, not only in the current member states but also in the ascension countries, the need for a change in the *perception* of the EU as stagnating, bureaucratic, and incompetent is evident.

The argument has been made elsewhere that political leaders are more often evaluated based on a *perception* of their performance rather than their real performance. The European Union and its leaders may therefore have more to worry about than political issues such as the ascension countries meeting the criteria for membership of the Union. If such issues are not communicated efficiently and convincingly, public perceptions of the costs and inadequacies of new member states may very well thrive regardless of the adoptions made by these new countries and rigorous tests by the EU.

This study demonstrated that characteristics of the media content, specifically the framing of European issues, have significant effects on how citizens process information and evaluate crucial agenda issues such as the enlargement. News media coverage influences the 'trains of thought' and can contribute to the public's political cynicism and negative issue interpretations. The study also showed, however, that though key perceptions of European affairs are susceptible to news frames, this does not immediately lead to changes in support for, for example, the enlargement of the EU. Does this imply that there is 'nothing to worry about' because media framing effects are, in the first instance, short-term and do not affect levels of EU-support? Such a diagnosis is probably both flawed and short sighted. After all, the observations that repeated exposure to similar messages and reinforcement of existing stereotypes is effective are not new (Lippmann, 1922; Fiske & Taylor, 1991). Future research needs to disentangle the long-term effects of news and information on public opinion about Europe to investigate cumulative effects of particular information environments.

What then needs to be done in the political arena to contribute positively towards this process? The answer is not likely to be simple. For a start, to intervene in the process of cynicism activation when citizens are faced with new information about European affairs, politicians are in need of refraining from using European politics to fight domestic battles. The regular EU summits, involving Prime Ministers from all EU countries, are used as battlegrounds for domestic political leaders. As discussed in Chapter 4, in the case of the Nice summit in December 2000, the EU was little more than a backdrop for British politicians against which domestic politics was discussed. When reviewing positive outcomes of international negotiations, politicians refer to having 'protected national interests' and 'won the battle' against the EU and other member countries. When reviewing less favorable results, national politicians refer to the ever-growing competence of the Union and absence of leeway for national interests and particularities. Using the European realm as a domestic political battleground in which blame can be assigned and credit taken – as discussed by van der Eijk and Franklin (1996) – fuels 'us' versus 'them' sentiments, skepticism, and political cynicism. Such strategic interpretations of European integration are therefore not likely to contribute positively to public opinion about European affairs.

Crucial issues such as the enlargement and the reorganization of EU institutions await in the near future. The importance of news and information in bridging the gap between the political arena and European citizens is not likely to diminish but rather grow. The last word has not yet been said about framing, European integration, and the role that journalists and politicians play in this process.

Notes

Chapter 1

1. In this book I refer to 'news about European affairs', public opinion about 'Europe' and 'European news' interchangeably. The term 'Europe' refers to issues of European integration.
2. Between 1994 and 1999 the turnout level in Britain dropped 12 percentage points. In Denmark this was three and in the Netherlands six points. The most significant drops were in Finland (down from 60% to 30%) and in Germany (down from 60% to 45%).
3. The Eurobarometer is the most consistent source of information about longitudinal developments in European public opinion and has been conducted since 1973 (sponsored by The European Commission). Since 1993 public support for the European single currency has been recorded as well and since 2001 public opinion is also monitored in the EU-candidate countries.
4. This classification is derived from Gabel (1998). He identifies five groups of studies, but there is considerable overlap between several of the categories. Consequently I distinguish three groups.
5. Recent research suggests that in addition to cost/benefit analyses, support for the EU can also be explained in terms of perceived cultural threats (see McLaren, 2002).
6. This interpretation of support for European integration has been challenged by studies of European referendum campaigns that suggest that predispositions on the question of European integration, sometimes referred to as the level of EU-skepticism or EU-attitudes, is a key predictor of the vote (Siune and Svensson 1993; Siune, Svensson & Tonsgaard 1994).
7. Research informed by a Habermasian notion of the necessity of a European public sphere has critically evaluated current media practices for being counter-productive to the ideal of a genuine public debate (e.g., Kunelius & Sparks, 2001).
8. The study also assessed the impact of other influences on the vote and found different levels of support for hypotheses concerning the influence of key variables such as ideology, economic evaluations, and government approval (de Vreese & Semetko, 2001; 2002c)
9. A few notable exceptions to this rule include the two Danish movements 'The June Movement' and 'The People's Movement' that both run for office in European elections and campaign in referendums on European issues, but are not part of domestic politics.
10. A number of studies discuss the changes in the last two decades (see e.g., Blumler & Hoffmann-Riem, 1992; Blumler & Nossiter, 1991; Blumler & Gurevitch, 1998; Hultén & Brants, 1992; Humpreys, 1996; McQuail, 1990; Siune & Hultén, 1998). Changes pertain to technology, market structures, media policies, and audience

preferences. Prior to the 1980s, European broadcasting was essentially publicly funded and controlled (with few exceptions such as Britain). The late 1980s and early 1990s marked a paradigmatic shift in the broadcasting scene and in the early 1990s the changes were coined by a distinction between public broadcasting monopolies and 'dual broadcasting systems' where public and commercial networks operate in the same markets. In 1980 all Western European countries (except Britain, Italy, and Luxembourg) had a public broadcasting monopoly. By 1990 this had changed so that only a few countries did not have a dual system of broadcasting with commercial and public broadcasters operating in the same market. By the end of the decade, all countries had entered a stage of dual broadcasting on liberalized market conditions.

11 *TV2* may become fully privatized if new broadcasting legislation is adopted. In addition, the Danish language private network *TV3* operates out of London.
12 In addition, *SBS* has two daily news bulletins.
13 Comparative studies of media and election campaigns (Blumler, 1983; Semetko et al., 1991; Semetko, 1996), European television news (Heinderyckx, 1993), and US versus European news (Hallin & Mancini, 1984) are key cross-national comparative studies from the last decades.
14 Other approaches to content analysis exist in which the emphasis on *systematic* analysis is less prominent (see McQuail (2000) for an overview).
15 Other 'classic' definitions of experimentation include Berelson (1952): "Any investigation that includes two criteria: (a) manipulation or control of some variable by the investigator and (b) systematic observation or measurement of other variables. In short, it means we actively intervene on the phenomena of interest to see what, if any, effects are produced by the intervention". Tannenbaum (1958, p. 67): "Research in which one or more independent variables that are assumed to be relevant are systematically manipulated and their effect, both independent and interactive on some dependent variables are observed under objective conditions with the possible contamination effect of other independent variables held constant".
16 However, it is possible that, despite random assignment, experimental conditions differ in their composition, and tests verifying successful random assignment are therefore appropriate.

Chapter 2

1 A substantial part of extant research focuses on election campaigns and the central role of (news) media (see, e.g., Altheide & Snow, 1979; Bennett, 1992; Blumler & Gurevitch, 1995; Norris et al., 1999; Patterson, 1993; Semetko et al., 1991; Swanson & Mancini, 1996).
2 Much research on framing is inspired by Goffman's observations that individual perceptions of events are cognitively processed and categorized (see, e.g., discussions in Gamson (1992; 1996), Pan and Kosicki (1993)).
3 The research by Loftus (1979) and later also by, for example, Kinder and Sanders (1996) address the effects of question wording. This is a long-standing research tradition in, for example, survey research. Specifically in relation to European integration, Saris (1997) demonstrated that subtle changes in question wording were capable of directing public opinion about the European Union.

4 It should be noted that the framing process as described here is different from the temporal perspective in Miller and Riechert (2001) where the framing process is discussed in terms of an 'emergence' phase, a 'definition/ conflict' phase, a 'resonance' phase, and an 'equilibrium/ resolution' phase.
5 Scheufele (2000) discussed individual-level consequences, but societal level consequences should be considered too.
6 Another overview of framing research (Simon, 2001) takes a more science philosophical approach and distinguishes between 'positivist studies of framing' (which compare to D'Angelo's (2002) cognitive paradigm) and 'constructionist studies of framing' that equal D'Angelo's (2002) constructionist paradigm.
7 D'Angelo (2002) argues that the three paradigms, much to the benefit of the field, co-exist.
8 A comparable classification to the issue-specific frame was recently suggested by McCombs and Ghanem (2001) who refer to issue-specific frames as 'ad hoc frames'.
9 The studies have appeared in international peer-reviewed journals or are large-scale internationally renowned research projects (e.g., Cappella & Jamieson, 1997; Iyengar, 1991; Neuman et al., 1992; Patterson, 1993). Some of these studies are parts of larger research endeavors that also include investigations of the effects of the news frames (e.g., Cappella & Jamieson, 1997; Iyengar, 1991; Semetko & Valkenburg, 2000). The effects studies are discussed in the subsequent section on framing effects.
10 In recent years several book chapters as well as dozens of conference presentations have been related to framing. At recent conferences of e.g. the International Communication Association (ICA) and the American Political Science Association (APSA) special sessions have been devoted to framing research.
11 In fact, some authors find the two news frames to be so closely related that the terms are used interchangeably (e.g., Lawrence, 2000).
12 The horse race frames has also been found to appear in election news coverage in a European context (e.g., Brants & van Praag, 1995; van Praag & Brants, 2000) without any indication of an increase in use during the 1990s.
13 The distinction between episodic and thematic frames is an example of a more generically driven news frame that transcends issue and time/ space limits. But this particular example is also problematic. There is some dispute as to whether the episodic and thematic 'frames' are in fact frames or whether what is described as a frame in the study is a *format* or a '*news bias*'. What Iyengar (1991) defined as 'episodic' has elsewhere been discussed in terms of a structural bias in the news towards 'personalization' and 'fragmentation' by which news becomes "hard to assemble in to a bigger picture and appear as rather self-contained, isolated happenings" (Bennett, 1996, p. 40).
14 Conceptually, the frames identified by Neuman et al. (1992) such as 'human impact' and 'conflict' share a lot of common ground with Bennett's (1996) distinction between four modes of news representation. Based on a discussion of news values he gauged a number of key characteristics of US news coverage by distinguishing between 'personalized', 'dramatized', 'fragmented', and 'normalized' strategies of news representation. Bennett (1996, p. 48) suggested that personalized news, for instance, can be defined as "the journalistic bias that gives preference to the individ-

ual actors and human interest angles in events while downplaying institutional and political considerations that establish their social context". This identification of a mode of reporting bears great resemblance with Neuman et al.'s (1992) 'human impact' frame.
15 The de Vreese et al. (2001) study is dealt with in length in Chapter 4.
16 McLeod et al. (1994, p. 136) and McLeod et al. (2002, p. 226) distinguish four types of individual level effects of political communication: opinion formation, cognitive changes, perceptions of the political system, and political participation. They classify framing as a 'cognitive change effect'. However, previous research suggests that framing effects may also be found on several attitudinal and behavioral measures.
17 No empirical research so far has provided evidence showing direct behavioral effects (such as political participation) following exposure to a specific frame. Initial steps have been taken by Shah et al. 1996 and Valentino et al. (2001a) who discuss effects on behavior intentions.
18 Some studies listed as drawing on 'issue-specific' frames deal with the framing of specific issues though the nature of the frame suggests that other issues may be framed along similar lines (e.g., McLeod & Detenber, 1999; Shah et al., 2001). This aspect is not discussed in the studies.
19 Druckman (2001b) additionally investigated the role of message endorser. He found that framing effects are most likely to occur if the frame is sponsored by a more credible source (e.g., the *New York Times*) than a less credible source (in his example the *National Enquirer*).
20 A dominant news frame, such as the episodic frame, may, for example in the case of covering terrorism, "encourage viewers to attribute causal responsibility for terrorism to personal qualities and of terrorists and inadequacy of sanctions" (Iyengar, 1991, p. 45). Similarly, episodic framing of poverty increases attributions of individual responsibility while thematic news frames increases attributions of societal responsibility.
21 Differences in definitions and discussions about the relationship between agenda-setting, priming, and framing (see Chapter 7) notwithstanding, agenda-setting can be defined the ability of media to increase to public perception of an issue's importance by devoting attention to that issue. Priming can be defined as the ability of the media to influence the importance attached to an issue or character trait when persons make evaluations of, for example, the president.
22 Agenda-setting emerged from McCombs and Shaw's (1972) exploratory study of the 1968 US election that synthesized the agenda-setting ideas into a systematic and testable hypothesis. They compared key issues in the media coverage of the election with a sample of undecided voters' perception of key issues in the campaign and found a strong positive correlation between the media and the public agenda. Agenda-setting has been explored and tested from a variety of research methods ranging from survey data (e.g., McCombs & Shaw, 1972), in-depth interviews (e.g. Neuman et al., 1992) to experiments (e.g., Iyengar & Kinder, 1987).
23 There is also considerable terminological inconsistency. Luskin (1990) refers to 'political sophistication', Fiske, Lau, and Smith (1990) to 'political expertise', Price and Zaller (1993) to 'public affairs knowledge', and Delli-Carpini and Keeter (1996) to 'political knowledge'.

24 Priming is known from research in cognitive psychology (Fiske & Taylor, 1991) and had earlier been identified in a political communication context by Patterson and McClure (1976) as an important potential effect of television political advertising. Priming has been defined as "the effect of a prior context on the interpretation and retrieval of information" (Fiske & Taylor, 1984, p. 231). In terms of news, priming refers to 'the ability of new information to alter the standards by which the public evaluates political leaders' (Krosnick & Kinder, 1990). When the US news media, for instance, covered the 1991 Gulf War extensively, US President Bush's performance was evaluated on his warfare abilities, but when the news media a year later focused on the American economy, Bush was evaluated on his economic performance (Jasperson et al., 1998)

25 Nelson et al. (1997) and Druckman (2001b) modeled a number of attitudes as mediators of framing. Frames in the news activated and made certain attitudes and considerations more salient which affected tolerance towards the KKK. No direct effect of exposure to the frames were found, but indirect, mediated effects were found across different studies.

26 In the study Cappella and Jamieson (1997) refer to knowledge as a surrogate for 'news reception' following the advice by Price and Zaller (1993).

27 In addition, Price et al. (1997) found 'residency status' to be a moderator of framing effects for perceptions of university funding so that students living in the state produced less consequence-related thoughts than out of state students who would be more affected by tuition increases according to the news material used in the study.

Chapter 3

1 Parts of the material from this chapter have been published in de Vreese (2003; 2001b; 2000).

2 One example is the agenda-setting approach with hundreds of studies investigating the relationship between the media agenda and the public agenda (Dearing & Rogers, 1996). Comparatively few studies have addresses the specific dynamics of agenda-building (Lang & Lang, 1991). Notable exceptions have studied the influence of politicians' agenda on the news agenda (e.g., Weaver & Swanzy, 1985) or by investigating the influence of routine sources on building the news agenda (e.g., Berkowitz, 1987).

3 One study discusses the negotiations taking place at the public service news program in Israel over how to frame a story about football fans at a victory celebration welcoming the Prime Minister (Liebes, 2000). Though stressing the importance of obtaining knowledge about "what goes on on the floor" the study does not rely on observations or in-depth interviews, but instead on a comparison between raw footage from the event and the broadcast news story supplemented by "unstructured discussions among a group of scholars and editors" (Liebes, 2000, p. 304).

4 The June 1999 elections took place in the aftermath of the introduction of the common European currency, the euro, in January 1999 and the resignation of the European Commission in March 1999. The 1999 turnout was significantly lower than in 1994 and in some countries the news media that repeated projections of low turnout were 'blamed' for contributing to this decline.

5   The general literature on production of news is too large to be discussed in detail here. One strand of research conceptualizes political news as the result of (1) the position of politics and politicians in a society, (2) journalists' and editors' orientation towards politics and politicians, (3) the degree of professionalization of politics, and (4) the degree media competition (adapted from Semetko et al. (1991)). These factors influence the autonomy and extent to which news media can exert discretion – that is independently defining their own policies and choices – in their coverage of politics. They thereby define the parameters within which news organizations operate.
In Europe significant cross-national variation is found on several of these parameters. The 'valuation' of politics differs between countries in the EU and citizens in these countries show very different levels of trust in government and political institutions (Nye, Zelikow & King, 1997). The orientation towards politics and politicians by news people also varies greatly in Europe and the journalistic culture in terms of covering politics differs between countries. The degree of professionalization of politics campaigns and the degree of competition in the media market show some trends of convergence in a European perspective. First, the European media landscape has profoundly changed during the past two decades so that all countries have full-blown competition in broadcasting and all operate in a dual system without a public service broadcasting monopoly (McQuail & Siune, 1998). Second, with respect to the professionalization of politics, shared European-wide trends are discernable at the national level of governance (see Chapter 1), although little is known about changes at the European level of governance.

6   The importance of the news organization in particular is stressed by Manheim (1998) who sees the newsroom as the key locale for defining news. He defines news as a product of internal behaviors and values of the institutional needs of the newsroom. Some studies suggest that news organizations are active players in defining the news agenda (e.g. Tuchman, 1978). Others studies suggest that news organizations are merely the place where culturally defined norms of news values and selection criteria are manifest (e.g., Galtung & Ruge, 1965; White, 1950).

7   The distinction between sacerdotal and pragmatic approaches refers to the approach to elections, but can also be applied to discuss and identify the approach to politics in general, outside a campaign period.

8   An additional source of information comes from newsroom observations at the television news programs in the three countries. This observational component consisted of periods of two or three days of presence in the newsroom. I attended central editorial meeting and monitored discussions between journalists, editors, and correspondents. The newsroom observations could not take place on the same days which makes any direct comparisons and conclusions at best tentative. In Denmark, the observations were carried out on June 7-8, 1999, in the Netherlands on June 10-11, 1999 and in Britain after the EP elections in late September 1999. The observations can therefore only be seen as illuminating background information for understanding the editorial decisions discussed in the interviews.

9   The interviewees appear in this study by title/ function in the newsroom rather than by name. These titles vary per program and comparable, and most concise titles are used here.

10 At the time of writing (October 2002), *BBC* has it's main evening news program at 10 p.m.
11 Until March 1999 (and again in 2002), *ITN* broadcast it's main news bulletin at 10 p.m.
12 It should be noted that some of the organizations and in particular the *BBC* are large organizations with many outlets and many staff involved in covering European affairs. The observations made in this study pertain specifically to the television news programs of these organizations and do not reflect, for example, radio news or current affairs magazines.
13 All interviews were transcribed prior to the analysis. Various strategies have been applied in analyzing interview material with journalists in other studies (see Kung-Shankleman, 2000). I only refer to themes if more interviewees addressed the same topic and provided 'consistent' answers. The findings are presented reflecting the situation at the time of the interviews.
14 *BBC* parliamentary journalists covering EU affairs, for example, serve no less than five radio stations, two terrestrial television channels (including the several daily *BBC* news bulletins), *BBC World*, and the 24-hour domestic news channel (source: Interview with senior *BBC* political correspondent).
15 Observation in the newsroom, June 1999.

Chapter 4

1 Parts of this chapter have been published in Peter & de Vreese (2002), Semetko et al. (2000), de Vreese (2001b; 2001d; 2001e), and de Vreese et al. (2001).
2 This was a general pattern, but included countries such as Italy and Spain where the coverage was either neutral or positive (Norris, 2000, p. 198).
3 Other scholars have stressed the crucial role that media play in shaping public opinion and creating a 'shared European identity' (e.g., Kunelius & Sparks, 2001). These studies have, by and large, acknowledged that pan-European projects aimed at promoting a common communicative space and European identity have failed (e.g., Schlesinger, 1997; Venturelli, 1993). National news media appear the more important forum and the making of "a common European culture and identity via trans-border flows of European-made television seems today an almost naïve aspiration" (Schlesinger, 1997, p. 13).
4 The results reported in Norris (2000) are based on the monitoring study conducted by the European Union itself. Norris (2000) deals only sporadically with the design of this study and does not address issues of data quality or the reliability of the coding.
5 See comments about changing schedules in Britain in Chapter 3. In the period between March 1999 and 2002 ITN broadcast at 6.30 p.m.. This bulletin is used in this study with the exception of the euro introdcution period where the *News at Ten* was used.
6 In this period, the following programs are omitted from the analysis due to technical problems: *BBC* 25-28 December, *ITN* 25-30 December, *TV2* 31 December, *NOS* 19, 21, 22, 26, 27 December, 5, 10 January and *RTL* 26, 27 December and 9, 10 January.
7 The routine period consisted of the following weekdays: January 5-8 and January 11, 1999.

8   During the EP campaign, the following programs are omitted from the analysis due to technical problems: *BBC* 28, 29 May, *ITN* 30, 31 May and 6 June, *DR* 29 May, *NOS* 31 May, 1 June, *RTL* 1 June.
9   For the summit period, the following programs are omitted from the analysis due to technical problems: *BBC* 25, 26 March 2000, 12, 13, 14 December 2000, *ITN* 25, 26 March 2000, 20, 22, 24 June 2000, *DR* 26 March 2000, 12 December 2000, *TV2* 26 March 2000, 19, 21 June 2000, 12 December 2000, *NOS* 17, 18, 19 March 2000, *RTL* 17, 81, 19 March 2000, 12, 13, 14 December 2000.
10 For the routine period, the following programs are omitted from the analysis due to technical problems: *BBC* 20 November 1999, 26 February 2000, 29, 30 July 2000, 22 August 2000, 23, 24 September 2000, *ITN* 20 November 1999, 26 February 2000, *DR* 26 February 2000, *TV2* 10 November 2000, *RTL* 14 May 2000.
11 The content analyses reported here are integral to a larger research program investigating news and public opinion about European affairs. For example, while this study focuses on Britain, Denmark, and the Netherlands, the analysis of the European election campaign covered all EU countries and involved a team of 37 native speakers of the 10 languages spoken in the EU. This study analyzed about 7,000 news stories. Additionally, the summit and routine news analyzed in this book is integral to a larger study also involving Germany and France for specific periods. For this study more than 16,000 news stories were analyzed.
12 Other studies of news content have focused on specific words (Jasperson et al., 1998) or segments of news stories (such as a 'communicator sequence', see Blumler, 1983). For the purpose of this study the news story was considered the most appropriate unit of analysis.
13 The total number of stories coded consisted of 3,134 British (*BBC* 1,597, *ITN* 1,537), 4,072 Danish (*DR* 2,012, *TV2* 2,060), and 3,582 Dutch (*NOS* 1,705, *RTL* 1,877) stories.
14 To identify political/economic news, a screening question about the political/economic nature of the topic was included. A story about cuts in the health sector, for example, may be a candidate for both the category 'Politics' (in terms of social politics) or 'Social welfare'. The additional screening question ensured that all political or economic stories were coded in the categories 'Introduction of the euro', 'Politics' and 'Economy' and that the remaining categories exclusively contained non-political/non-economic stories.
15 The other items were: "Does one party/ individual/group/country reproach another?", "Does the story refer to two sides or to more than two sides of the problem/issue?", and "Does the story emphasize the achievements and/or actions of an individual/party versus the achievements and/or actions of another individual/party?". Semetko and Valkenburg (2000) did not use the final item in their analysis. Others, however, argue the centrality of assessments of publicly elected figures' achievements in news (e.g., Cappella & Jamieson, 1997). This is why this item was included after pre-tests.
16 The other items were: "Is there a reference to economic consequences of pursuing or not pursuing a course of action?", and "Is there a mention of financial losses or gains now or in the future?".
17 An actor is not necessarily a person, but may also be a government, an institution, organization or another type of entity. An actor does not have to act, that is func-

tion in the news story as actively doing something. An actor can also be the object or target of actions. Journalists are only actors in the story if the news report is about the journalist. Spokespersons are always coded according to the person/ entity whom they represent. An actor was coded only once per news story.

18 In other analyses (see Peter & de Vreese, 2002), the tone measure is calculated as a percentage-based measure because it, in this case, had to be taken into account that the absolute number of EU representatives differed considerably not only within but also between the countries analyzed there. The evaluation differential was therefore to be preferred to a mean evaluation.

19 The measures of news frames and focus of the news utilized in the euro study are not applied.

20 For the European elections new candidates for the European Parliament were also coded as EU actors. However, these candidates were assigned a special code, as they are in essence domestic politicians and it is therefore interesting too see whether the Parliamentary election coverage consisted of national candidates or EU level actors. For each actor, it was coded whether the actor was as an individual or group, related to the EU or any other level than the EU (e.g., regional, domestic, or world). For the current analysis this distinction is not applied as it is elsewhere (Peter & de Vreese, 2002).

21 'Other political news' was identified by a screening question asking: "Does this story address local/ national/ international politics, political institutions/ actors?"

22 In the content analysis of the summit coverage and the routine weeks the fourth item was omitted from the conflict scale.

23 The indicators for strategic news coverage used in this study are limited. Jamieson (1992) defines strategic news as consisting of five components (see Chapter 2). Scholars have argued that the presence of polls should not be considered part of an index of strategic news coverage as the mere presence of polls does not affect audience responses to the news (Valentino et al., 2001a). Of the remaining four indicators, only two are used in this analysis. This, however, is not considered a problem because the aim in this study is not to assess the level of strategic news and compare this to, for example, US news.

24 Sports and weather was also a common component of both the routine news period, as well as the event period, with the amount of time during the routine period at a low of 7% in Denmark and a high of 13% in the Netherlands with Britain (8%) in between. Weather and sports are placed within the news bulletin in some programs and in special independent segments in other programs.

25 The Dutchman was appointed to lead the European Central Bank for a term of eight years, and he took office at the time the euro was launched. His appointment had been the subject of much debate because he was supported strongly by the Germans but initially rejected by the French, who insisted that a Frenchman have the seat after only four years.

26 This observation should be intepreted with caution given the modest number of cases ranging from 8 EU actors in Denmark to 33 in the Netherlands.

27 On Election Day the British and Danish networks carried exit polls. On June 11 and 12, 1999 most programs made only brief reference to the European elections. The actual results of the elections were publicly available until Monday June 14, 1999. This time lag was due to a regulation stating that all election results in the EU

member countries were to be made public simultaneously. The remaining countries all went to the polls on Sunday June 13, 1999.
28 This aggregate list of topics in the news should be interpreted with caution because the six news periods are presented together.
29 This number is an average. Some summits received significantly more coverage than others. The Nice summit (2000) for example received almost 20% of the news in Denmark and between 10-15% in Britain and the Netherlands (see de Vreese, 2001b).
30 While the content analysis in this study supports the claim that 'expected low turnout' was a prominent theme on the news agenda, often initiated by the news media themselves, no clear conclusions about negative real-life effects can be drawn from the literature. On the one hand there is hardly any evidence to suggest that polls predicting the level of turnout in elections has large effects. Studies of demobilizing effects of the publication of polls yield either minimal or no effects on voters to turn out to vote (Ansolabehere and Iyengar, 1994; Sudman, 1986). On the other hand, Zaller (1992) has suggested that the most significant effects of media content are likely to occur in a situation where the information environment is dominated by coverage of an issue with a consistent directional bias. It is therefore unclear, and also beyond the scope of this study, to assess what (if any) effects the prevalence of the 'turnout' theme in the campaign news coverage had.
31 It should be noted, however, that the coding relied upon by Norris (2000) allows for multiple codings of topics in a news story whereas this current study assigned one, dominant topic per news story.

Chapter 5

1 Parts of this chapter were presented at the 2001 ICA annual meetings (de Vreese, 2001c).
2 KLO [Kijk- en Luisteronderzoek] is the Audience Research Department of the Dutch public broadcasters.
3 The author thanks reporters at *NOS Journaal* (in particular former editor-in-chief Nico Haasbroek).
4 An overview of all the stories in the experimental bulletin can be obtained from the author. A post-test item asked participants to evaluate the trustworthiness of the experimental and other stories. The evaluation of the experimental story did not deviate from other stories.
5 The cross-talk and field report versions were made to explore effects of format differences on appreciation of news. The traditional field report and the live cross-talk version contained identical information. The correspondent, in the cross-talk versions, not only paraphrased, but in fact cited literally what the MPs and the President of the Dutch Bank had stated in front of the camera in the field report versions. The full script of each story can be obtained from the author. For more details on the effects of format differences, see Snoeijer et al. (2002).
6 The essence of an experiment is the elimination of intervening variables through random assignment to experimental condition. To check whether the randomization procedure was successful, an ANOVA was conducted for a number of individual characteristics such as gender, age, education level, political knowledge, and

political interest. This revealed no significant differences between participants in the experimental conditions on any of the measures, suggesting a successful randomization.

7   A control group would have to be treated to a 'frameless' television news story which would violate the conventions for the nature of television news stories. To omit a control group in the design is in line with the procedures used in experimental framing research by, for example, Domke et al. (1999), Iyengar (1991), McLeod & Detenber (1999), and Nelson et al. (1997).

8   This procedure was chosen because the final questionnaires provided information that could cue participants to alter answers to previous questions. A single questionnaire would enable participants to go back in the questionnaire whereas the chosen procedure with separate questionnaires and envelopes made this impossible.

9   The other items are, for the conflict frame: "Does the answer refer to one or more parties reproaching each other?"; "does the answer refer to two or more sides of the issue/ problem?"; "does the answer refer to the performance of an individual/ group/ country?"; "does the answer refer to political disputes over the issue?". For the economic consequences frame the items were: "Does the answer refer to financial consequences of pursuing or not pursuing an action?"; "does the answer mention financial losses/ gains, nor or in the future?"; "does the answer mention the impact of Dutch economy/ tax payers?".

10 A GLS factor analysis confirmed the loading of the items on the two factors. The factor analysis explained 44% of the variance and resulted in a non-significant χ^2 (χ^2 = 22.08 (19), p = .28) indicating a satisfactory fit.

11 The question read: "*We are also interested in what you can remember from the story about the enlargement of the European Union. Please write below how you would tell this story to a friend that has not seen the story. You can think of, for example, persons and countries mentioned, what happened, why it happened, and what the consequences are. Please write down everything you can remember*".

12 The question wording of the three items was: '*The European Union should be enlarged with central and eastern European countries such as the Check republic, Hungary, and Rumania*', '*It is a good thing that the Netherlands participates in the euro*', '*Turkey should become member of the EU*'.

13 To check for potential interaction effects, a MANOVA with frame (conflict versus economic consequences) and format (live cross-talk versus field report) as between-subject factors and use of frames (as identified in the participants thoughts) as within-subject factor yielded a main effect for frame condition for the conflict scale ($F(1, 144)$ = 48.45, p < .001) and for the economic consequences scale ($F(1, 144)$ = 86.52, p < .001). The MANOVA showed no significant main effect for format (live cross-talk versus field report) neither for the conflict scale ($F(1, 144)$ = 3.62, p = .06) nor for the economic consequences scale ($F(1, 144)$ = 0.31, p = .86). The MANOVA also showed no significant interaction effect between frame and format, neither for the conflict scale ($F(1,144)$ = 2.01, p = .16) nor for the economic consequences scale ($F(1, 144)$ = .43, p = .51). Post-hoc Scheffé tests for the framing condition yielded a clear structure in homogeneous subsets, revealing that the experimental framing condition had a significant effect on viewers' use of frames in their thoughts.

14 An ANOVA controlling for potential interaction effects with the two formats yielded no significant main effect for condition neither for the core part ($F(3,145)$ = .70,

p = .55), the part pertaining to the conflict frame ($F(3,144)$ = .82, p = .49), nor the part pertaining to the economic consequences part ($F(3,144)$ = .01, p = 1.00).
15 The effect of the frame was significant in both the conflict condition ($F(1, 144)$ = 59.92, partial η^2 = .30, p < .001) and in the economic consequences condition ($F(1, 144)$ = 96.82, partial η^2 = .41, p < .001).
16 Political knowledge ($F(1, 144)$ = 2.82, partial η^2 = .02, p < .10), verbosity ($F(1, 144)$ = 3.75, partial η^2 = .03, p < .05).
17 An ANOVA controlling for potential interaction effects with the different formats yielded no significant main effect for condition for the level of European integration support ($F(3, 144)$ = .62, p = .60).

Chapter 6

1 Parts of this chapter have been presented at the annual meetings of the American Political Science Association, Boston, August 29 - September 2, 2002 (de Vreese, 2002b).
2 Cappella and Jamieson (1997) investigated the effects of strategy news in two contexts. The first series of experiments assessed the effects of issue and strategy frames in the news coverage of a 1991 mayoral political campaign. The second series of experiments investigated the effects of the two frames during the 1993-94 Health Care reform debate in the U.S. In both contexts they found the strategic news frame to fuel public cynicism about politics.
3 Brants and van Kempen (2002) discuss their findings in the light of the different composition of the audience for the two news programs in terms of, for example, education which point to a process of self-selection.
4 Experiments with a temporal component in the design are not common in other areas of communication research either. One recent study drawing on a 'prolonged-exposure design' found cultivation effects of repeated exposure to talk shows with specific content (Rössler & Brosius, 2001).
5 The authors do not directly address this potentially confounding aspect of their design. They draw on aggregate-level time-series analysis to further substantiate their arguments about the persistent and cumulative effect of agenda-setting (Iyengar & Kinder, 1987, pp. 26-33), but these analyses are correlational and do not include individual level exposure and attention measures or any information about topics salient in news to which the respondents were exposed to.
6 The design does not include a control group which would have to be treated to a 'frameless' television news story which would violate the conventions for the nature of television news stories. To omit a control group in the design is in line with the procedures used in most experimental framing research (Domke et al., 1999; Iyengar, 1991; McLeod & Detenber, 1999; Nelson et al., 1997; Valentino et al., 2001a). Since this study is designed to test the effects of strategic news coverage on a variety of dependent measures, the other group (exposed to issue-driven news) may effectively be considered the functional equivalent of a control group (Brown & Melamed, 1990).
7 The key feature of experimentation is the elimination of intervening variables through random assignment to experimental conditions. In this study the randomization procedure was successful: chi-square tests revealed no significant differences

between the different conditions on demographic dimensions: gender ($\chi^2 = .33$, $df = 1$, $p = 57$), age ($\chi^2 = 50.53$, $df = 45$, $p = .26$), education ($\chi^2 = 7.53$, $df = 8$, $p = .48$).

8   The experimental bulletin was somewhat shorter (six minutes) than a regular 8 o'clock news bulletin. Participants were informed that the remaining time would be news about the aftermath of the September 11 events in the U.S. They were informed that this news was changing so rapidly that it was not possible to include it in the proof recording.

9   Measures of political cynicism have been the focus of much scholarly attention, but there is little agreement on how to conceptualize and tap political cynicism. Some scholars have linked discussion of cynicism to measures of political efficacy (Acock & Clarke, 1990; Acock, Clark & Stewart, 1985; Craig, Niemi & Silver, 1990; Niemi, Craig & Mattei, 1991). At the core of cynicism is an absence of trust (Agger, Goldstein & Pearl, 1961). However, conventional measures of political trust, such as those used in the American National election studies, are often criticized (see, for example, Lodge & Tursky, 1979; Muller & Jukam, 1977). Moreover, equating standard measures of political trust, alienation, and efficacy, is not appropriate in the attempt to gauge specific dimensions of cynicism about politics (Cappella & Jamieson, 1997). I build on the research by Cappella & Jamieson (1997) and therefore use their items to investigate effects of the strategic news frame on political cynicism. The items in this study are worded slightly differently to apply to a policy debate rather than a specific election campaign.

10 The questions were: 'Sometimes politics is so complex that people like me do not understand what is going on', 'People like me have no influence what the government does', and 'I think I am better informed about politics than most others'.

11 The news outlets were: television: *NOS, RTL, SBS*. Current affairs weeklies: *Elsevier, Vrij Nederland,* HP de Tijd. Newspapers: *de Volkskrant,* NRC *Handelsblad, Telegraaf, AD, Trouw, Metro,* and *Spits*

12 The stories were: European Parliament asks Commissioner for rectification (*RTL*, October 4, 2001); New fake-euro coins found (*SBS*, October 5, 2001).

13 The stories were: EU makes list of terrorists (*Metro*, October 2, 2001); Preparation for the euro in supermarket (*Telegraaf,* October 5, 2001); ESF funds to the Netherlands (*NRC* October 6, 2001).

14 Self-reported exposure measures are often criticized. Participants were cued with the day, date, and time of broadcast (in the case of television) to obtain as reliable estimates as possible. Participants were re-interviewed over three consecutive weeknights, depending on which day they took part in the experiments. Participants interviewed on the last day were additionally probed for exposure to the previous evening's news as this included a EU story.

15 A regression model with political cynicism as the dependent variable and 'exposure to strategic news', 'political knowledge', 'political efficacy' and interaction terms (exposure x knowledge) and (exposure x efficacy) was also tested. Since the interaction terms were not significant the simple but more parsimonious model is used here and presented as an ANCOVA.

16 Ten percent of the participants reported having seen either of the two television news programs containing EU news. A total of 44% of the participants reported reading a newspaper that in that week contained EU news on the front page.

17 Regression analyses with political cynicism and the number of positive, neutral, and negative comments respectively as the dependent variable and exposure to strategic news, political knowledge, political efficacy, and verbosity as well as the interaction term exposure x knowledge as predictor variables were also conducted. Since the coefficients were similar and none of the interaction terms significant, the reduced and more parsimonious models are presented here as ANCOVAs.
18 The week's news was heavily dominated by news about the aftermath of the September 11, 2001 events.
19 It should be noted, however, that Miller and Krosnick (2000) report an interaction effect between exposure and knowledge on their dependent measures whereas this study finds a main effect of knowledge.

Chapter 7

1 Peter (2002) moreover finds that the *difference* between positive and negative evaluations of EU actors is larger in countries with anti-EU parties or polarized elite opinion climate.
2 Agenda-setting addresses the relationship between the media agenda and the public agenda. Cohen (1963, p. 13) succinctly stated the core of the theory in his study of foreign affairs and noted that the press "may not be successful much of the time in telling people what to think, but it is stunningly successful in telling people what to think about". Following McCombs and Shaw (1972), more than two hundred studies have investigated the basic propositions of the theory (McCombs et al., 1997b; McLeod et al., 1994). Research on agenda-setting has expanded to include the full range of dynamic processes between party, policy, media, and public agendas (Dearing & Rogers, 1996).
3 For a review of the two approaches, see Cappella and Jamieson (1997, pp. 70-77).
4 The research for this project was carried out in Austria, Sweden, Denmark, Switzerland, and The Netherlands. Interviews with newsmakers, directors of key teaching and training institutions and with policy makers as well as members of the unions and the employers' organizations were held in each of these five countries.

References

Aarts, K. & Semetko, H. A. (2003). The divided electorate: media use and political involvement. *Journal of Politics* (forthcoming).

Abramson, P. R. & Aldrich, J. H. (1982). The decline of electoral participation in America. *American Political Science Review, 76 (3)*, 502-521.

Acock, A. & Clarke, H. D. (1990). Alternative measures of political efficacy: Models and means. *Quality & Quantity, 24*, 87-105.

Acock, A., Clarke, H. D. & Stewart, M. C. (1985). A news model for old measures: A co-variance structure analysis of political efficacy. *Journal of Politics, 47*, 1062-1084.

Agger, R. E., Goldstein, M. N. & Pearl, S. A. (1961). Political cynicism: Measurement and meaning. *Journal of Politics, 23 (3)*, 477-506.

Althaus, S. L., Edy, J. A. & Phalen, P. F. (2001). Using substitutes for full-text news stories in content analysis: Which text is best? *American Journal of Political Science, 45 (3)*, 707-723.

Altheide, D. L. & Snow, R. P. (1979). *Media logic*. London: Sage.

Andersen, J., Borre, O., Goul-Andersen, J. & Nielsen, H. J. (1999). *Vaelgere med omtanke. En analyse af folketingsvalget 1998* [Thoughtful electorate: An analysis of the general elections 1998]. Aarhus: Systime.

Anderson, C. & Reichert, M. S. (1996). Economic benefits and support for membership in the EU: A cross-national analysis. *Journal of Public Policy, 15*, 231-249.

Anderson, P. J. & Weymouth, T. (1999). *Insulting the public? The British press and the European Union*. London: Longman.

Ansolabehere, S. & Iyengar, S. (1994). Of horseshoes and horse races: Experimental studies of the impact of poll results on electoral behavior. *Political Communication, 11*, 413-430.

Ansolabehere, S., Iyengar, S., Simon, A. & Valentino, N. A. (1994). Does attack advertisement demobilize the electorate? *American Political Science Review, 88 (4)*, 829-838.

Asp, K. (1983). The struggle for the agenda. Party agenda, media agenda, and voter agenda in the 1979 Swedish election campaign, *Communication Research 10*, 333-355.

Ball-Rokeach, S. (1985). The origins of individual media-systems dependency: A sociological framework. *Communication Research, 12*, 485-510.

Ball-Rokeach, S., Power, G. J., Guhrie, K. K. & Waring, H. R. (1990). Value-framing abortion in the United States: An application of media system dependency theory. *International Journal of Public Opinion Research, 2*, 249-273.

Banducci, S., Karp, J. & Lauf, E. (2002). *Elite leadership, media coverage and support for European integration*. Paper presented to the annual conference of the International Communication Association. Seoul, Korea. ICA.

Banks, S. M., Salovey, P., Greener, S., Rothman, A. J., Moyer, A., Beauvais, J & Epel, E. (1995). The effects of message framing on mammography utilization. *Health Psychology, 14 (2),* 178-184.

Baron, R. M. & Kenny, D. A. (1986). The moderator-mediator variable distinction in social psychological research: Conceptual, strategic, and statistical considerations. *Journal of Personality and Social Psychology, 51,* 1173-1182.

Beck, P. A., Dalton, R. J., Greene, S. & Huckfeldt, R. (2002). The social calculus of voting: Interpersonal, media, and organizational influences on Presidential choices. *American Political Science Review, 96,* 57-74.

Benford, R. D. & Snow, D. A. (2000). Framing processes and social movements: An overview and assessment. *Annual Review of Sociology, 26,* 611-639.

Bennett, S. E., Rhine, S. L., Flickinger, R. S. & Bennett, L. M. (1999). "Video malaise" revisited. Public trust in the media and government. *Harvard International Journal of Press/ Politics, 4 (4),* 8-23.

Bennett, W. L. (1992). *The governing crisis: Media, money, and marketing in American elections.* New York: St. Martin's Press.

Bennett, W. L. (1996). *News: the politics of illusion.* New York: Longman.

Bennett, W. L. & Entman, R. M. (2001). *Mediated politics. Communication and the future of democracy.* Cambridge: Cambridge University Press.

Berelson, B. (1952). *Content analysis in communications research.* New York: Free Press.

Berelson, B., Lazersfeld, P. F. & MacPhee, W. N. (1954). *Voting: A study of opinion formation in a presidential campaign.* Chicago: Chicago University Press.

Berkowiz, D. (1987). TV news sources and news channels. *Journalism Quarterly 3,* 508-513.

Bierhoff, J., Deuze, M. & de Vreese, C. H. (2001). *Media Innovation, Professional Debate and Training. A European Analysis.* European Journalism Centre. Maastricht, the Netherlands.

Bleiss, H., Betsch, T. & Franzen, A. (1998). Framing the framing effect: The impact of context cues on solutions to the 'Asian disease' problem. *European Journal of Social Psychology, 28,* 287-291.

Blumler, J. G. (Ed.) (1983). *Communicating to voters. Television in the first European parliamentary elections.* London: Sage.

Blumler, J. G. & Gurevitch, M. (1995). *The crisis of public communication.* London: Routledge.

Blumler, J. G. & Gurevitch, M. (1998). Campaign journalism at the BBC, 1997. In I. Crewe, B. Gosschalk & J. Bartle (Eds.). *Why Labour won the general election of 1997.* London: Frank Cass.

Blumler, J. G. & Gurevitch, M. (2001). "Americanization" reconsidered: UK-US campaign communication comparisons across time. In. W. L. Bennett & B. Entman (Eds.). *Mediated politics. Communication and the future of democracy* (pp. 390-403). Cambridge: Cambridge University Press.

Blumler, J. G. & Hoffmann-Riem, W. (1992). New roles for public television in Western Europe: Challenges and prospects. *Journal of Communication, 42,* 20-36.

Blumler, J. G. & Kavanagh, D. (1999). The third age of political communication. Influences and features, *Political Communication, 16,* 209-231.

Blumler, J. G. & Nossiter, T.J. (1991). Broadcasting finance in transaction: An international comparison. In J. Blumler and T.J. Nossiter (Eds.). *Broadcasting finance in transition. A comparative handbook.* New York: Oxford University Press.

Blumler, J. G., Gurevitch, M. & Ives, J. (1978). *The challenge of election broadcasting.* Leeds: Leeds University Press.

Blumler, J. G., Gurevitch, M. & Nossitier, T. (1986). Setting the television news agenda: campaign observation at the BBC. In I. Crewe & M. Harrop (Eds.). *Political communication: The general election campaign of 1983* (pp. 104-124). Cambridge: Cambridge University Press.

Blumler, J. G., Gurevitch, M. & Nossitier, T. (1989). The earnest vs. the determined: election newsmaking at the BBC, 1987. In I. Crewe & M. Harrop (Eds.). *Political communication: The general election campaign of 1987* (pp. 157-174). Cambridge: Cambridge University Press.

Blumler, J. G., McLeod, J. & Rosengren, K. E. (1992). *Comparatively speaking.* Newbury Park, CA: Sage.

Boomgaarden, H. & de Vreese, C. H. (2002). *Valenced news frames and public support for EU: Linking content analysis and experimental data.* Paper presented to the annual meetings of the Netherlands School of Communications Research, Utrecht, November.

Bosch, A. & Newton, K. (1995). Economic calculus or familiarity breeds content? In O. Niedermeyer & R. Sinnott (Eds.). *Public opinion and internationalized governance* (pp. 73-104). Oxford: Oxford University Press.

Brants, K. & van Kempen, H. (2002). The ambivalent watchdog. The changing culture of political journalism and its effects. In R. Kuhn & E. Neveu (Eds) *Political journalism. New challenges, new practices* (pp. 168-185). London: Routledge.

Brants, K. & McQuail, D. (1997). The Netherlands. In B. Oestergaard (Ed.). *The media in Western Europe* (pp. 152-166). London: Sage.

Brants, K. & van Praag, P. (Eds.) (1995). *Verkoop van de politiek. De verkiezingscampagne van 1994.* ['Selling politics: The 1994 election campaign']. Amsterdam: Het Spinhuis.

Breed, W. (1955). Social control in the newsroom: A functional analysis. *Social Forces* 53, 109-116.

Brettschneider, F. (1997). The press and the polls in Germany, 1980-1994. Poll coverage as an essential part of election campaign reporting. *International Journal of Public Opinion Research,* 9, 248-265.

Brosius, H. B., Donsbach, W. & Birk, M. (1996). How do text-picture relations affect the informational effectiveness of television newscasts? *Journal of Broadcasting and Electronic Media,* 40, 180-195.

Brown, S. R. & Melamed, L. E. (1990). *Experimental design and analysis.* Newbury Park: CA: Sage.

Cameron, G. T. & Frieske, D. A. (1994). The time needed to answer: Measurement of memory response latency. In A. Lang (Ed.). *Measuring psychological responses to media* (pp.149-165). Hillsdale, NJ: Lawrence Erlbaum.

Cappella, J. N. & Jamieson, K. H. (1996). News frames, political cynicism, and media cynicism. *The Annals of the American Academy, 546,* 71-84.

Cappella, J. N. & Jamieson, K. H. (1997). *Spiral of cynicism. The press and the public good.* New York: Oxford University Press.

Caspari, M., Schoenbach, K. & Lauf, E. (1999). Bewertung politischer Akteure in den Fernsehnachrichten: Analyse der Berichterstattung in Bundestagswahlkaempfen der 90er Jahre [The evaluation of political actors on television news: An analysis of news in federal-election campaigns of the 1990s]. *Media Perspektiven, 5,* 270-274.

Cayrol, R. (1983). Media use and campaign evaluations. Social and political stratification of the European electorate. In J.G. Blumler (Ed.). *Communicating to voters. Television in the first European parliamentary elections* (pp. 163-179). London: Sage.

Cayrol, R. (1983). Broadcasters and the election campaign: Attitudes to Europe and professional orientations. In J.G. Blumler (Ed.). *Communicating to voters. Television in the first European parliamentary elections* (pp. 213-222). London: Sage.

Chaffee, S. & Kanihan, S. F. (1997). Learning about politics from the mass media. *Political Communication, 17,* 421-430.

Cobb, M. D. & Kuklinski, J. H. (1997). Changing minds: Political arguments and political persuasion. *American Journal of Political Science, 41 (1),* 88-121.

Cohen, A. A. (1996). *Global newsroom, local audiences: A study of Eurovision news exchange.* London: John Libbey.

Cohen, B. C. (1963). *The press and foreign policy.* Princeton, NJ: Princeton University Press.

Cooper, A. H. (2002). Media framing and social movement mobilization. German peace protest against INF missiles, the Gulf War and NATO peace enforcement in Bosnia. *European Journal of Political Research, 41,* 37-80.

Craig, S. C., Niemi, R. G. & Silver, G. E. (1990). Political efficacy and trust: A report on the NES pilot study items. *Political Behavior, 12,* 289-314.

Crigler, A. N., Just, M. & Belt, T. (2002). *The three faces of negative campaigning.* Paper presented to the annual conference of the American Political Science Association, Boston, MA.

Crigler, A. N. (Ed.) (1996). *The psychology of political communication.* Ann Arbor: University of Michigan Press.

D'Angelo, P. (2002). News framing as a multi-paradigmatic research program: A response to Entman. *Journal of Communication,* forthcoming.

Dearing, J. W. & Rogers, E. M. (1996): *Agenda-setting. Communication concepts 6.* Thousand Oaks, CA: Sage.

Delli-Carpini, M. X. & Keeter, S. (1996). *What Americans know about politics and why it matters.* New Haven: Yale University Press.

Deuze, M. (2002). *Journalists in the Netherlands. An analysis of the people, the issues and the (inter-)national environment.* Amsterdam: Aksant Academic Publishers.

Domke, D., McCoy, K. & Torres, M. (1999). News media, racial perceptions, and political cognition. *Communication Research, 26,* 570-607.

Domke, D., Shah, D. & Wackman, D. B. (1998). "Morel referendums": Values, news media, and the process of candidate choice. *Political Communication, 15,* 301-321.

Druckman, J. N. (2001a). The implication of framing effects for citizen competence. *Political Behavior, 23,* 225-256.

Druckman, J. N. (2001b). On the limits of framing effects: Who can frame? *Journal of Politics, 63,* 1041-1066.

Durham, F. D. (1998). News frames as social narratives: TWA Flight 800. *Journal of Communication, 48 (4),* 100-117.

van der Eijk, C. & Franklin, M. N. (Eds.) (1996): *Choosing Europe. The European electorate and national politics in the face of union.* Michigan: The University of Michigan Press.

van der Eijk, C., Franklin, M. N. & Oppenhuis, E. (1996). The strategic context: Party choice. In C. van der Eijk & M. N. Franklin (Eds.). *Choosing Europe. The European electorate and national politics in the face of union* (pp. 332-365). Michigan: The University of Michigan Press.

Eilders, C. (1997). *Nachrichtenfaktoren und Rezeption. Eine empirische Analyse zur Auswahl und Verarbeitung politischer Information.* [News factors and reception. An empirical analysis on the selection and processing of political information]. Opladen: Westdeutscher Verlag.

Entman, R. B. (1989). *Democracy without citizens: media and the decay of American politics.* New York: Oxford University Press.

Entman, R. B. (1991). Framing US coverage of international news: Contrasts in narratives of the KAL and Iran air incidents. *Journal of Communication, 41,* 6-27.

Entman, R. B. (1993). Framing: Toward clarification of a fractured paradigm. *Journal of Communication, 43,* 51-58.

Epstein, E. J. (1973). *News from nowhere. Television and the news.* Chicago: Ivan R. Dee.

Erber, R. & Lau, R. R. (1990). Political cynicism revisited: An information-processing reconciliation of policy-based and incumbency-based interpretations of changes in trust in government. *American Journal of Political Science Review, 34,* 236-253.

Esser, F., Reinemann, C. & Fan, D. (2001). Spin-doctors in the United States, Great Britain and Germany. Meta-communication about media manipulation. *Harvard Journal of Press/Politics, 6 (1),* 16-45.

Ettema, J. S. & Whitney, D. C. (Eds.) (1982). *Individuals in mass media organizations: creativity and constraint.* Beverly Hills, CA: Sage.

European Commission (1997). *Euromedia Monitoring 1995-1997.* Union for Public Opinion and Research. Brussels, Belgium: Directorate-General X.A.2.

European Commission. (1998). *Eurobarometer: Public opinion in the European union.* (Rep. No. 48). Brussels, Belgium: Directorate-General X.

European Commission. (1999). *Eurobarometer: Public opinion in the European union.* (Rep. No. 50). Brussels, Belgium: Directorate-General X.

Eurobarometer/European Commission. (2002). *Eurobarometer: Public opinion in the European union.* (Rep. No. 56). Brussels, Belgium: Directorate-General X.

Eurobarometer Candidate countries/European Commission. (2002). Public opinion in the candidate countries. (Rep. No. 1). Brussels, Belgium: Directorate-General X.

Fallows, J. (1996). *Breaking the news. How the media undermine American democracy.* New York, NY: Pantheon Books.

Farrell, D. (1996). Campaign strategies and tactics. In L. LeDuc, R. G. Niemi & P. Norris (Eds.). *Comparing democracies. Elections and voting in global perspective* (pp. 160-183). Thousand Oaks, CA: Sage.

Finkel, S. E. & Geer, J. G. (1998). Spot check: casting doubt on the demobilizing effect of attack advertising. *American Journal of Political Science, 42,* 573-595.

Fishbein, M. & Ajzen, I. (1975). *Belief, attitude, intention and behavior: an introduction to theory and research.* Reading: Addison-Wesley.

Fiske, S. T. & Taylor, S. (1984): *Social cognition.* New York: Random House.

Fiske, S. T. & Taylor, S. (1991): *Social cognition.* New York: Random House.

Fiske, S. T., Kinder, D. R. & Larter, W. M. (1983). The novice and the expert: Knowledge-based strategies in political cognition. *Journal of Experimental and Social Psychology, 19,* 318-400.

Fiske, S. T., Lau, R. R. & Smith, R. A. (1990). On the varieties and utilities of political expertise. *Social Cognition, 8*, 31-48.

Franklin, M., van der Eijk, C. & Marsh, M. (1995). Referendum outcome and trust in government: Public support for Europe in the wake of Maastricht. *West European Politics, 18*, 101-107.

Franklin, M., Marsh, M. & Wlezien, C. (1994). Attitudes toward Europe and referendum votes: A response to Siune and Svensson. *Electoral Studies, 13*, 117-121.

Franklin, M., Mackie, T., Valen, H. et al. (1992). *Electoral change: Responses to evolving social and attitudinal structures in Western democracies.* Cambridge: Cambridge University Press.

Freedman, P. & Goldstein, K. (1999). Measuring media exposure and effects of negative campaign ads. *American Journal of Political Science, 43 (4)*, 1189 - 1208.

Frisch, D. (1993). Reasons for framing effects. *Organizational Behavior and Human Decision Processes, 56*, 274-302.

Fundesco/AEJ Annual Report (1997). *The European Union in the media, 1996*, Madrid.

Gabel, M. (1998). Public support for European integration: An empirical test of five theories. *Journal of Politics, 60*, 333-354.

Gabel, M. & Palmer, H. (1995). Understanding variation in public support for European integration. *European Journal of Political Research, 27*, 3-19.

Galtung, J. & Ruge, M. H. (1965). The structure of foreign news. The presentation of the Congo, Cuba, and Cyprus crises in four Norwegian newspapers. *Journal of Peace Research, 1*, 64-91.

Gamson, W. A. (1992): *Talking politics.* New York: Cambridge University Press.

Gamson, W. A. (1996). Media discourse as a framing resource. In A.N. Crigler (Ed.). *The psychology of political communication* (pp. 111-132). Ann Arbor: University of Michigan Press.

Gamson, W. A. & Modigliani, A. (1989). Media discourse and public opinion on nuclear power: A constructionist approach. *American Journal of Sociology, 95*, 1-37.

Gans, H. J. (1979). *Deciding what's news.* New York: Pantheon Books.

Gavin, N.T. (Ed.) (1998). *The economy, media and public knowledge.* Leicester: Leicester University Press.

Gavin, N. T. (2000). Imagining Europe: Political identity and British television coverage of the European economy, *The British Journal of Politics and International Relations, 2 (3)*, 353-73.

Gavin, N. T. (2001). British journalists in the spotlight. Europe and media research, *Journalism, 2*, 299-314.

Gavin, N. T. & Goddard, P. (1998). Television news and the economy: Inflation in Britain. *Media, Culture & Society 20*, 451-470.

Gitlin, T. (1980). *The whole world is watching.* Berkeley: University of California Press.

Goddard, P., Corner, J., Gavin, N. T. & Richardson, K. (1998). Economic news and the dynamics of understanding: the Liverpool project. In N. T. Gavin (Ed.) *The economy, media and public knowledge* (pp. 9-37). Leicester: Leicester University Press.

Goffman, E. (1974). *Frame analysis: An essay on the organisation of experience.* Cambridge: Harvard University Press.

Golding, P. & Elliott, P. (1979). *Making the news.* New York: Longman.

Graber, D. A. (1988). *Processing the news. How people tame the information tide.* Second edition. New York: Longman.

Graber, D. A. (1990). Seeing is remembering: How visuals contribute to learning from television news. *Journal of Communication, 40,* 134-155.
Graber, D. A. (2001). *Processing politics. Learning from television in the internet age.* Chicago: University of Chicago Press.
Gunther, B. (1997). *Measuring bias on television.* Luton: University of Luton Press.
Gurevitch, M. & Blumler, J. G. (1981). The construction of election news at the BBC. In J.S. Ettema & Whitney, D. C. (Eds.) *Individuals in mass media organizations: Creativity and constraints* (pp. 179-204). Beverly Hills: Sage.
Gurevitch, M. & Blumler, J. G. (1990). Comparative research: The extending frontier. In D. L. Swanson & Nimmo, D. (Eds.) *New directions in political communication. A resource book* (pp. 305-325). Newbury Park: Sage.
D'Haenens, L. & de Lange, M. (2001). Framing of asylums seekers in Dutch regional newspapers. *Media, Culture & Society, 23,* 847-860.
Hallin, D. & Mancini, P. (1984). Speaking of the president: Political structure and representational form in U.S. and Italian television news. *Theory & Society,* 829-850.
Hart, R. P. (1994). *Seducing America: How television charms the American voter.* 2nd Edition. Thousand Oaks, CA: Sage.
Heinderyckx, F. (1993). Television news programmes in Western Europe: A comparative. *European Journal of Communication 8 (4).*
Herbst, S. (1998). *Reading public opinion. How political actors view the democratic process.* Chicago: Chicago University Press.
Herr, J. P. (2002). The impact of campaign appearances in the 1996 election. *Journal of Politics, 64,* 904-913.
Hertog, J. K. & McLeod, D. M. (2001). A multiperspectival approach to framing analysis: A field guide. In S. D. Reese, O.H. Gandy & A. E. Grant (Eds.) *Framing public life* (pp. 139-162). Mahwah, NJ: Lawrence Erlbaum.
Hetherington, M. (1998). The political relevance of political trust. *American Political Science Review, 92,* 791-808.
Hetherington, M. (2001). Declining trust and a shrinking policy agenda: Why the media scholars should care. In R. Hart & D. R. Shaw (Eds.) *Communication in U.S. elections. New agendas* (pp. 105-121). Lanham, MA: Rowman & Littlefield.
Hewstone, M. (1986). *Understanding attitudes to the European Community. A social-psychological study in four member states.* Cambridge: Cambridge University Press.
Hjarvard, S. (1999). *Nyheder i konkurrence* [News in competition]. Copenhagen: Samfundslitteratur.
Hodess, R. B. (1997). The role of news media in European integration: A framework of analysis for political science. *Res Publica, 39,* 215-227.
Holtz-Bacha, C. (1999). Mass media and elections: An impressive body of research. In Brosius, H-B. & Holtz-Bacha, C. (Eds.) *German communication yearbook* (pp. 39-68). Cresskill, NJ: Hampton Press.
Holtz-Bacha, C. & Norris, P. (2001). "To entertain, inform and educate": Still the role of public television. *Political Communication, 18,* 123-140.
Hovland, C. (1959). Reconciling conflicting results derived from experimental and survey studies of attitude change. *American Psychologist,* 8-17.
Hsu, M-L. & Price, V. (1993). Political expertise and affect: Effects on news processing. *Communication Research, 20,* 671-695.

Hultén, O. & Brants, K. (1992). Public service broadcasting: Reactions to competition. In K. Siune and W. Truetzschler (Eds.). *Dynamics of media politics. Broadcast and electronic media in Western Europe.* London: Sage.

Humpreys, P. J. (1996). *Mass media and media policy in Western Europe.* Manchester: Manchester University Press.

Inglehart, R. (1970). Cognitive mobilization and European identity. *Comparative Politics, 3,* 45-70.

Inglehart, R. (1984). *Continuity and change in the attitudes of the European Community public, 1970-1984.* Research report. Brussels: European Commission.

Inglehart, R. (1990). *Culture shift in advanced industrial societies.* Princeton, NJ: Princeton University Press.

Inglehart, R., Rabier, J. R. & Reif, K. (1991). The evolution of public attitudes towards European integration 1970-86. In Reif., K. & Inglehart, R. (Eds.). *Eurobarometer: The dynamics of European public opinion.* London: Macmillan.

Iyengar, S. (1991). *Is anyone responsible? How television frames political issues.* Chicago, IL: University of Chicago Press.

Iyengar, S. (1996). Framing responsibility for political issues. *Annals of the American Academy,* 59-70.

Iyengar, S. & Kinder, D. R. (1987). *News that matters: Television and American opinion.* Chicago: University of Chicago Press.

Jackson, S. (1992). *Message effects research.* New York: The Guilford Press.

Jamieson, K. H. (1992). *Dirty politics: Deception, distraction, and democracy.* New York: Oxford University Press.

Jasperson, A. E., Shah, D. V., Watts, M., Faber, R. J. & Fan, D. P. (1998). Framing the public agenda: Media effects on the importance of the federal budget deficit. *Political Communication, 15,* 205-224.

Kahneman, D. & Tversky, A. (1983): Choices, Values, and Frames. *American Psychologist, 39, (4),* 341-350.

Kahneman, D. A., Tversky, A. & Slovic, P. (1984). *Judgment under uncertainty.* Cambridge: Cambridge University Press.

Kelly, M. & Siune, K. (1983). Television and campaign structures. In Blumler, J. (Ed.) *Communicating to voters. Television in the first European parliamentary elections* (pp. 41-64). London: Sage.

Kepplinger, H. M. (1998). *Die Demontage der Politik in der Informationsgesellschaft.* [The dismantling of politics in the information society]. Freiburg: Alber.

Kepplinger, H. M. & Weissbecker, H. (1991). Negativität als Nachrichtenideologie [Negativity as news ideology]. *Publizistik, 36,* 330-342.

Kevin, D. (2001). Coverage of the European Parliament Elections of 1999: National public spheres and European debates. *Javanost – The Public, 8 (1).*

Kinder, D. R. & Palfrey, T. (Eds.) (1993). *Experimental foundations of political science.* Ann Arbor: University of Michigan Press.

Kinder, D. R. & Sanders, L. M. (1990). Mimicking political debate with survey questions: The case of white opinion on affirmative action for blacks. *Social Cognition, 8,* 73-103.

Kinder, D. R. & Sanders, L. M. (1996). *Divided by color. Racial politics and democratic ideals.* Chicago: Chicago University Press.

Kiousis, S., Bantimaroudis, P. & Ban, H. (1999). Candidate image attributes. Experiments on the substantive dimension of second level agenda setting. *Communication Research, 26*, 414-428.

Kleinnijenhuis, J., Maurer, M., Kepplinger, H. M. & Oegema. D. (2001). Issues and personalities in German and Dutch television news: Patterns and effects. *European Journal of Communication, 16*, 337-359.

Kleinnijenhuis, J., Oegema, D., de Ridder, J. A. & Ruigrok, P. C. (1998). *Paarse polarisatie: de slag om de kiezer in de media* [Purple polarisation: The battle over the voter in the media]. Aalphen aan den Rijn: Samson.

Köcher, R. (1986). Bloodhounds or missionaries: Role definitions of Germans and British journalists', *European Journal of Communication 1*, 43-64.

Kolarska-Bobinska, L., Dolinska, X., et al. (2001). *Before the great change. Polish public opinion and EU enlargement.* Warsaw: Institute of Public Affairs.

Kosicki, G. (1993). Problems and opportunities in agenda-setting research. *Journal of Communication, 43 (2)*, 100-127.

Krippendorf, K. (1980). *Content analysis: An introduction.* Thousand Oaks, CA: Sage.

Krosnick, J. A. & Brannon, L. A. (1993). The impact of the Gulf War on the ingredients of presidential evaluations: Multidimensional effects of political involvement. *American Political Science Review, 87 (4)*, 963-978.

Krosnick, J. A. & Kinder, D. R. (1990). Altering the foundations for support for the president through priming. *American Political Science Review, 84 (2)*, 173-190.

Kuhberger, A. (1995). The framing of decisions: A new look at old problems. *Organizational Behavior and Human Decision Making, 62*, 230-240.

Kunelius, R. & Sparks, C. (2001). The European public sphere: Dreams and realities. *Javanost – The Public, 8 (1)*, 5-20.

Küng-Schankleman, L. (2000). *Inside the BBC and CNN. Managing media organizations.* London: Routledge.

Lang, G. E. & Lang, K. (1991). Watergate: An exploration of the agenda-building process. In D. L. Protess & M. McCombs (Eds.). *Agenda setting. Readings on media, public opinion, and policymaking* (pp. 277-289). Hillsdale, NJ: Lawrence Erlbaum.

Lau, R. R. & Smith, R. A. (1991). Political beliefs, policy interpretations, and political persuasion. *Journal of Politics, 53*, 6-44.

Lau, R. R., Sigelman, L., Heldman, C. & Babbitt, P. (1999). Do negative campaigns mobilize or suppress turnout? Clarifying the relationship between negativity and participation. *American Political Science Review, 93 (4)*, 851-875.

Lavrakas, P. & Traugott, M. W. (Eds.) (2000). *Election polls, the news media, and democracy.* New York: Chatham House.

Lawrence, R. (2000). Game-framing the issues: Tracking the strategy frame in public policy news. *Political Communication, 17*, 93-114.

Leroy, P. & Siune, K. (1994). The role of television in European elections: The cases of Belgium and Denmark. *European Journal of Communication, 9*, 47-69.

Lichter, R. & Noyes, R. E. (1996). *Good intentions make bad news: Why Americans hate campaign journalism.* Lanham: Rowan & Littlefield.

Liebes, T. (2000). Inside a news item: A dispute over framing. *Political Communication, 17*, 205-305.

Lippmann, W. (1922 [1965]). *Public opinion.* New York: Free Press.

Lodge, M. & Tursky, B. (1979). Comparisons between category and magnitude scaling of public opinion employing SRC/CPS items. *American Political Science Review, 73*, 50-66.

Loftus, E. F. (1979). *Eyewitness testimony*. Cambridge, MA: Harvard University Press.

Loftus, E. F., Klinger, M. R., Smith, K. D. & Fielder, J. (1990). A tale of two questions: Benefits of asking more than one question. *Public Opinion Quarterly, 54 (3)*, 330-345.

Lopez-Escobar, E., Llamas, J. P., McCombs, M. & Lennon, F. R. (1998). Two level of agenda setting among advertising and news in the 1995 Spanish elections. *Political Communication, 15*, 225-238.

Luskin, R. C. (1990). Measuring political sophistication. *American Journal of Political Science, 31 (4)*, 856-872.

McCombs, M. E. (1981). The Agenda-setting approach. In D. D. Nimmo & K. R. Sanders (Eds.). *Handbook of political communication*. Beverly Hills: Sage.

McCombs, M. E. & Ghanem, S. I. (2001). The convergence of agenda setting and framing, in S. D. Reese, O.H. Gandy & A. E. Grant (Eds.). *Framing public life* (pp. 67-82). Mahwah, NJ: Lawrence Erlbaum.

McCombs, M. E. & Shaw, D. L. (1972). The agenda-setting function of mass media. *Public Opinion Quarterly 36*, 176-187.

McCombs, M. E., Lopez-Escobar, E. & Llamas, J. P. (2000). Setting the agenda of attributes in the 1996 Spanish general election. *Journal of Communication, 50 (2)*, 77-92.

McCombs, M. E., Shaw, D. L. & Weaver, D. (Eds.) (1997b). *Communication and democracy. Exploring the intellectual frontiers in agenda-setting theory*. Hillsdale, NJ: Lawrence Erlbaum.

McCombs, M. E., Llamas, J.P., Lopez-Escobar, E. & Rey, F. (1997a). Candidate images in Spanish elections: Second-level agenda-setting effects. *Journalism and Mass Communication Quarterly, 74*, 703-717.

McLaren, L. M. (2002). Public support for the European Union: Cost/benefit analysis or perceived cultural threat? *Journal of Politics, 64*, 551-566.

McLeod, D. M. & Detenber, B. H. (1999). Framing effects of television news coverage of social protest. *Journal of Communication, 1999, 49*(3), 3-23.

McLeod, D. M., Kosicki, G. M. & McLeod, J. M. (2002). Resurveying the boundaries of political communication effects. In J. Bryant & D. Zillmann (Eds.) *Media effects. Advances in theory and research* (pp. 215-268). Mahwah, NJ: Erlbaum.

McLeod, J. M., Kosicki, G. M. & McLeod, D. M. (1994). The expanding boundaries of political communication effects. In J. Bryant and D. Zillmann (Eds.). *Media effects* (pp. 123-162). Hillsdale, NJ: Erlbaum.

McLeod, J. M., Becker, L. B. & Byrnes, J. E. (1974). Another look at the agenda-setting function of the press. *Communication Research, 1*, 131-166.

McLeod, J. M., Scheufele, D. A., Moy, P. et al. (1999). Understanding deliberation: The effects of discussion networks on participation in a public forum. *Communication Research, 26*, 743-774.

McManus, J. H. (1994). *Market-driven journalism. Let the citizen beware*. Thousand Oaks, CA: Sage.

McQuail. D. (1992). *Media performance*. London: Sage.

McQuail, D. (1994). *Mass communication theory*. 3rd edition. London: Sage.

McQuail, D. (2000). *McQuail's mass communication theory*. 4th edition. London: Sage.

McQuail, D. & Siune, K. (1998). *Media policy: convergence, concentration and commerce.* London: Sage.
Mair, P. (2000). The limited impact of Europe on national party systems. *West European Politics, 23 (4),* 27-51.
Mancini, P. (1999). New frontiers in political professionalism. *Political Communication, 16,* 231-246.
Manheim, J. B. (1998). The news shapers: Strategic communication as a third force in news making. In D. Graber, D. McQuail & P. Norris (Eds.). *The politics of news. The news of politics* (pp. 94-109). Washington, DC: CQ Press.
Martin, C. R. & Oshagan, H. (1997). Disciplining the workforce: The news media frame a General Motors plant closing. *Communication Research, 24,* 669-697.
Mazzoleni, G. & Schulz, W. (1999). "Mediatization" of politics: A challenge for democracy. *Political Communication, 16,* 247-262.
Mendelson, M. (1993). Television frames in the 1988 Canadian election. *Canadian Journal of Communication, 18,* 149-171.
Meurs, E, van Praag, Ph. & Brants, K. (1995). De produktie van het campagnenieuws. NOS-journaal en RTL-nieuws. ['The production of campaign news: The NOS Journaal and RTL News'] In K. Brants & Ph. van Praag (Eds.). *Verkoop van de politiek. De verkiezings-campagne van 1994.* ['Selling politics. The 1994 election campaign'] (pp. 131-149). Amsterdam: Het Spinhuis.
Meyer, C. (1999). Political legitimacy and the invisibility of politics: Exploring the European Union's communication deficit. *Journal of Common Market Studies, 37,* 617-639.
Miller, A. H. (1974). Political issues and trust in government: 1946-1970. *American Political Science Review, 68,* 951-972.
Miller, A. H., Goldenberg, E. N. & Erbing, L. (1979). Type-set politics: Impact of newspapers on public confidence. *The American Political Science Review, 73 (1),* 67-84.
Miller, J. M. & Krosnick, J. A. (2000). News media impact on the ingredients of presidential evaluations: Politically knowledgeable citizens are guided by a trusted source. *American Journal of Political Science, 44,* 301-315.
Miller, M. M. & Riechert, B. P. (2001). The spiral of opportunity and frame resonance: Mapping the issue cycle in news and public discourse. In S. D. Reese, O. H. Gandy & A. E. Grant (Eds.). *Framing public life* (pp. 67-82). Mahwah, NJ: Lawrence Erlbaum.
Mondak, J. J. (2001). Developing valid knowledge scales. *American Journal of Political Science, 45,* 224-241.
Morgan, D. (1995). British news and European Union news: The Brussels news beast and its problems. *European Journal of Communication, 10,* 321-343.
Moy, P. & Pfau, M. (2000). *With malice toward all? The media and public confidence in democratic institutions.* Westport, CT: Praeger.
Moy, P. & Scheufele, D. A. (2000). Media effects on political and social trust. *Journalism and Mass Communication Quarterly, 77,* 744-759.
Muller, E. & Jukam, T. O. (1977). On the meaning of political support. *American Political Science Review, 71,* 1561-1595.
Neale, J. M. & Libert, R. M. (1986). *Science and behaviour. An introduction to methods of research,* 3rd edition. Englewood Cliffs: Prentice-Hall.
Nelson, T. E. & Oxley, Z. M. (1999). Issue framing effects on belief importance and opinion. *Journal of Politics, 61,* 1040-1061.

Nelson, T. E. & Kinder, D. R. (1996). Issue frames and group-centrism in American public opinion. *Journal of Politics, 58*, 1055-1078.

Nelson, T. E., Clawson, R. A. & Oxley, Z. M. (1997). Media framing of a civil liberties conflict and its effect on tolerance. *American Political Science Review, 91*, 567-584.

Neuman, W. R., Just, M. R. & Crigler, A. N. (1992). *Common knowledge. News and the construction of political meaning.* Chicago: The University of Chicago Press.

Newman, B. (2000). *Handbook of political marketing.* Thousand Oaks, CA: Sage.

Newton, K. (1999). Social and political trust in established democracies. In P. Norris (Ed.). *Critical citizens* (pp. 169-187). Oxford: Oxford University Press.

Niemi, R. G., Craig, S. C. & Mattei, F. (1991). Measuring internal political efficacy in the 1988 National Election Study. *American Political Science Review, 85*, 1407-1413.

Noël-Aranda, M-C. (1983). Projecting a European election: The challenge faced by the communicators. In J. G. Blumler (Ed.). *Communicating to voters. Television in the first European parliamentary elections* (pp. 83-100). London: Sage.

Norris, P. (1995). The restless searchlight. Network news framing of the post-cold war. *Political Communication 12*, 357-370.

Norris, P. (1999). *Critical citizens.* Oxford: Oxford University Press.

Norris, P. (2000). *A virtuous circle. Political communications in postindustrial societies.* Cambridge: Cambridge University Press.

Norris, P., Curtice, J., Sanders, D., Scammell, M. & Semetko, H. A. (1999). *On message. Communicating the campaign.* London: Sage.

Nye, J. S. Jr., Zelikow, P. D. & King, D. C. (Eds.) (1997). *Why people don't trust government.* Cambridge: Harvard University Press.

Page, B. I. & Shapiro, R. Y. (1992). *The rational public: Fifty years of trends in Americans' policy preferences.* Chicago: Chicago University Press.

Pan, Z. & Kosicki, G. (1993). Framing analysis: An approach to news discourse. *Political Communication, 10*, 59-79.

Pan, Z. & Kosicki, G. M. (2001). Framing as a strategic action in public deliberation. In S. D. Reese, O.H. Gandy & A. E. Grant (Eds.) *Framing public life* (pp. 35-66). Mahwah, NJ: Lawrence Erlbaum.

Patterson, T. E. (1993). *Out of order.* New York: Alfred A. Knopf.

Patterson, T. E. & McClure, R. D. (1976). *The unseeing eye. The myth of television power in national elections.* Putnam.

Pepermans, R. & Verleye, G. (1998). A unified Europe? How euro-attitudes relate to psychological differences between countries. *Journal of Economic Psychology, 19*, 681-699.

Peter, J. (2002). *Why the television coverage of the European Union matters.* Unpublished PhD dissertation. Amsterdam: University of Amsterdam.

Peter, J. & Lauf, E. (2003). The impact of coder characteristics on cross-national assessment of reliability. *Journalism and Mass Communication Quarterly* (forthcoming).

Peter, J. & de Vreese, C. H. (2002). *A faceless European Union: A cross-national comparative investigation of the television news coverage of EU representatives.* Paper presented at the annual meetings of the International Communication Association, ICA, Seoul, Korea.

Pinkleton, B. E. & Austin, E. W. (2001). Individual motivations, perceived media importance and political disaffection. *Political Communication, 18*, 321-334.

Pinkleton, B. E. & Austin, E. W. (2002). Exploring relationships among media use frequency, perceived media importance, and media satisfaction in political disaffection and efficacy. *Mass Communication & Society, 5,* 113-140.

Plasser, F., Scheucher, C. & Senft, C. (2000). Is there a European style of political marketing?. In B. Newman (Ed.). *Handbook of political marketing* (pp. 89-112). Thousand Oaks, CA: Sage.

van Praag, P. & v/d Eijk, C. (1998). News content and effects in a historic campaign. *Political Communication, 15,* 165-183.

van Praag, P. & Brants, K. (2000). Politieke communicatie in een consensusdemocratie [Political communication in a consensus democracy]. In P. van Praag & K. Brants (Eds.). *Tussen beeld en inhoud. Politiek en media in de verkiezingen van 1998* [Between image and content. Politics and the media in the 1998 elections] (pp. 243-257). Amsterdam: Het Spinhuis.

Przeworski, A. & Teune, H. (1970). *The logic of comparative social inquiry.* New York: Wiley-Interscience.

Price, V. & Tewksbury, D. (1997). News values and public opinion. A theoretical account of media priming and framing. In: G. Barnett & F.J. Boster (Eds.) *Progress in communication science* (173-212). Greenwich, CT: Abiex.

Price, V. & Zaller, J. (1993). Who gets the news? Alternative measures of news reception and their implications for research. *Public Opinion Quarterly, 57,* 133-164.

Price, V., Tewksbury, D. & Powers, E. (1997). Switching trains of thought. The impact of news frames on readers' cognitive responses. *Communication Research, 24,* 481-506.

Putnam, R. D. (1995). Bowling alone: America's declining social capital. *Journal of Democracy, 6 (1),* 65-78.

Putnam, R. D. (2000). *Bowling alone: the collapse and revival of American community.* New York: Simon & Schuster.

Reese, S. D. (1984). Visual-verbal redundancy effects on television news learning. *Journal of Broadcasting, 28,* 79-87.

Reese, S. D. & Ballinger, J. (2001). History of Theory: The roots of a sociology of news: Remembering Mr. Gates and Social Control in the newsroom. *Journalism & Mass Communication Quarterly, 78 (4),* 641-658.

Reese, S. D. & Buckalew, B. (1995). The militarism of local television: The routine framing of the Persian Gulf War. *Critical Studies in Mass Communication, 12,* 40-59.

Reese, S. D., Gandy, O. H. & Grant, A. E. (Eds.) (2001). *Framing public life: Perspectives on media and our understanding of the social world.* Mahwah, NJ: Lawrence Erlbaum.

Reeves, B. & Geiger, S. (1994). Designing experiments that assess psychological responses to media messages. In A. Lang (Ed.) *Measuring psychological responses to media* (pp. 165-180). Hillsdale, NJ: Lawrence Erlbaum.

Rhee, J. W. (1997). Strategy and issue frames in election campaign coverage: A social cognitive account of framing effects. *Journal of Communication, 47(3),* 26-48.

Rhee, J. W. & Cappella, J. N. (1997). The role of political sophistication in learning from news: Measuring schema development. *Communication Research, 24,* 197-223.

Riffe, D., Lacy, S. & Fico, F. G. (1998). *Analyzing media messages: using quantitative content analysis in research.* Mahwah, NJ: Lawrence Erlbaum.

Riffe, D. & Freitag, A. (1997). A content analysis of content analyses: Twenty-five years of journalism. *Journalism & Mass Communication Quarterly, 74 (4),* 873-882.

Robinson, M. (1976). Public affairs television and the growth of political malaise. *American Political Science Review, 70,* 409-432.
Rogers, E. M. & Dearing, J. W. (1988). Agenda-setting research: Where has it been? Where is it going? In J. A. Anderson (Ed.). *Communication Yearbook, 11* (pp. 555-594). Newbury Park, CA: Sage.
Romer, D., Jamieson, K. H. & Cappella, J. N. (2000). Does attack advertising affect turnout? In K. H. Jamieson (Ed.). *Everything you think you know about politics... and why you are wrong.* New York: Basic Books.
Rosengren, K. E. (1993). From field to frog ponds. *Journal of Communication. 43 (3),* 6-17.
Rössler, R. & Brosius, H-B. (2001). Do talk shows cultivate adolescents' view of the world? A prolonged-exposure experiment. *Journal of Communication, 51 (1),* 143-163.
Rothman, A. J. & Salovey, P. (1997). Shaping perceptions to motivate healthy behavior: The role of message framing. *Psychological Bulletin, 121,* 3-19.
Saris, W. E. (1997). The public opinion about the EU can easily be swayed in different directions. *Acta Politica: International Journal of Political Science, 32,* 406-435.
Scheufele, D. A. (1999). Framing as a theory of media effects. *Journal of Communication, 49(1),* 103-122.
Scheufele, D. A. (2000). Agenda-setting, priming, and framing revisited. Another look at cognitive effects of political communication. *Mass Communication & Society, 3,* 297-316.
Schlesinger, P. (1997). From cultural defense to political culture: media, politics, and collective identity in the European Union. *Media, Culture & Society, 19 (3),* 369-391.
Schönbach, K. (1983). What and how voters learned. In J. G. Blumler (Ed.). *Communicating to voters. Television in the first European parliamentary elections* (pp. 299-318). London: Sage.
Schönbach, K. & Semetko, H. A. (1992). Agenda-setting, agenda reinforcing or agenda-deflating? A study of the 1990 German national election. *Journalism Quarterly, 69 (4),* 837-846.
Schönbach, K., de Ridder, J. & Lauf, E. (2001). Politicians on TV: Getting attention in Dutch and German election campaigns. *European Journal of Political Research, 39 (4),* 519-531.
Schudson, M. (1995). *The power of news.* Cambridge, MA: Harvard University Press.
Schudson, M. (2000). The sociology of news production revisited (again). In J. Curran & M. Gurevitch (Eds.). *Mass media and society* (pp. 175-200). London: Arnold.
Semetko, H. A. (1996). Political balance on television: Campaigns in the US, Britain and Germany. *Harvard International Journal of Press/Politics 1,* 51-71.
Semetko, H. A. & Canel, M. J. (1997). Agenda-senders versus agenda-setter: Television in Spain's 1996 election campaign. *Political Communication, 14,* 459-479.
Semetko, H. A. & Schönbach, K. (1994). *Germany's unity election: Voters and the media.* Cresskill, NJ: Hampton Press.
Semetko, H. A. & Valkenburg, P. M. (2000). Framing European politics: A content analysis of press and television news. *Journal of Communication, 50 (2),* 93-109.
Semetko, H. A., de Vreese, C. H. & Peter, J. (2000). Europeanised politics – Europeanised media? European integration and political communication. *West European Politics, 23 (4),* 121-142.

Semetko, H. A., Blumler, J. G., Gurevitch, M. & Weaver, D.H. (1991). *The formation of campaign agendas: A comparative analysis of party and media role in recent American and British Elections.* Hillsdale, NJ: Lawrence Erlbaum.
Severin, W. J. & Tankard, J. W. Jr. (1997). *Communication theories. Origins, methods, and uses in the mass media* (4th edition). New York: Longman.
Shah, D., Domke, D. & Wackman, D. B. (1996). "To Thin Own Self Be True". Values, framing, and voter decision-making strategies. *Communication Research, 23*, 509-560.
Shah, D., Domke, D. & Wackman, D. B. (2001). The effects of value-framing on political judgment and reasoning. In S. D. Reese, O.H. Gandy & A. E. Grant (Eds.) *Framing public life* (pp. 227-244). Mahwah, NJ: Lawrence Erlbaum.
Shah, D., Watts, M. D., Domke, D. & Fan, D. (2002). News framing and cueing of issue regimes. Explaining Clinton's public approval in spite of scandal. *Public Opinion Quarterly, 66*, 339-370.
Shapiro, M. A. (1994). Think-aloud and though-list procedures in investigating mental processes. In A. Lang (Ed.). *Measuring psychological responses to media* (pp. 1-14) Hillsdale, NJ: Lawrence Erlbaum.
Shoemaker, P. J. & Reese, S. D. (1996). *Mediating the message. Theories of influences on mass media content.* 2nd edition. White Plains: Longman.
Simon, A. F. (2001). A unified method for analyzing media framing. In R. Hart & D. R. Shaw (Eds.) *Communication in U.S. elections. New agendas* (pp. 75-89). Lanham, MA: Rowman & Littlefield.
Simon, A. & Xenos, M. (2000). Media framing and effective public deliberation. *Political Communication, 17*, 363-376.
Siune, K. (1983). The campaign on television: What was said and who said it? In Blumler, J. (Ed.) *Communicating to voters. Television in the first European parliamentary elections* (pp. 223-240). London: Sage.
Siune, K. & Borre, O. (1975). Setting the agenda for a Danish election, *Journal of Communication 1*, 65-73.
Siune, K. & Hultén, O. (1998). Does public broadcasting have a future? In D. McQuail & K. Siune (Eds.) *Media policy. Convergence, concentration, commerce* (pp. 23-37). London: Sage.
Siune, K. & Svensson, P. (1993). The Danes and the Maastricht Treaty: The Danish EC referendum of June 1992, *Electoral Studies, 12 (2),* 99-111.
Siune, K., Svensson, P. & Tonsgaard, O. (1994). The European Union: The Danes said NO in 1992 but YES in 1993: How and why. *Electoral Studies, 13 (2),* 107-116.
Slaatta, T. (1998). *Europeanisation and the Norwegian news media. Political discourse and news production in the transnational field.* Oslo: University of Oslo.
Slater, M. D. (1991). Use of message stimuli in mass communication experiments: A methodological assessment and discussion. *Journalism Quarterly, 68 (3),* 412-421.
Smith, K. A. (1985). America's most important problem: A trend analysis, 1946-1976. *Public Opinion Quarterly, 44,* 164-180.
Smith, G. E. & Wortzel, L. H. (1997). Prior knowledge and the effect of suggested frames of reference in advertising. *Psychology and Marketing, 14,* 121-143.

Sniderman, P. M. & Theriault, S. M. (2002). The dynamics of political argument and the logic of issue framing. In W. E. Saris & P. Sniderman, P. (Eds.). *The issue of belief: Essays in the intersection of non-attitudes and attitude change.* Princeton: Princeton University Press.

Snoeijer, R., de Vreese, C. H. & Semetko, H. A. (2002). The effects of live TV reporting on recall and appreciation of political news. *European Journal of Communication 17, 1,* 85-101.

Snow, D. A. & Benford, R. D. (1992). Master frames and cycles of protest. In A.D. Morris & C.M. Mueller (Eds.). *Frontiers in social movement theory.* New Haven, CT: Yale University Press.

Sotirovic, M. (2000). Effects of media use on audience framing and support for welfare. *Mass Communication & Society, 3,* 269-296.

Staab, J. F. (1990). *Nachrichtenwert-Theorie. Formale Struktur and empirischer Gehalt.* [News value theory. Formal structure and empirical content]. Freiburg: Alber.

Stephan, E. (1998). *Judgmental heuristics and biases in decision making.* Paper presented to the 'Seminar on Financial and Economic Expectations', The Royal Dutch Academy of Arts and Sciences (KNAW), Amsterdam, The Netherlands, September 1998.

Stephens, M. (1980). *Broadcast news.* New York: Holt, Rinehart & Winston.

Stevens, J. (1996). *Applied multivariate statistics for the social sciences.* 3rd edition. Mahwah, NJ: Lawrence Erlbaum.

Sudman, S. (1986). Do exit polls influence voting behavior? *Public Opinion Quarterly, 50,* 331-339.

Swanson, D. L. & Mancini, P. (1996). *Politics, media, and modern democracy: An international study of innovations in electoral campaigning and their consequences.* Westport: Praeger.

Tankard, J. W. (2001). The empirical approach to the study of media framing. In S. D. Reese, O. H. Gandy & A. E. Grant (Eds.). *Framing public life* (pp. 95-106). Mahwah, NJ: Lawrence Erlbaum.

Tannenbaum, P. H. (1958). Experimental method in communication research. In R. O. Nafziger & D. M. White (Eds.) *Introduction to mass communication research.* Baton Rouge, LA: Louisiana State University Press.

Terkildsen, N., Schnell, F. I. & Ling, C. (1998). Interest groups, the media, and policy debate formation. *Political Communication, 15,* 45-61.

Tewksbury, D., Jones, J., Peske, M. W., Raymond, A. & Vig, W. (2000). The interaction of news and advocate frames: Manipulating audience perceptions of a local policy issue. *Journalism and Mass Communication Quarterly, 77,* 804-830.

Tuchman, G. (1978). *Making news. A study in the construction of reality.* New York: Free Press.

Tumber, H. (1995). Marketing Maastricht: The EU and news management. *Media, Culture & Society, 17 (3),* 511-520.

Valentino, N. A., Beckmann, M. N. & Buhr, T. A. (2001a). A spiral for of cynicism for some: The contingent effects of campaign news frames on participation and confidence in government. *Political Communication, 18,* 347-367.

Valentino, N. A., Buhr, T. A. & Beckmann, M. N. (2001b): When the frame is the game: Revisiting the impact of "strategic" campaign coverage on citizen's information retention. *Journalism and Mass Communication Quarterly, 78,* 93-112.

Valkenburg, P. M., Semetko, H. A. & de Vreese, C. H. (1999). The effects of news frames on readers' thoughts and recall. *Communication Research, 26,* 550-568.

Vallone, R. P., Ross, L. & Lepper M. R. (1985). The hostile media phenomenon: Biased perception and perceptions of media bias in coverage of the Beirut massacre. *Journal of Personality and Social Psychology, 49,* 577-585.

de Vreese, C. H. (1999). *News and European integration. News content and effects in cross-national comparative perspective.* Research Report. The Amsterdam School of Communications Research. Amsterdam: University of Amsterdam.

de Vreese, C. H. (2000). *The Battle over the News Agenda. A Cross-national Analysis of Political Television Journalism in the 1999 European Parliamentary Elections.* Paper presented to the Annual Meeting of the American Political Science Association, August, Washington DC.

de Vreese, C. H. (2001a). Election coverage – new directions for public broadcasting: The Netherlands and beyond. *European Journal of Communication 16, 2,* 155-179.

de Vreese, C. H. (2001b). Europe in the News: A cross-national comparative study of the news coverage of key EU events. *European Union Politics, 2,* 283-307.

de Vreese, C. H. (2001c). *Defining the issue: The effects of frames in television news on public understanding of political issues.* Paper presented at the annual meetings of the International Communication Association, ICA, Washington D.C.

de Vreese, C. H. (2001d). Frames in television news. British, Danish, and Dutch television news coverage of the introduction of the euro. In S. Hjarvard (Ed.). *News in a globalized society.* Gothenburg: Nordicom.

de Vreese, C. H. (2001e). Le elezioni del parlamento Europeo 1999. Dinamarca: Un' elezione al margine dell'Europa [The 1999 European parliamentary elections. Denmark: Voting a the rim of Europe) (pp. 223-258). In R. Marini (Ed). *L'Europa dell'euro e della Guerra* [A Europe of euro and war]. Rome: RAI.

de Vreese, C. H. (2002a). *The effects of frames in political television news on issue interpretation and frame salience.* Manuscript submitted for publication.

de Vreese, C. H. (2002b). *The effects of strategic news on political cynicism, issue evaluations and policy support: A two-wave experiment.* Paper presented to the Annual Meeting of the American Political Science Association, August, Boston.

de Vreese, C. H. (2003). "Space and time permitting": Television reporting of second-order elections. *Journalism Studies,* (forthcoming).

de Vreese, C. H. & Semetko, H. A. (2001). *Why the Danes said NO to the euro: A panel study of the dynamics of opinion and the vote.* Paper presented at the annual meetings of the American Political Science Association, San Francisco, CA.

de Vreese, C. H. & Semetko, H. A. (2002a). Public perception of polls and support for restrictions on publication of polls: Denmark's 2000 euro referendum. *International Journal of Public Opinion Research, 14,* 410-433.

de Vreese, C. H. & Semetko, H. A. (2002b). Cynical and engaged: strategic campaign coverage, public opinion and mobilization in a referendum. *Communication Research, 29 (6),* 615-641.

de Vreese, C. H. & Semetko, H. A. (2002c). *News matters: Influences on the vote in a referendum campaign.* Manuscript conditionally accepted for publication.

de Vreese, C. H., Peter, J. & Semetko, H. A. (2001). Framing politics at the launch of the euro: A cross-national comparative study of frames in the news. *Political Communication, 18 (2),* 107-122.

Wang, X. T. (1996). Framing effects: Dynamics and task domains. *Organizational Behavior and Human Decision Processes, 68*, 145-157.

Wattenberg, M. P. & Brians, C. L. (1999). Negative campaign advertising: Demobilizer or mobilizer? *American Political Science Review, 93*, 891-900.

Weaver, D. H. (1977). Political issues and voter need for orientation. In D. L. Shaw & M. McCombs (Eds.). *The emergence of American political issues: The agenda-setting function of the press* (pp. 107-119). St. Paul, MN: West.

Weaver, D. H. (1998). *Reply to Kosicki's column: Framing should not supplant agenda-setting.* Newsletter of the Communication Theory & Methodology Division of AEJMC. Vol. 27, 2.

Weaver, D. H. & Swanzy, N. E. (1985). Who sets the agenda for the media? A study of local agenda-building. *Journalism Quarterly 63*, 88-94.

Weaver, D. H. & Wilhoit, G. C. (1996). *The American journalist: A portrait of US news people and their work.* Bloomington: Indiana University Press.

Weaver, D. H., Graber, D. A., McCombs, M. & Eyal, C. H. (1981). *Media agenda-setting in a presidential election.* New Yok: Praeger.

Weischenberg, S., Löffelholz, M. & Scholl, A. (1998). Journalism in Germany. In D. H. Weaver (Ed.), *The global journalist* (pp. 229-256). Bloomington: Indiana University Press.

Werder, O. (2002). Debating the euro – Media agenda-setting in a cross-national environment. *Gazette, 64*, 219-234.

White, D. M. (1950). The gatekeeper: A case-study in the selection of news. *Journalism Quarterly, 34*, 31-38.

Wilke, J. & Reinemann, C. (2001). Do the candidates matter? Long-term trends of campaign coverage: A study of German press since 1949. *European Journal of Communication, 16 (3)*, 291-314.

Zaller, J. (1992). *The nature and origins of mass opinion.* New York: Cambridge University Press.

Zaller, J. (1998). Monica Lewinsky's contribution to political science. *PS: Politics Science and Politics 31 (2)*, 182-189.

Zaller, J. (2002). The statistical power of election studies to detect media exposure effects in political campaigns. *Electoral Studies, 21 (2)*, 297-330.

Zhao, X. & Chaffee, S. H. (1995). Campaign advertisements versus television news as sources of political issue information. *Public Opinion Quarterly, 59*, 41-65.

Zucker, H. G. (1978). The variable nature of news media influence. In B. D. Ruben (Ed.). *Communication Yearbook, 2* (pp. 235-246). New Brunswick, NJ: Transaction.

Appendices

Appendix A. Overview of experimental research on framing effects

Study	P/TV	Sample	Number studies	Effect type C/P	Effect type A/A	Effect type B	Comparison Independent variable (framing manipulation)	Measures Dependent variable (framing effect)	Main results
Cappella & Jamieson (1997)	P/TV	349 + 276	2	X	X		Strategic vs. issue framing of health care and 1991 mayoral race in Philadelphia	Political cynicism (fc and scale); cynical learning (scale)	Strategy frame activates political cynicism (both for health care and campaign issue, both print and TV); Issue frame does not affect cynicism (campaign), and activates cynicism (health care); Frames do not affect learning.
Cobb & Kuklinski (1997)	P	435 s	1		X		Pro vs. con framing of NAFTA and health care in easy vs. hard to comprehend versions	Support NAFTA and health care (scale), mediators: political awareness and partisanship	Con/hard frame cause negative attitude change for NAFTA issue and con/easy frame for health care. Retest suggest that con/hard frame effects are pervasive
Domke, McCoy & Torres (1999)	P		1		X		Ethical vs. material framing of immigration	Assessment of US economy (three item index)	Material frame activates immigrant considerations
Domke, Shah & Wackman (1998)	P	172 + 201 s	1	X			Ethical vs. material framing of abortion, euthanasia, and health care	Issue interpretation and decision-making strategy (thought listing procedure)	Ethical frame produces non-compensatory decision making strategy, material frame compensatory
Druckman (2001)	P	151 s	1†	X	X		Free speech vs. public safety v high vs. low source credibility	Tolerance towards KKK mediated by importance of free speech, public safety, and opposing racism (scale)	Frame (in NY Times) activated importance of free speech and opposing racism as consideration that in turn shaped the overall tolerance. Frame had no significant main effect, only mediated.
Iyengar (1991)	TV	772	9		X		Episodic vs. thematic television news coverage of crime, terror poverty, unemployment, and racial inequality	Responsibility attributes (causal / treatment) (thought-listing procedure)	Terrorism: episodic frames leads to causal attribution of responsibility and punitive measure, same (though less strong) pattern for crime. Poverty, unemployment, and racial inequality: episodic frame leads to individualistic attribution of responsibility, thematic frame to societal attribution of responsibility
McLeod & Detenber (1999)	TV	212 s	1		X		Low vs. medium vs. strong status quo framing of anarchist protest	Criticism of protesters / police, impression of protest, id with protesters (all scale)	Affects audience impressions of protest depending on degree of frame present in the news
Nelson & Kinder (1996) a	P	84 s	1		X		Stereotypical vs. non-stereotypical visual framing of blacks	Attitude towards affirmative action programs (scale)	Stereotypical images lead to racial prejudice considerations that negatively affect support for affirmative action
Nelson & Oxley (1999)	P	57 s	2		X		Environmental vs. economic framing of land development	Issue opinion (approval plan); Belief content (expectations for plan); Belief importance (rank order ideas)	- Economic frame leads to favorable opinion towards plan; Economic beliefs more important if exposed to economic frame, v.v. for environmental frame; Modest effect on belief content
	P	121 s			X		Personal responsibility vs. threat to children framing of welfare	Issue opinion (approval welfare cut); Belief content (beliefs about welfare); Belief importance; (rating ideas)	- Frames influence belief importance which mediates issue opinion; Modest effect of both frames on belief content
Nelson, Clawson & Oxley (1997)	TV/P	222 s + 71 s	2	X	X		Free speech vs. public order framing of KKK rally	Tolerance towards KKK (scale); accessibility (reaction time task); task rating, value rating (study 2)	Free speech frame leads to greater tolerance towards KKK; frames do not influence cognitive accessibility; public order frame increases public order values importance for tolerance

Appendix A. Overview of experimental research on framing effects (continued)

Study	P/TV	Sample	Number studies	Effect type C/P	Effect type A/A	Effect type B	Comparison *Independent variable (framing manipulation)*	Measures *Dependent variable (framing effect)*	Main results
Price, Tewksbury & Powers (1997)	P	278 s	2	x	x		Conflict vs. human interest vs. personal consequences framing of university funding	Issue interpretation (thought-listing procedure); affective valence (thl); policy support and person evaluations (feeling thermometers)	Frames affect topical focus of thoughts, no main frame effect on policy support and person evaluation, only interaction between frame and residency at university for funding
Rhee (1997) b	P/TV	276	1	x			Strategy vs. issue framing of 1991 Philadelphia mayoral campaign	Issue interpretation (letters)	Strategy frame leads to strategic interpretation of campaign (found for print, not for TV); knowledgeable persons make more references to the media frames.
Schenk-Hamlin, Procter & Rumsey (2000)	P	360 s	2		x		Candidate frame vs. ad hoc issue advertisements	Political cynicism and politician accountability (thought listing procedure)	Candidate framed ads leads to more political cynicism and increases politician based accountability for societal problems compared to ad hoc issue framed ads.
Shah, Domke & Wackman (2001)	P	172 + 201 s	1	x		x	Ethical vs. material framing of economy, education, government cuts, health care)	Candidate choice (FC); issue interpretation (thought-listing procedure)	News frames influence issue interpretation; news frames marginal direct impact on vote choice decision making strategy, mediated by participants' individual issue interpretation
Tewksbury, Jones, Peske, Raymond & Vig (2000)	P	510 s	1	x			Moderate vs. strong degree of presence of advocate frame in hog farm news coverage	Issue interpretation (thought listing procedure); evaluation and regulation hog farms (scale)	Relative emphasis given to news frame influences issue interpretation and evaluation of hog farms in immediate post-test. Retest after 3 weeks showed muted effect of frame on issue interpretation
Valentino, Beckman & Buhr (2001)	P	301	1	x	x	x	Strategy vs. sincere framing of political campaigns	Campaign evaluation (thought listing procedure); vote intention; civic duty perception (scale); political trust (scale); political meaningfulness	Strategy frame produces strategic comments and sincere frame sincere comments; strategy frame reduces vote intention and feeling of civic duty for low educated; strategy frame reduces trust and political meaningfulness for non-partisans
Valentino, Buhr & Beckman (2001) c	P			x	x		Strategy vs. sincere framing of political campaigns	Campaign perception (thought listing procedure); recall (MC)	Strategy frame produces more negative reactions to campaign than sincere frame; strategy frame produces lower recall than sincere frame
Valkenburg, Semetko & de Vreese (1999)	P	169 s	1	x			Conflict vs. human interest vs. economic consequences vs. responsibility framing of (a) the euro and (b) crime	Issue interpretation (thought-listing procedure; recall (mc)	Frames give direction to readers' thoughts about both issues; human interest frame for crime issue reduces recall

Notes: P/TV refers to print (P) versus television (TV) based studies. The s notation listed under sample refers to student sample. C/P refers to studies focusing on cognitive / information processing effects, A/A to studies focusing on attitudinal and/ or affective effects, B to studies focusing on behavioral (intentional) effects. FC refers to 'forced choice' options, MC to multiple choice, thl to thought-listing procedures, scale to scaled Likert-type item response options. † this article reports two studies but only one focused on media (newspapers) role in framing. 'a' this study also reports three studies based on survey question framing experiments from the NES studies. These are not included as they do not deal specifically with media framing effects. 'b' this study reports on the same data as Cappella & Jamieson (1997), but uses different dependent measures and methods of data analysis. 'c' this study draws on the same experiment as reported in Valentino, Buhr and Beckman (2001).

Appendix B

Technical appendix content analysis

EURO LAUNCH STUDY. For the *euro* study, coders were trained during January and February 1999 and coding took place between February and April 1999. Inter-coder reliability tests were conducted on a randomly selected sub-sample of 10% of the news stories in the 10 days sub-sample period.

Topic: The main categories were: 'Introduction of the euro' (e.g. preparations for the euro, exchange rate, European Monetary Union); 'Politics without introduction of the euro' (e.g. elections, social politics, relations between states); 'Economy without introduction of the euro' (e.g. unemployment, budget, wages and earnings); 'Society' (e.g. crime, trials, culture); 'Social welfare/ education/ science/ technology' (e.g. welfare cuts; schooling; inventions); 'Agriculture/ environment/ energy/ traffic' (e.g. farming; nuclear energy; public transport); '(Natural) disasters' (e.g. earthquakes; epidemics); 'Sports/Weather' and 'Other topics'. The percentage of inter-coder agreement for the topic measures was 95% for the British stories, 92% for the Danish, 82% for the Dutch stories.

Focus: No reliabilities can be reported for this measure.

News frames: The percentage of agreement between coders for the conflict frame items ranged from 73% to 100% for the British news, from 92% to 100% for the Danish, and from 85% to 100% for the Dutch news. The percentage of agreement between coders for the economic consequences frame items were between 89% and 100% for the British news, between 82% and 100% for the Danish, and between 88% and 92% for the Dutch news. Cronbach's alpha was used to assess the internal consistency of the scales. The alphas for the conflict frame were: Britain: $\alpha = .67$; Denmark $\alpha = .74$; Netherlands: $\alpha = .81$. The alphas for the economic consequences frame were: Britain: $\alpha = .57$; Denmark $\alpha = .70$; Netherlands: $\alpha = .61$. With three items and consistently positive item-total correlations the alpha for Britain was considered acceptable for the purpose of our study (Stevens, 1996).

ELECTION ELECTION STUDY. For the *election* study, coders were recruited in both Netherlands and abroad. Coding of Greek, Italian, Portuguese, and Finnish news was administrated locally after intensive training by the principal researchers at the coding locations Coding of British, Danish, and Dutch news took place at the University of Amsterdam. Coders were trained during six weeks before coding and supervised throughout the whole coding period. For the reliability test, coders had to code at least 18 randomly selected television stories per channel, except Danish news which was coded by one coder only, but was closely monitored by the coder trainer.

Topic: The inter-coder agreement was r = .76 in the Netherlands and r = .86 in Britain.

Actors: The inter-coder agreement was r = .52 in Britain and r = .86 in the Netherlands.

Actor evaluation: The inter-coder was r = .44 in Britain and r = .37 in the Netherlands.

SUMMIT AND ROUTINE STUDY. The coding of *summit* and *routine* weeks was completed simultaneously. Training took place in January and February 2001 and coding from February – June 2001. Coding of this material took place in two waves. First, each story in all bulletins was coded for topic, length, and formal characteristics (surface coding). Based on a screening question whether the news story was about the EU, its policies or institutions, these news stories were coded for a number of characteristics (in-depth coding). To assess the quality of the coding, two reliability tests were performed. For the surface coding between 31 and 45 randomly selected news stories were coded by two to four coders. For the in-depth coding of EU-stories, two British coders coded 12 and four Danish coders coded 20 randomly selected stories. All Dutch stories were double-coded by a coder and a coder trainer.

Topic: The inter-coder agreements using the detailed topic list were: Britain 82%, Denmark 86%, and the Netherlands 77% The inter-coder agreement reported here is a conservative estimate based on an analysis of the agreement of coding detailed and specific topics. The agreement between coders is higher when looking at the collapsed categories. The screening question read: "Is this story about the EU?". "About the EU" was defined as a story mentioning at least twice in complete, independent sentences either the EU, its institutions, policies, or politics. A story only referring to the EU marginally, for example mentioning the EU once at the end of the news story, does not pass the screening and is thus not included in subsequent analyses. This implies that the measure of EU coverage is rather conservative and that a broader, more inclusive definition would lead to slightly higher visibility of EU news. A less conservative screening question (Does the story mention EU level politics/ institutions/ actors) was also included in the analysis and only few stories that passed the inclusive screening, did not pass the stricter "about" screening. However, in the analysis the "about" screening question is used to ensure that the news stories dealt substantially with EU affairs.

Focus: The inter-coder agreements were: Britain 100%, Denmark 100% and the Netherlands 95%. The inter-coder agreements for the two screening questions were: Britain 99 and 100%, Denmark 98 and 100%, and the Netherlands 98 and 99%.

Frames: The percentage of agreement between coders for the conflict frame items ranged from 73 to 92% for the British news, from 85 to 95% for the Danish, and from 67 to 80% for the Dutch news. For the summit stories the country-wise internal consistency (Cronbach's alpha) of the conflict scale was: Britain: $\alpha = .66$; Denmark $\alpha = .69$; and Netherlands: $\alpha = .57$. For the routine news stories the alphas were: Denmark $\alpha = .60$; and Netherlands: $\alpha = .63$. No reliability measure is reported for Britain given the low number of cases. As reported in the results section only 11 news stories in Britain (both *BBC* and *ITN*) dealt with EU affairs. In each of the analyses item-correlations were consistently positive.

Strategy: The inter-coder agreements for the items were: Britain 83 and 92%, Denmark 71 and 74%, and the Netherlands 93 and 100%.

Actor: The inter-coder reliabilities were measured as the average agreement between the coders. The inter-coder agreement was: Britain 74%, Denmark 85% and the Netherlands 90%.

Actor evaluation: inter-coder reliabilities measured as the average agreement between the coders in percent were Britain 90%, Denmark 96%, and the Netherlands 97%.

Appendix C. Text EU story (issue and strategy version)

Anchor introduction (identical for both conditions)

Poland should enter the European Union within one and a half year. And not in 2004, which was originally planned. This is the conclusion of a report published today by the European Union.

The report has been received with enthusiasm by the winners of the recent Polish elections: the Democratic Left-Alliance. The enlargement of the Union will be discussed in more detail by the end of October during the EU summit in Brussels.

Text news report strategy

(Italics denote difference in the news text from the issue news report)

But the European Commission wants Poland to enter a year earlier, on January 1 2003. *A political power play has begun in Brussels.*

According to the report from the Commission, Poland is politically and economically ready for membership of the EU. And that is even though the agriculture has not been modernized and though the diary production does not yet comply with the strict hygiene norms of the EU. Surveys show that more citizens from the current EU countries are increasingly skeptical about the enlargement. *A political charm campaign is awaiting. So far the initiative of the Commission resembles a strategic plan rather than a concrete policy plan.*

Benschop (Secretary of State): "I consider it an interesting political step by the Commission. It is appealing and Poland has accomplished a lot, but the question is whether membership now is responsible. We will have to do our best to convince the EU citizens about the necessity of this step".

In 1951 the foundation for today's European Union was established. Six countries joined forces in coal and steel. Now there is a common market and in January that one currency. And the Union is getting bigger. A total of 13 countries will join. Six of them are the top of the list: Cyprus, and the former East-bloc countries the check republic, Poland, Estonia, Hungary, and Slovenia. The European Commission has concluded that Poland in the past years has demonstrated that it can join the Union earlier.

Reporter: "Is this report not going to cause annoyance with the other candidate countries who want to enter? Benschop: "It seems that Poland has *won the first battle. A tough task is to in fact live up to these expectations".*

The European Commission is facing a hard time with this proposal because in the European Parliament, the political parties are divided over the hasty enlargement. Some member countries are even against the enlargement. Ireland, for example, rejected the Treaty of Nice last year. And that Treaty was meant to create the possibility for enlargement.

Benschop knows that public opinion is of crucial importance and has thus launch a 'charm campaign'. The question is whether Brussels and Benschop succeed in mobilizing public support.

Text news report issue

But the European Commission wants Poland to enter a year earlier, on January 1 2003.

According to the report from the Commission, Poland is politically and economically ready for membership of the EU. And that is even though the agriculture has not been modernized and though the diary production does not yet comply with the strict hygiene norms of the EU.

But the Commission and the Polish authorities are working on concrete policies for to be implemented to modernize the agricultural sector and invest in less developed cities and regions.

Benschop (Secretary of State): "I consider it an interesting political step by the Commission. It is appealing and Poland has accomplished a lot, but the question is whether membership now is responsible. We will have to do our best to convince the EU citizens about the necessity of this step".

In 1951 the foundation for today's European Union was established. Six countries joined forces in coal and steel. Now there is a common market and in January that one currency. And the Union is getting bigger. A total of 13 countries will join. Six of them are the top of the list: Cyprus, and the former East-bloc countries the check republic, Poland, Estonia, Hungary, and Slovenia. The European Commission has concluded that Poland in the past years has demonstrated that it can join the Union earlier.

Reporter: "Is this report not going to cause annoyance with the other candidate countries who want to enter?

Benschop: "It seems that Poland has shown that a country can get there by working hard and focused. They send a signal to the rest".

The European Commission is facing a hard time with this proposal because in the European Parliament, the political parties are divided over the hasty enlargement. Some member countries are even against the enlargement. Ireland, for example, rejected the Treaty of Nice last year. And that Treaty was meant to create the possibility for enlargement.

Benschop and his colleagues are joining effort to focus on the policies. If successful, the Polish flag will join the rest of the 15 nations in Brussels one and a half year from now.

Author index

Aarts, K., 48, 142
Abramson, P. R., 140
Acock, A., 197
Agger, R. E., 197
Ajzen, I., 34
Aldrich, J. H., 140
Althaus, S. L., 31
Altheide, D. L., 186
Andersen, J., 3, 10, 80
Anderson, C., 7
Anderson, P. J., 8, 58
Ansolabehere, S., 140, 141, 171, 194
Asp, K., 158
Austin, E. W., 142, 143, 151, 158, 169

Babbitt, P., 141
Ballinger, J., 54
Ball-Rokeach, S., 1, 121
Ban, H., 82, 174, 175
Banducci, S., 113, 166
Banks, S. M., 23
Bantimaroudis, P., 82, 174, 175
Baron, R. M., 47
Beauvais, J., 23
Beck, P. A., 57
Becker, L. B., 47
Beckmann, M. N., 18, 34, 35, 37, 40, 49, 140, 142-145, 150, 157, 158, 188, 196
Belt, T., 139, 140, 142, 144
Benford, R. D., 24
Bennett, L. M., 141
Bennett, S. E., 141
Bennett, W. L., 10, 43, 140, 141, 186, 187
Berelson, B., 140, 186
Berkowiz, D., 187
Betsch, T., 23

Bierhoff, J., 61, 180
Birk, M., 126
Bleiss, H., 23
Blumler, J. G., 4 10, 12-15, 54-59, 62, 64, 68, 71, 74, 77, 142, 163, 164, 183, 185, 186, 190
Boomgaarden, H., 181
Borre, O., 3, 10, 58, 80
Bosch, A., 8
Brannon, L. A., 48, 159
Brants, K., 12, 55, 80, 139, 142, 185, 187, 196
Breed, W., 54
Brettschneider, F., 5
Brians, C. L., 141
Brosius, H. B., 126, 196
Brown, S. R., 7, 144, 167, 196
Buckalew, B., 26
Buhr, T. A., 18, 34, 35, 37, 40, 49, 140, 142-145, 150, 157, 158, 188, 196
Byrnes, J. E., 47

Cameron, G. T., 178
Canel, M. J., 12, 15, 55, 58, 59
Cappella, J. N., 18, 26-28, 30, 33-35, 37, 39, 40, 44, 45, 49, 50, 89, 118, 120, 122-124, 136, 139, 140-145, 147, 149, 157, 158, 169, 174, 177, 179, 187, 189, 192, 196-198
Caspari, M., 82
Cayrol, R., 9
Chaffee, S., 122, 141, 146
Clarke, H. D., 197
Clawson, R. A., 18, 25, 27, 37, 38, 49, 50, 121, 123, 136, 142, 143, 176-178, 189, 194, 196

Cobb, M. D., 35, 37
Cohen, A. A., 115
Cohen, B. C., 198
Cooper, A. H., 24, 43
Corner, J., 79
Craig, S. C., 197
Crigler, A. N., 14, 25, 28, 33-36, 43, 46, 81, 116, 118, 122, 123, 135, 139, 140, 142, 144, 178, 187, 188
Curtice, J., 3, 58, 78, 79, 82, 142, 186

D'Angelo, P., 21, 24-26, 187
D'Haenens, L., 28, 32
Dalton, R. J., 57
Dearing, J. W., 147, 189, 198
Delli-Carpini, M. X., 188
Detenber, B. H., 18, 35, 39, 49, 122-124, 137, 143, 145, 168, 174, 188, 194, 196
Deuze, M., 12, 61, 113, 180
Dolinska, X., 6
Domke, D., 27, 29, 33, 35-37, 49, 121, 122, 171, 174, 188, 194, 196
Donsbach, W., 126
Druckman, J. N., 25, 37, 38, 46, 49, 50, 121, 122, 136, 176-178, 188, 189
Durham, F. D., 24, 28

Edy, J. A., 31
Eilders, C., 113
Elliott, P., 54, 59
Entman, R. M., 10, 21, 24, 27-29, 122, 136, 140, 173, 174
Epel, E., 23
Erber, R., 171
Esser, F., 10, 43
Ettema, J. S., 54
Eurobarometer Candidate countries, 6
Eurobarometer, 1, 4, 6, 9, 21, 77, 122, 126, 137, 146, 147, 167, 172
Eyal, C. H., 48

Faber, R. J., 28, 35, 36, 189
Fallows, J., 140
Fan, D., 10, 28, 29, 33, 35, 36, 43, 189

Farrell, D., 10
Fico, F. G., 173
Fielder, J., 22
Finkel, S. E., 141
Fishbein, M., 34
Fiske, S. T., 24, 48, 182, 188, 189
Flickinger, R. S., 141
Franklin, M. N., 8, 10, 183
Franzen, A., 23
Freedman, P., 141
Freitag, A., 85
Frieske, D. A., 178
Frisch, D., 23
Fundesco/AEJ, 79, 115

Gabel, M., 7, 8, 126, 146, 167, 182, 185
Galtung, J., 190
Gamson, W. A., 25-30, 33, 34, 36, 43, 46, 122, 178, 186
Gandy, O. H., 21
Gans, H. J., 24, 54
Gavin, N. T., 1, 12, 15, 44, 51, 56, 58, 77, 79, 81
Geer, J. G., 141
Geiger, S., 17, 125, 147
Ghanem, S. I., 187
Gitlin, T., 26
Goddard, P., 79
Goffman, E., 22
Golding, P., 54, 59
Goldstein, K., 141
Goldstein, M. N., 197
Goul-Andersen, J., 3, 10, 80
Graber, D. A., 35, 36, 45, 46, 48, 122, 126, 130, 15, 178
Grant, A. E., 21
Greene, S., 23, 57
Guhrie, K. K., 121
Gunther, B., 59
Gurevitch, M., 12, 13, 15, 35, 36, 54-59, 62, 64, 68, 71, 74, 77, 142, 163, 164, 185, 186, 190

Hallin, D., 186
Hart, R. P., 140

AUTHOR INDEX

Heinderyckx, F., 186
Heldman, C., 141
Herbst, S., 1
Herr, J. P., 82
Hertog, J. K., 28, 33
Hetherington, M., 140, 182
Hewstone, M., 8, 172
Hjarvard, S., 58, 115
Hodess, R. B., 4, 81
Hoffmann-Riem, W., 185
Holtz-Bacha, C., 15, 48
Hovland, C., 14
Hsu, M-L., 136
Huckfeldt, R., 57
Hultén, O., 185
Humpreys, P. J., 185

Inglehart, R., 6, 8, 181, 182
Ives, J., 15, 62
Iyengar, S., 18, 27, 28, 31, 34, 35, 37, 40, 46, 48, 49, 122, 124, 127, 129, 140, 141, 143, 150, 171, 174, 177, 187, 188, 194, 196

Jackson, S., 17,
Jamieson, K. H., 18, 26-28, 30, 33-35, 37, 39, 40, 44, 45, 49, 50, 82, 89, 118, 120, 122-124, 136, 139, 140-145, 147, 149, 157, 158, 169, 174, 177, 179, 183, 187, 189, 192,196-198
Jasperson, A. E., 28, 35, 36, 189
Jones, J., 37, 39, 121, 123-125, 136, 144, 145, 150, 168, 176
Jukam, T. O., 197
Just, M. R., 14, 28, 31, 33-36, 43, 46, 81, 116, 118, 122, 123, 135, 139, 140, 142, 144, 178, 187, 188

Kahneman, D., 22, 23, 27
Kanihan, S. F., 122, 141
Karp, J., 113, 166
Kavanagh, D., 10
Keeter, S., 188
Kenny, D. A., 47

Kepplinger, H. M., 82, 83, 118, 166
Kevin, D., 4, 81, 114, 171
Kinder, D. R., 4, 17, 24, 27, 46, 48, 49, 81, 114, 122, 125, 142-144, 146, 178, 186, 189, 196
King, D. C., 140, 189
Kiousis, S., 82, 174, 175
Kleinnijenhuis, J., 82
Klinger, M. R., 22
Köcher, R., 12
Kolarska-Bobinska, L., 6
Kosicki, G. M., 28, 34, 42, 44, 120, 123, 135, 174, 175, 186, 188, 198
Krippendorf, K., 15
Krosnick, J. A., 48, 50, 159, 170, 189, 198
Kuhberger, A., 23
Kuklinski, J. H., 35, 37
Kunelius, R., 81, 114, 116, 185, 191
Küng-Schankleman, L., 191

Lacy, S., 173
Lang, G. E., 189
Lang, K., 189
de Lange, M., 28, 32
Larter, W. M., 48
Lau, R. R., 171, 188
Lauf, E., 82, 84, 113, 116, 141
Lavrakas, P., 5
Lawrence, R., 28, 30, 44, 139, 174, 189
Lazersfeld, P. F., 140
Lennon, F. R., 174, 175
Lepper M. R., 137
Leroy, P., 78, 79, 115
Libert, R. M., 17
Lichter, R., 140
Liebes, T., 174, 189
Lippmann, W., 21, 182
Llamas, J. P., 174-176
Lodge, M., 197
Löffelholz, M., 117
Loftus, E. F., 22, 186
Lopez-Escobar, E., 82, 174-176
Luskin, R. C., 188

Mackie, T., 10
MacPhee, W. N., 140
Mair, P., 10
Mancini, P., 10, 186
Manheim, J. B., 54, 190
Marsh, M., 8
Martin, C. R., 28, 29
Mattei, F., 197
Maurer, M., 82
Mazzoleni, G., 10
McClure, R. D., 189
McCombs, M. E., 47, 48, 82, 174-176, 187, 188, 198
McCoy, K., 37, 38, 122, 174, 194, 196
McLaren, L. M., 185
McLeod, D. M., 18, 28, 33-35, 39, 42, 49, 122-124, 137, 143, 145, 168, 174, 188, 194, 196, 198
McLeod, J. M., 13, 14, 34, 42, 47, 172, 174, 188, 198
McManus, J. H., 43, 113, 122
McQuail, D., 11, 12, 15, 21, 42, 59, 185, 186, 190
Melamed, L. E., 17, 144, 167, 196
Mendelson, M., 28-30
Meurs, E., 55
Meyer, C., 11, 44, 66, 116, 173
Miller, A. H., 140, 171
Miller, J. M., 48, 50, 159, 198
Miller, M. M., 187
Modigliani, A., 25-30, 34, 36, 122
Mondak, J. J., 48
Morgan, D., 12, 44, 56-58, 66, 78
Moy, P., 142, 172
Moyer, A., 23
Muller, E., 197

Neale, J. M., 17
Nelson, T. E., 18, 25, 27, 37, 38, 46, 49, 50, 121, 123, 125, 136, 137, 142, 143, 176-178, 189, 194, 196
Neuman, W. R., 14, 28, 31, 33-36, 43, 46, 81, 116, 118, 122, 123, 135, 178, 188, 189
Newman, B., 10
Newton, K., 8

Nielsen, H. J., 3, 10, 80
Niemi, R. G., 197
Noël-Aranda, M-C., 15, 56, 59, 75, 113, 163
Norris, P., 3, 9, 10, 12, 15, 28-30, 48, 58, 77-79, 80, 83, 82, 85, 101, 107, 115, 141, 142, 166, 167, 171, 174, 186, 194
Nossiter, T. J., 15, 55, 57, 58, 74, 163, 185
Noyes, R. E., 140
Nye, J. S. Jr., 140, 189

Oegema. D., 82
Oppenhuis, E., 8, 183
Oshagan, H., 28, 29
Oxley, Z. M., 18, 25, 27, 37, 38, 46, 49, 50, 121, 123, 125, 136, 137, 142, 143, 176-178, 189, 194, 196

Page, B. I., 1, 77
Palfrey, T., 17, 125, 144, 146
Palmer, H., 7
Pan, Z., 28, 34, 42, 44, 123, 135, 175, 186
Patterson, T. E., 28, 30, 78, 122, 139, 141, 187, 189
Pearl, S. A., 197
Pepermans, R., 7
Peske, M. W., 37, 39, 121, 123-125, 136, 144, 145, 150, 168, 176
Peter, J., 10, 13, 28, 32, 44, 82, 84, 113, 116, 117, 166, 167, 173, 188, 191, 198
Pfau, M., 142
Phalen, P. F., 31
Pinkleton, B. E., 142, 143, 151, 158, 161
Plasser, F., 11
Power, G. J., 121
Powers, E., 25, 26, 33-37, 40, 44, 50, 81, 121-124, 129, 131, 135, 142, 150, 151, 168, 171, 178, 189
Price, V., 25, 26, 33-37, 40, 43, 44, 48, 50, 81, 121-124, 127, 129, 131, 135-137, 142, 150, 151, 168, 174, 177, 178, 188, 189
Przeworski, A., 13
Putnam, R. D., 141

AUTHOR INDEX

Rabier, J. R., 6
Raymond, A., 37, 39, 121, 123-125, 136, 144, 145, 150, 168, 176
Reese, S. D., 14, 24, 21, 26, 43, 54, 56, 85, 113, 115, 126, 165, 173
Reeves, B., 17, 125, 147
Reichert, M. S., 7
Reif, K., 6
Reinemann, C., 10, 43, 82
Rey, F., 174, 175
Rhee, J. W., 35, 37, 40, 50, 131, 135, 136, 140, 142, 145, 151, 158, 159, 179
Rhine, S. L., 141
Richardson, K., 79
de Ridder, J. A., 82
Riechert, B. P., 187
Riffe, D., 85, 173
Robinson, M., 140
Rogers, E. M., 47, 189, 198
Romer, D., 141
Rosengren, K. E., 13, 14, 25
Ross, L., 137
Rössler, R., 196
Rothman, A. J., 23
Ruge, M. H., 190
Ruigrok, P. C., 82

Salovey, P., 23
Sanders, D., 3, 58, 78, 79, 82, 142, 186
Sanders, L. M., 24, 27, 49, 122, 142, 186
Saris, W. E., 137, 186
Scammell, M., 3, 58, 78, 79, 82, 142, 186
Scheucher, C., 11
Scheufele, D. A., 21, 24, 25, 27, 42, 44, 48, 53, 136, 142, 172-177, 187
Schlesinger, P., 81, 191
Scholl, A., 117
Schönbach, K., 9, 15, 55, 82
Schudson, M., 43, 54, 56
Schulz, W., 10
Semetko, H. A., 3, 9, 10, 12, 13, 15,28, 32, 33, 35, 37, 40, 44, 48, 54-59, 68, 77-79, 81, 82, 86, 107, 109, 117, 121, 124, 128, 129, 130, 135, 139, 142, 144, 150, 168, 170, 174, 185, 186, 188, 190-192, 194
Senft, C., 11

Shah, D. V., 27-29, 33, 35-38, 49, 121, 122 171, 174, 188, 189, 194, 196
Shapiro, M. A., 130
Shapiro, R. Y., 1, 77
Shaw, D. L., 188, 198
Shoemaker, P. J., 14, 24, 43, 53, 54, 56, 85, 113, 115, 165, 173
Sigelman, L., 141
Silver, G. E., 197
Simon, A. F., 21, 28, 29, 140, 141, 171, 187
Siune, K., 11, 58, 78, 79, 115, 185, 190
Slaatta, T., 56, 57, 74
Slater, M. D., 17, 18, 125, 147
Slovic, P., 23
Smith, K. A., 48
Smith, K. D., 22
Smith, R. A., 188
Sniderman, P. M., 27
Snoeijer, R., 128, 194
Snow, D. A., 24
Snow, R. P., 186
Sotirovic, M., 130
Sparks, C., 81, 114, 116, 185, 191
Staab, J. F., 113
Stephan, E., 23
Stewart, M. C., 197
Sudman, S., 194
Svensson, P., 185
Swanson, D. L., 10, 186
Swanzy, N. E., 189

Tankard, J. W., 45, 82, 122, 123, 168
Tannenbaum, P. H., 186
Taylor, S., 24, 182, 189
Teune, H., 13
Tewksbury, D., 25, 26, 33-37, 39, 40, 44, 50, 81, 121-124, 123-125, 129, 131, 135, 136, 142, 144, 145, 150, 151, 168, 171, 176, 178, 189
Theriault, S. M., 27
Tonsgaard, O., 185
Torres, M., 37, 38, 122, 174, 194, 196
Traugott, M. W., 5
Tuchman, G., 23, 43, 54, 190
Tumber, H., 11, 116

Tursky, B., 197
Tversky, A., 22, 23, 27

Valen, H., 10
Valentino, N. A., 18, 34, 35, 37, 40, 49, 140-145, 150, 157, 158, 171, 188, 196
Valkenburg, P. M., 28, 32, 33, 35, 37, 40, 44, 81, 86, 121, 124, 129, 130, 135, 150, 168, 174, 187, 192
Vallone, R. P., 137
van der Eijk, C., 8, 55, 183
van Kempen, H., 139, 142, 196
van Praag, P., 55, 80, 139, 187
Verleye, G., 7
Vig, W., 37, 39, 121, 123-125, 136, 144, 145, 150, 168, 176
de Vreese, C. H., 3, 9, 10, 13, 24, 28, 32, 35, 37, 40, 44, 55, 58, 61, 82, 107, 109, 117, 121, 124, 128, 129, 130, 135, 139, 150, 166-168, 170, 180, 181, 185, 188, 191, 193, 194, 196

Wackman, D. B., 27, 35, 37, 38, 49, 121, 171, 188
Wang, X. T., 23
Waring, H. R., 121
Wattenberg, M. P., 141
Watts, M. D., 28, 29, 33, 35, 36, 189
Weaver, D. H., 12, 43, 47, 48, 54-56, 58, 68, 77, 174, 175, 189, 190, 198
Weischenberg, S., 117
Weissbecker, H., 118, 166
Werder, O., 4
Weymouth, T., 8, 58
White, D. M., 54, 190
Whitney, D. C., 54
Wilhoit, G. C., 43
Wilke, J., 82
Wlezien, C., 8

Xenos, M., 28, 29

Zaller, J., 15, 27, 48, 122, 157, 171, 188, 189, 194
Zelikow, P. D., 140, 189
Zhao, X., 141, 146
Zucker, H. G., 47

Subject index

Accessibility, 176-178 (see also *framing effects, mediators*)
Agenda-building, 189
Agenda setting, 47, 174-176
    Second-level 136, 174-176
Audience frames 24 (see also *framing effects*)

Balance, 57, 59, 73, 118, 166
BBC, 11, 15, 55, 60, 61, 63, 64, 66-68, 70, 72, 97, 104, 164
Bias, see *balance*
Britain, 6, 79

Comparative design, 13, 56
Conflict, see *frames*
Content analysis, 16, 77-120, 151, 165-167, 173 (see also *news*)
Cynicism, see *political cynicism*

Denmark, 2, 3, 6, 78, 80, 107, 109, 110
DR, 11, 60, 63, 64, 65, 66, 68, 69, 71, 72, 74, 75, 97, 98, 164

Economic consequences, see *frames*
Efficacy, 142, 153, 158, 169-171
Elections
    Sacerdotal approach to, 54, 55, 58, 68, 163, 164
    Pragmatic approach to, 54, 55, 58, 68, 74, 163
EU summits
    In the news, 88, 89, 101-106, 165
Euro
    In the news, 83, 85, 89-96, 111, 112
European Commission, 3

European elections, 3, 9, 56, 64-66, 68-72, 75, 78, 81, 83, 87, 96-101, 113, 163
European Parliament, 8, 56, 165
European public sphere, 81
Experiments, 17, 18, 37, 125-128, 147-149, 167

Frame-building, 24, 53, 75, 76, 162-165, 173
Frame-setting 24, 121, 167-170 (see also *framing effects*)
Frames, 26-34, 44, 81, 82, 86, 93, 117
    Cold War frame, 29
    Conflict frame, 32, 41, 44, 71, 73, 81, 93, 104, 109, 117, 122, 132, 133, 135, 165, 167, 168
    Economic consequences frame, 32, 41, 44, 73, 81, 93, 122, 132, 133, 135, 167, 168
    Episodic/ thematic frame, 31
    Free speech/ public disorder frame, 37, 38
    Game frame, 30
    Generic frames, 28
    Human interest/ impact frame, 31, 32
    Issue specific frames, 28
    Material/ ethical frame, 38
    Strategy/ issue frame, 30, 39, 40, 45, 81, 105, 110, 117, 139, 140, 149, 152, 154, 156, 168, 176, 177
    Valenced frames, 181
Framing, 5, 21-52, 173
    As a process, 42
    In the newsroom, 42, 75, 76
Framing devices, 42, 174

Framing effects, 35-41, 45, 46, 121, 122, 167-170
  Mediators of, 46-50, 178, 179
  Moderators of, 46-50, 142, 178, 179
  Typology, 35

Horse race, see *frames*

Information processing, see *framing effects, typology*
Interviews, 15
ITN, 11, 60, 63, 67, 70, 71, 74, 104, 164

Journalism, 12, 179, 180 (see also *frame-building*)
Journalist roles, 55-56, 163

Knowledge, see *political knowledge*

Media effects, see *agenda-setting, priming,* and *framing effects*
Media frames 24 (see also *frames*)
Media organizations, see *BBC, DR, ITN, NOS, RTL, TV2*
Mobilization
  Effect of news frames on, 140, 150, 159, 169, 171

Netherlands, the, 6, 79
News content
  Actors in EU news, 82, 83, 86, 95, 100, 106, 111, 118, 166
  Tone of news coverage, 82, 83, 87, 96, 101, 106, 111, 118, 166
  Visibility EU news, 90, 91, 97, 102, 107, 116, 16
News production, 53-76, 190
News values, 43, 59, 70-73, 75, 165
NOS, 12, 60, 61, 63, 65, 68, 69, 72, 75, 97, 104, 126, 127, 147, 148, 164

Objectivity, see *balance*

Political actors, see *news, actors in EU news*
Political awareness, 48

Political cynicism, 140, 143, 149, 150, 152, 153
Political knowledge, 48, 49, 142, 153, 155, 156, 158, 169 (see also *political sophistication*)
Political parties, 10, 166
  Professionalization of 10
Political sophistication, 48, 49, 171, 179 (see also *political knowledge*)
Priming, 47, 159, 176
Public opinion, 1, 3, 5-7, 16, 77, 121, 135, 150, 156, 159, 167, 173
Public broadcasting, 11, 12

Referendum, 4, 105, 109, 110
Reliability
  Of content analysis, 84
RTL, 12, 60, 63, 65, 104, 164

Salience
  Of news frames, 123, 124, 133, 134, 136
Schema, 45

Television, 4, 9, 77, 122, 161 (see also *BBC, DR, ITN, NOS, RTL, TV2*)
Television news, see *news*
TV2, 11, 60, 63, 65, 70, 98, 164

Validity
  Of experiments, 17-18, 125-128, 147-149